MARATHON

MARATHON

THE ULTIMATE TRAINING GUIDE

HAL HIGDON,
CONTRIBUTING EDITOR *RUNNER'S WORLD* MAGAZINE

RODALE

Book design by Anthony Serge

Front cover photographs © bubbles-columbus04, © Reuters/CORBIS,
and © Gail Mooney/CORBIS

"High-Carbohydrate Foods" on pages 234–235 was adapted from *Nancy Clark's
Sports Nutrition Guidebook* by Nancy Clark with permission from the author.
"Oxygen Power Table" on pages 258–259 was adapted from *Oxygen Power* by
Jack Tupper Daniels and Jimmy Rhett Gilbert with permission from the authors.

Library of Congress Cataloging-in-Publication Data

Higdon, Hal.
    Marathon : the ultimate training guide / Hal Higdon.— 3rd ed.
        p.   cm.
    Includes index.
    ISBN-13 978–1–59486–199–4 paperback
    ISBN-10 1–59486–199–4 paperback
    1. Marathon running—Training.   I. Title.
    GV1065.17.T73H55   2005
    796.42'52—dc22   2005014083

Distributed to the trade by Holtzbrinck Publishers

    10   paperback

LIVE YOUR WHOLE LIFE™

We inspire and enable people to improve their lives and the world around them

For more of our products visit **rodalestore.com** or call 800-848-4735

FOR THE V-TEAM, THE MERRY GROUP
OF MARATHONERS WHO POST MESSAGES
TO MY INTER*ACTIVE* FORUMS

CONTENTS

INTRODUCTION

MARATHONING FOR A NEW MILLENNIUM

On a sunny afternoon in June, I went for a run in Oak Forest, a suburb southwest of Chicago. It was a Wednesday in the 2nd week of my 18-week training program leading to the LaSalle Bank Chicago Marathon in October. That morning, along with thousands of other runners using my programs to train for Chicago, I had received an e-mail message (from myself) telling me to run 3 miles.

So I did, running a loop through the forest preserve, as instructed, at a pleasantly comfortable pace. I measured the course with a watch that used the global positioning satellites overhead to precisely tell me how far I ran: 3.09 miles. Later that evening, one of the group leaders of the class I lectured to at a nearby high school confirmed the watch's accuracy.

It was one of five lectures I gave that week at five separate locations around the city of Chicago. Nearly 2,000 runners, most of them running their first marathons, had signed up for the class, which was sponsored by the Chicago Area Running Association (CARA). They did so partly to attend lectures such as mine, but also to participate in training runs on the weekend in a dozen different locations. Almost every one of those 2,000 runners would have run 3 miles that day and would do 7 miles on the weekend either because I had told them so in an e-mail message similar to the one I received, because they'd logged into my Web site to access my free training programs, or because they were following the program in this book (in an earlier edition).

I say this with some pride: Hundreds of thousands of runners

have run marathons using my training programs. Many have fol-
lowed my novice program to finish their first marathons. Once having achieved that suc-cess, they often migrate upward to use one of my intermediate

HUNDREDS OF THOUSANDS OF RUNNERS HAVE RUN MARATHONS USING MY TRAINING PROGRAMS.

or advanced programs, running more miles or adding speedwork to improve their times, to set personal records, even to qualify for the prestigious Boston Marathon, which accepts only runners who qualify by running fast times.

DRAMATIC CHANGES

The first edition of this book was published in 1993, but within a half dozen years, the sport of long-distance running had changed so dramatically—with more and more people running marathons, with more and more of them women, and with pacing teams and gels and computerized timing—that I felt a revision was necessary for the book to remain relevant. The second edition appeared in 1999, and now, a half dozen years later, the sport has taken another quantum leap into the future, demanding of me a third edition. Since the first two editions found their way into the hands of more than 110,000 eager readers, I had little difficulty convincing Rodale to allow me to update and revise my work.

Certainly the e-mail message I and so many other runners had re-ceived that morning telling us to run 3 miles was part of the tech-nological change that had come to the marathon in the new millennium. Add to that the GPS watch, which not only precisely measured the length of my run but also allowed me to upload that and other data into my computer log after I returned home.

At my lectures throughout Chicago and its suburbs that week, I answered dozens of questions typically asked by first timers: "How can I expect to run 26 miles when your longest training run is only 20?" and "What's the best kind of cross-training?" or "Should I add weight lifting to my training routine?" Typical, so very typical, and I honestly don't object to answering them again and again because I respond to the joy (and fear) I see in the eyes of people training for their first marathons.

But new runners in Chicago and elsewhere need not wait for me to appear at a clinic near them. They could go online and access one of my free Inter*Active* Training Forums to ask a question and receive a direct answer—often within minutes—from me and other experienced marathoners who surf into my forums while at work or at home or at school or as a break from their daily routines. This is my "V-Team," a group of runners who enjoy the camaraderie that comes from communicating with other like-minded people. For example, looking for a training partner or course where you can run a planned 12-miler while visiting another city? You can find one online. I run one of the more popular online forums, often responding to several dozen questions a day, but I am not alone. There are other training programs available through the Internet, and many other coaches offer advice to beginners, some free and others for pay. In the past half dozen years, the Internet has dramatically changed how runners learn how to train for marathons.

Also during this period since publication of the second edition of this book, there have been other, nontechnological changes in the sport. Marathons have continued to grow in size, Chicago being one of four world marathons (the others: New York, London, and Berlin) that attract fields larger than 30,000 runners. Within the United States, according to figures from the USATF Road Running Information Center, the number of runners finishing marathons has grown from 170,000 to 400,000 in two decades. Those finishers are slightly older and somewhat slower; their motivation in entering a marathon (often their first road race of any distance) being mainly to finish it, not to finish it fast.

In an article on the *Forbes* magazine Web site titled "The Slowing of the Marathon," columnist Dan Ackman cited figures to show

CHANGING DEMOGRAPHICS

Major changes in the demographics of marathons and marathoners occurred toward the end of the 20th century, as documented by the USA Track and Field Road Running Information Center. In 1976 (the year Jack Fultz won the Boston Marathon in 2:20:19), the estimated number of U.S. marathon finishers was 25,000. By 2003, that number had grown to 400,000.

That coincides with the "invasion" by females of the previously male-only sport. In 1966, Roberta Gibb Bingay became the first woman to run the Boston Marathon, and she did so without a number, jumping into the race in Hopkinton after the approximately 500 male starters had passed. It was only after 6 years of increased female participation that the sponsoring Boston Athletic Association finally welcomed women as official entries. By 1975, female finishers at Boston represented 1.5 percent of the field (28 of 1,846 overall finishers).

In the quarter century that followed, the marathon experienced many dramatic changes, none more dramatic than the emergence of

how dramatically marathon fields had slowed over a period of two decades. Male runners in the 1983 New York City Marathon had a median time of 3:41:49, an 8:27-minute-per-mile pace. Ten years later, they had slowed to 4:14:27, or a 9:43 pace. And 10 years after that, the median male time dropped further, to 4:28:41, or 10:25 per mile. "In other words," wrote Ackman, "when the median 1983 runner was finishing the race, today's runner still had 5 miles to go."

Not everyone has welcomed this downward slide. The medical director of one major marathon in the Southwest described this phenomenon to *Forbes* as "the dumbing down of the marathon." He suggested that a 10-minute pace was arguably not running, adding: "In a way, it's an insult to the distance."

women running 26 miles 385 yards. By 2003, female finishers at Boston were 37 percent of the 17,030 total. In all U.S. marathons, women now comprise approximately 40 percent of the fields, a figure that has not varied much in a half dozen years, according to Ryan Lamppa of the Road Running Information Center. Understandably, some marathons show higher or lower percentages. The New York City Marathon, which attracts a large number of foreign runners, had only 34 percent female finishers in 2003, while the Portland Marathon in Oregon attracted 57 percent.

The Boston Marathon is among the few marathons in the world that requires runners to submit fast times in order to enter. Because of the way its qualification system is structured, Boston attracts the "oldest" field, with 53 percent "masters," signifying runners 40 or older. Among major marathons, Chicago has the "youngest" field, with only 33 percent masters, while the City of Los Angeles Marathon attracts the most runners under age 19 (11 percent) because of its successful Students Run L.A. training program.

GUARANTEED FINISH

I certainly disagree. Rather than its demonstrating the "dumbing down" of the marathon, I submit that the drop in median times might portend a "smarting up." Today's marathoners have slightly different goals from those of the preceding generation and certainly different from the generation before that. When I ran my first Boston Marathon, in 1959, I entered planning to win that race, or at least stay close to the leaders and finish near the front. I did stay close to those leaders for nearly two-thirds of the distance, but I failed to finish. I repeated that dismal performance in the next two marathons I ran, running in the lead but not making it to the finish line. Finally, in my fourth attempt, I finished my first marathon in just under 3 hours, despite having walked most of the last several miles.

In contrast, among those enrolled in the CARA Marathon Training Class, the finishing rate is something like 99 percent. This is because members listen to me when I tell them to run their first marathons to have a good time rather than to run a fast time. This is one of the main themes of my lectures to first timers. I suggest they pick

TODAY'S MARATHONERS HAVE SLIGHTLY DIFFERENT GOALS FROM THOSE OF THE PRECEDING GENERATION AND CERTAINLY DIFFERENT FROM THE GENERATION BEFORE THAT.

a time goal ½ hour slower than their potential because it guarantees two things: 1) they will finish the race with smiles on their faces, enjoying the experience, and 2) if they ever run a second marathon, they will be guaranteed to set a personal record because they ran so slowly the first time.

Those words of advice never fail to cause appreciative laughter, but they are true. I wish someone had offered me that advice when I first ran Boston nearly a half century ago. I wish someone had written a book such as this, offering training advice. There were few marathon coaches when I got my start. I learned almost all I knew about running by trial and error: making a mistake in training or racing and then correcting it. Sometimes we have to find our own way to the finish line—although it helps if you have someone offering proper directions so you don't get lost.

That is the purpose of this third edition of this book. I want to show you the way to a comfortable finish if you are running your first marathon, or to an improved performance if that is your goal in a latter marathon. Please join me on the starting line.

—*Hal Higdon, Long Beach, Indiana*

CHAPTER 1

THE MYSTIQUE OF THE MARATHON

THERE'S A CERTAIN MAGIC TO RUNNING 26 MILES 385 YARDS

I heard the comment in passing, approximately 8 miles into the Twin Cities Marathon one year. "To think," said a woman spectator, "they paid to do this." Her comment floated out of the crowd, but by the time I turned to look, my stride had carried me past where she stood beside the course.

I understood what she meant. Twenty-six miles is a long way. Adding 385 more yards makes the distance even longer and further confuses people who don't understand what motivates us to run marathons. Even thinking about running that far takes a certain amount of endurance. And courage. And maybe even arrogance. Yet somehow those of us who call ourselves marathoners do it again, and again, and again.

The woman's comment didn't disturb me at first. First of all, I thought there was some truth to what she said. Second, I was too busy running as fast as I could to worry about what the spectators were thinking.

Only later would her remark return to haunt me. It was obvious that she failed to comprehend the mystique of the marathon. Yet how do you fully explain to spectators the joy and pain that go into running 26 miles and 385 yards? The woman certainly would have found ludicrous some of the goals I had used through a long career to motivate myself. As a younger runner, I had focused my training on making an Olympic Team and winning the Boston Marathon. Even though I had failed in achieving both goals, I had come close enough to make the quest worthwhile.

As I aged, I often chose more quixotic goals to keep myself moving from day to day and year to year. Sometimes, these goals were outside the competitive arena. One summer, Steve Kearney, a close friend of mine from Chesterton, Indiana, and I decided to run the length of the state of Indiana. We convinced eight other runners to join us. When people asked afterward why we wanted to do such a crazy stunt, Steve and I would shrug and say, "It seemed like a neat thing to do."

As I write these words, I have run 111 marathons. Each of those marathons presented its own challenge, the motivation to run each being slightly different from the one before and the one after. About a year before the 100th running of the Boston Marathon, in 1996, I realized that given the number of marathons I previously had run and with a bit of extra effort, I could run my 100th marathon at the 100th Boston. The problem (and challenge) was that I would need to run 10 marathons within the space of a year to achieve that goal.

Run 10 I did, using the 100/100 challenge to motivate my training for more than a year, a very enjoyable year as I ran marathons from Memphis, Tennessee; to Hamilton, Bermuda; to Seaside, Oregon. That 99th marathon in Oregon, 1 month before the 100th Boston, fittingly was called the Trail's End Marathon, although Trail's Pause might have been a more appropriate name in my case, given the dozen more marathons that followed to bring me to my current total of 111.

On two occasions, I have run multiple marathons as a way of marking landmark birthdays. On turning 60, I ran 6 marathons in 6 weeks to celebrate the birthday. I called that my 6/6/60 Challenge. The Twin Cities Marathon mentioned in the opening paragraph of this chapter was the first of the six, and I cruised the distance almost effortlessly, finishing in close to 3 hours and winning my age group and with it $250 in prize money. But several other marathons in that 6/6/60 effort almost finished me rather than my finishing them. The week after Twin Cities, I ran my next marathon in Milwaukee and pulled a muscle 4 miles into the race. My wife, Rose, waiting at the finish line, was ready to send out a search party when finally I came limping across the finish line in a time slower than 5 hours. I did finish all six marathons, but nowhere near as fast as I had planned.

I should have learned my lesson but a decade later decided to replicate that effort and not only run seven marathons in 7 months to celebrate my 70th birthday but also raise $700,000 for seven separate charities. I actually raised $914,000, but that was the easy part, compared with running the marathons. I figured that allowing a month between marathons for 7/7/70 would make it easier than doing them only a week apart. And this proved true, but flying home from my sixth marathon in Honolulu, my wife and I heard someone coughing in the row behind us. After our trip, we both came down with bronchitis. That was less a problem for her, since antibiotics provided their usual miracle cure, but I was scheduled to run my seventh and final marathon within 4 weeks at Walt Disney World. I finished, but only with the help of a friend who paced me and didn't complain when we walked most of the last half dozen miles.

For my 80th birthday, I've figured an easier challenge: eight marathons in the 8 succeeding years. That will take care of 8/8/80, but I haven't yet figured out how to celebrate my 90th birthday.

CHOOSING GOALS

Not everybody who arrives at the starting line of a marathon (hopefully after having followed one of my training programs for the preceding 18 weeks) will have motivated themselves by choosing goals as ludicrous as some of mine. Indeed, a large percentage of people entering at least the most popular marathons are running their first marathons—and it may turn into their only marathon. Forty percent of those who run Chicago each year are first timers. Nevertheless, each one of those nouveau marathoners will have chosen goals as carefully as I have chosen mine.

For most of them, the goal is only to finish the 26 miles 385 yards. And that is how it should be. But those of us who have been running more than a few years often choose different goals. If you follow my advice and run your first marathon in a sensibly slow time aimed mainly at getting yourself to the finish line, you may want to pick bettering that time as a goal for your second or third marathon. Certain numbers contain their own magic; thus, runners attempt to break 6 hours or 5 hours or 4 hours. To be asked your time for the marathon and be able to begin your answer by saying "three" puts you in an almost elite ego-building category, even if your time was only 3:59:59. Respond with a time that begins with "two," and if the person asking a question also is a marathoner, his eyebrows will rise, his jaw will drop. I know because I possess a marathon personal record of 2:21:55, and I see the reaction of people when I tell them my time: "What planet were you born on?"

That may sound fast—and it was in its day—but consider that were I able to re-create that time today, I would finish nearly 3 miles behind today's world elite. That's the men; I

FOR MANY EXPERIENCED RUNNERS, IT'S NOT MERELY THE RACE ITSELF BUT THE EXPERIENCE THAT GOES INTO THE RACE.

would also finish more than a mile behind the fastest women.

But finishing times mean much less to me today than they did decades ago, and it's not entirely because I know my best times are behind me. For me, and for so many other experienced runners, it's not merely the race itself but also the preparation that goes into the race: the steady buildup of miles, the long runs on Sundays, the inevitable taper, the ceremonial aspects of the total experience. Two positive aspects of marathoning are that it provides focus for your training and offers a recognizable goal.

If you love to run, you appreciate the motivation the marathon provides for those long Sunday runs and those fast midweek track workouts. Marathon training focuses the mind, and that may be the best excuse for racing this distance.

I continue to run daily, not to improve my times at the marathon and at other distances but simply because I enjoy running. When possible, I pick scenic courses that provide me with enjoyable sights and sounds. Races are just a by-product.

Alastair Calder of Warren, Michigan, agrees. Calder says he uses entry into a marathon as an incentive to get out and run, increase his mileage, and feel good. "The marathon medal simply signifies the successful completion of training, not just the finishing of a race."

THE MARATHON LIFESTYLE

Another positive by-product of marathons is improved health. Marathon running has the potential to significantly increase your life span and to impact positively the quality of your life. Again, it's not so much the running of the race that affects your health but the lifestyle changes that often accompany the commitment to run a marathon. To become a successful runner/marathoner, you need to: (1) follow a proper diet, (2) eliminate extra body fat, (3) refrain from smoking and avoid heavy drinking, (4) get adequate sleep, and (5) exercise regularly. Epidemiologists such as Ralph E. Paffenbarger, MD, who analyzed the data of Harvard University alumni, have determined that these five lifestyle changes have the potential to add several years to our lives. In fact, Kenneth H. Cooper, MD, the renowned author of *Aerobics*, suggests that researchers at his Cooper Institute in Dallas believe that the proper combination of diet and exercise plus preventative health maintenance can extend life by as much as 6 to 9 years! The marathon lifestyle is definitely a healthy lifestyle.

We have known this at least since the mid-1970s, when the first running boom got under way. One of the first individuals responsible for promoting marathon running as a healthy activity—or at least not a dangerous activity—was Thomas J. Bassler, MD, a pathologist at Centinella Valley Community Hospital in California, and one of the founders of the American Medical Joggers Association. Dr. Bassler proposed the theory that if you could train for and complete a marathon, you would become immune to death by heart attack for at least 6 months. He later extended that immunity to a year—then beyond a year.

Dr. Bassler's marathon immunity theory ignited an instant controversy. Many people, including members of the medical establishment, considered his theory not only unfounded but outrageous. A few considered it dangerous because they thought it would lure ill-prepared people to the starting line.

The criticism centered on Dr. Bassler's lack of evidence. He had not done a controlled study. All he had done was propose a theory and ask medical experts to prove him wrong, and that is not how serious medical research is conducted.

Over a period of years, eminent cardiologists attempted to dispute Dr. Bassler's theory. They would cite evidence of a runner who died of a heart attack, and Dr. Bassler would point out that the runner hadn't run marathons. They would cite a marathoner who had collapsed in the last mile, and Dr. Bassler would note that the runner hadn't finished the race. Dr. Bassler refused to accept anecdotal evidence of coronary deaths, demanding to see x-rays. In several apparent marathon coronary deaths, he identified the culprit as dehydration or a cardiac arrhythmia, rather than the standard heart attack caused by blocked arteries. On several occasions, when seemingly pinned into a corner with his theory disproved, Dr. Bassler would modify the theory just enough to maintain the controversy.

On numerous occasions over the years, I interviewed Dr. Bassler for books and articles and found him almost pixielike. His face was serious, but his eyes twinkled. Although he always professed to be 100 percent committed to his theory of marathon immunity, I was never quite certain whether he was serious or merely putting us on.

But Dr. Bassler certainly succeeded in convincing the general public that running distances of 26 miles and 385 yards was not fraught with danger; that marathoners were not routinely collapsing, clutching their hearts; and that marathon running should not be banned from city streets as a matter of public safety. By digging deep to uncover examples of supposed marathon deaths, each critic of Dr. Bassler was inadvertently proving what I consider to be the doctor's main message: that marathon running is a relatively safe sport and a benign activity as long as you train intelligently, behave rationally, and take proper precautions (such as drinking plenty of liquids on hot and humid days).

I'm not sure if cardiologists ever succeeded in disproving the Bassler theory of marathon immunity. More likely, everybody simply lost interest as marathons became a fixture of contemporary life. Certainly, as the number of people running marathons annually increased from 25,000 in 1976 to 400,000 in 2003, the odds that someone might have a negative medical experience while running also increased. "We're unquestionably more at risk the hour a day that we run," suggests Paul D. Thompson, MD, director of preventive cardiology at Hartford Hospital in Connecticut, "but the other 23 hours in the day, we are much less at risk. In balance, you're much safer exercising than not exercising."

As we moved into the new millennium, enough marathons had been run and enough runners had survived marathons that an occasional cardiac death in a race was considered no more or less alarming than someone's dying while attending a symphony concert

RISKY RUNNERS?

How risky is running? Paul D. Thompson, MD, director of preventive cardiology at Hartford Hospital in Connecticut and a 2:28:15 marathoner, concedes that runners incur some risk. While delivering a lecture titled "Historical Concepts of the Athlete's Heart" at the annual meeting of the American College of Sports Medicine, Dr. Thompson cited several seminal studies quantifying the risks of exercise, beginning with one of his own that suggested sudden cardiac death was seven times more likely during jogging than at rest. He estimated the incidence as 1 death annually for every 15,240 healthy joggers.

Another study, published in the *New England Journal of Medicine*, offered similar statistics: 1 cardiac arrest for every 18,000 previously healthy men. A national fitness chain, however, claimed 1 death per 82,000 members or per 2.6 million workouts. And at Dr. Kenneth H. Cooper's Aerobics Center in Dallas, which has 3,500 members, there have been only 5 cardiac events with 2 deaths in 34 years of operation.

"There is cardiac risk from exercise," concedes Dr. Thompson, "but this risk is small and, at least in adults, most common among those who exercise least."

What safety precautions should you take before becoming a runner or signing up for your first marathon? If you are older than 35, if you are overweight, if you smoke or once smoked, if you have high blood pressure or high cholesterol, if you follow a fast-food diet, if you have a family history of heart attacks, if you don't already exercise, your degree of risk is greater than someone without those "ifs." Check with your family physician before starting to run, and once out the door, follow a sensible training program, such as those in this book.

(which I once saw occur). Dr. Bassler faded into the backwaters of marathon celebrity, but his immunity theory certainly should be credited for helping create the marathon mystique.

BIGGER AND BETTER

There definitely is a mystique about running a marathon—no doubt about it. You can run 5-K races until your dresser drawers overflow with T-shirts, but it's not quite the same as going to the starting line of a marathon. Marathons, on average, seem to be bigger events than 5-K or 10-K races, even when those shorter-distance events attract large fields.

> YOU CAN RUN 5-K RACES UNTIL YOUR DRESSER DRAWERS OVERFLOW WITH T-SHIRTS, BUT IT'S NOT QUITE THE SAME AS GOING TO THE STARTING LINE OF A MARATHON.

Arrive several days in advance of a marathon and you know you're at a Big Event, regardless of how many people are entered. Maybe the excitement is partly anticipation among those who have entered. Each runner has committed so many miles in training for this one event that the race takes on a level of importance above and beyond the ordinary, regardless of the size of the field. One year I visited Toledo, Ohio, to lecture the night before the Glass City Marathon, which attracted about 500 runners. Compared with marathons in New York or Chicago or London or Berlin, with their fields of 30,000 runners, that's pretty small potatoes. Yet despite Glass City's relatively small field, the same pre-marathon excitement was present. I could feel it around me as I spoke. People often talk about there being a "glow" around pregnant women. That's certainly true, but there's a similar glow around expectant marathoners. If not 9 months, many of them have devoted 18 weeks of preparation for their big event. All the people in my audience at Toledo had worked hard to get ready for the race. Looking at their faces, I envied them.

After my talk, I climbed into my car and drove home to Long Beach, Indiana. The trip took me 3 or 4 hours and wasn't much fun. But the marathon my audience would run the next morning—which would also take 3 or 4 hours or more—would be fun. Meanwhile, I had to wait 8 more weeks before I would run the marathon I was training for.

What is it about the marathon? Is it the race's history? Its traditions? The many fine runners who have run it? The marathon is all of that, but there's also a mystique about the distance itself. Would the race have the same appeal if it were a more logical 25 miles? Or 40 kilometers?

FOOTSTEPS OF PHEIDIPPIDES

The establishment of the marathon at the unquestionably odd distance of 26 miles and 385 yards (or 42.2 kilometers) certainly adds to the mystique. It's a familiar joke among many marathoners that a frequent question they often get from their nonrunning friends is "How far is this marathon?" The fact is that, technically speaking, all marathons are precisely 26 miles 385 yards. Anything longer and the race is considered an ultramarathon. Anything less and either the course was mismeasured or it's something else. The first event to be called a marathon was held in 1896 at the first modern Olympic Games in Athens, Greece. This long-distance footrace was staged at the end of those games to re-create and commemorate the legendary run of Pheidippides in 490 BC.

In that year, the Persians invaded Greece, landing near the plains of Marathon on Greece's eastern coast. According to the legend, an Athenian general dispatched Pheidippides, a hemerodromo, or runner-messenger, to Sparta (150 miles away) to seek help. It reportedly took Pheidippides 2 days to reach Sparta. The Spartans never did arrive in time to help, but the Athenians eventually overwhelmed their enemy, killing 6,400 Persian troops while losing only

192 of their own men. Or so it was recorded by Greek historians of the time.

Some historians dispute those numbers, suspecting they are the typically exaggerated claims of the victors. Then there is the question of whether the messenger dispatched to Athens with news of the victory was the same Pheidippides who ran to and from Sparta.

A hemerodromo by that or another name apparently did run a route that took him south along the coast and up and across a series of coastal foothills before descending into Athens, a distance of about 25 miles from the plains of Marathon. According to legend, Pheidippides announced, "Rejoice. We conquer!" as he arrived in Athens—then fell dead.

Ah, legends. Latter-day historians doubt the total accuracy of the legend. That includes the late Jim Fixx, who traced Pheidippides' journey for a *Sports Illustrated* article that became part of *Jim Fixx's Second Book of Running*. If there was a hemerodromo, claimed Fixx, he may not have been the same one known to have relayed the request for troops to Sparta. There may or may not have been a hemerodromo by the name of Pheidippides who died following a postbattle run to Athens. Fixx and others noted that Herodotus, who first described the Battle of Marathon, failed to mention a hemerodromo; the story appeared 4 centuries later, when the history of the battle was retold by Plutarch.

Nevertheless, the legend took on the imprint of historical fact and was certainly no less worthy of respect than legends involving mythical Greek gods such as Hermes or Aphrodite. It seemed perfectly suitable at the 1896 Olympic Games to run a race in Pheidippides' honor from the plains of Marathon to the Olympic stadium in downtown Athens. It was particularly fitting that a Greek shepherd named Spiridon Loues won that event, the only gold medal in track and field won by the Greeks on their home turf. Among the American clubs represented at those first Games was the Boston Athletic

Association (BAA), whose team manager was John Graham. So impressed was Graham with this race that he decided to sponsor a similar event in his hometown the following year. Races of approximately 25 miles (40 kilometers) had been held before in Europe, including one held in France before the Olympics. But nobody had attached the name marathon to these races, and there was not yet a marathon mystique.

Fifteen runners lined up at the start of the first Boston Athletic Association Marathon in 1897 to race from a side road in suburban Ashland into downtown Boston, and a new legend was born. (A previous American marathon was run in the fall of 1896 from Stamford, Connecticut, to Columbus Circle, near the finish line of the current New York City Marathon, but it failed to survive.) The Boston Marathon remains the oldest continuously held marathon. It continues to retain its status and prestige, and it attracted a record 35,868 finishers in 1996, its 100th running.

DETERMINING THE DISTANCE

For a dozen years, the official marathon distance was approximately 25 miles. That was the distance run in the 1900 Olympic Games in Paris and the 1904 Games in St. Louis, as well as in the Boston Marathon for its first 28 years. Then in 1908, in London, the British designed a marathon course that started at Windsor Castle and finished at the Olympic stadium. This was long before course certification experts measured race distances to an accuracy of plus or minus a few feet. Nobody challenged the British course design, which reportedly was laid out so that the royal family could see the start of the race. The distance from start to finish for that marathon was precisely 26 miles and 385 yards. For whatever reason, that distance eventually became the standard for future marathons. The Boston Athletic Association waited until 1924 to lengthen its course, moving the starting line from Ashland to the nearby town of Hopkinton, where it is today.

Frank Shorter tells the story of running the marathon trials for the 1971 Pan American Games. At 21 miles, he was lockstep with Kenny Moore, a 1968 Olympian. "Why couldn't Pheidippides have died here?" Shorter groaned to Moore. In that case, it was Shorter who "died" and Moore who went on to win the race. Shorter one-upped Moore the following year at the Olympic Games in Munich, Germany, winning the gold medal while Moore placed fourth and Jack Bachelor placed ninth. That was the best recent showing by American marathoners in the Olympics until Meb Keflezighi and Deena Drossin won silver and bronze medals in Athens in 2004.

The running event that is so popular today might not have been the same if the plains of Marathon had been closer to Athens. Exercise physiologists tell us that it is only after about 2 hours of running—or about 20 miles for an accomplished runner—that the body begins to fully deplete its stores of glycogen, the energy source that fuels the muscles. Once glycogen is depleted, the body must rely more on fat, a less efficient fuel source. This is one of the reasons runners hit the wall at 20 miles, and successfully getting past that obstacle is what makes a marathon such a special event.

Twenty miles is the longest distance that I ask people using my training programs to run in practice for the marathon. Particularly for those training for their first marathons, I want them to touch the edge of the wall, not collide with it. You significantly increase your risk of injury and overtraining, both of which may negatively impact your race day performance, if you run much farther in practice. Nevertheless, many of us who consider ourselves accomplished runners run 20-milers as part of our marathon buildup without excessive pain and with little fanfare. It is only when we stretch beyond that point that people sit up and take notice. Would a million people line the roads along the Boston and New York City marathon routes if the distance were only 20 miles and if there were no wall to conquer? No, they want to see us tempt the fate of Pheidippides. They come to see us suffer, although inevitably both spectator and runner

GLYCOGEN AND THE WALL

A term frequently used by marathoners is "hitting the wall." This usually occurs around 20 miles, about the time the body runs out of energy. Often this happens so suddenly that runners feel as though they crashed into a brick wall. Their pace slows. Their breath becomes labored. They struggle to finish. It can be said that the first half of the marathon is 20 miles long; the second half, 6 more.

Physiologically, runners hit the wall when they deplete their muscles of glycogen. Glycogen is the sugarlike substance that serves as the main fuel for our muscles when we exercise. It is stored in the liver and in the muscles. When you run long distances, you deplete your glycogen stores and eventually run out of energy. With glycogen gone, the body begins burning fat, a much less efficient fuel source.

But not all runners hit the wall. With proper training, you can teach your body to burn fat more efficiently. Refueling on the run with sports drinks and gels adds to your glycogen supply. Proper pacing also will allow you to hurdle the feared wall and achieve a peak performance.

leave fulfilled only if we demonstrate through our successful crashing through the wall and crossing of the finish line that we are victorious.

CHANGING YOUR LIFE

For many runners, completing one marathon is enough. They cross the line and, overwhelmed with the experience, think, "Never again!" Only 13 miles into the Chicago Marathon and struggling, Nicole Kunz of McHenry, Illinois, swore to herself that she never—absolutely never—would run another marathon. Within 24 hours after finishing, however, Kunz already had begun to consider training for the Flying Pig Marathon in Cincinnati the following spring.

Marathoners may change their minds the next day, the next week, the next month, or sometimes as soon as they get to the end of the finishing chute, but nobody can deny that a marathon—particularly a first marathon—is a very special event. A very, very special event. Finishing a marathon changes your life forever. Professional photographers who take pictures of runners crossing the finish line find marathoners make much better customers than those finishing shorter-distance events. "Runners tend to buy many more photos of themselves from events that they regard as important milestones in their running careers," states Gerald Swanson, vice president for business development at MarathonFoto, the leading race photography organization. "Marathon photos outsell shorter-event photos by at least two to three times. People also buy multiple photos of themselves at the same marathon, compared to only a single photo at a shorter race."

COMPLETING A MARATHON IS LIKE TACKING A PHD AT THE END OF YOUR NAME, GETTING MARRIED, HAVING A BABY. YOU'RE SPECIAL.

Why? It's the same reason that people order more pictures at weddings. Completing a marathon is like tacking a PhD at the end of your name, getting married, having a baby. You're special, and whether anyone else knows it or not, you certainly do. Your life will never again be quite the same, and regardless of what the future brings, you can look back and say, "I finished a marathon." Regardless of the large number of people running marathons today, you're still part of an elite crowd.

Some runners finish their first marathon, place their medal in a drawer, hang their photo on the wall of their office cubicle, and go on to different challenges. For many, however, that first marathon is merely the beginning of a lifetime journey. Running marathons becomes a continuing challenge of numbers: personal records (or PRs), which exist to be bettered at each race. Even when aging brings the inevitable decline in performance, new challenges arise as the lifetime marathoner moves from one 5-year bracket to another. In the area of performance, success breeds success.

It is also possible to run marathons recreationally, not caring about time or finishing position but participating merely for the joy of attending a Great Event with all its accompanying pleasures. I have run many marathons in this manner, running within myself and finishing far back from where I might have had I pushed the pace harder. One year at the Honolulu Marathon, I started in the back row and made a game out of passing as many people as possible—but doing it at a pace barely faster than theirs so as not to call attention to my speed. I didn't want it to seem that I was trying to show them up. Beginning with the 1995 St. George (Utah) Marathon and prompted by an article I wrote ranking the marathon courses most likely to yield fast times so people could qualify for the 100th Boston Marathon, *Runner's World* began to organize pacing teams led by editors running slower than usual while shepherding others. I've led pacing teams on several occasions. It's fun, and it's rewarding to help others meet their goals. At Chicago, we now have nearly 100 pace team leaders, shepherding runners to finishing times from 2:50 through 6:00. Many other marathons offer the same.

I've also run marathons in which I stopped at planned dropout points, using the race as a workout to prepare for later marathons. At the World Masters Championships in Rome in 1985, I ran the marathon at the end of a week's track competition mainly so I could enjoy the sights and sounds of the Eternal City. In the last miles of the race, as I entered a piazza with a panoramic view of St. Peter's Cathedral across the Tiber River, I paused for several minutes to absorb that view, and only then continued toward the finish line in a stadium used for the 1960 Olympic Games. How fast I ran and how well I placed were the last things on my mind. Crossing the finish line, more refreshed than fatigued, I was approached by an Australian runner, who announced, "This is the first time I ever beat you."

I felt obliged to correct him: "You didn't beat me. You merely finished in front of me."

The Australian stammered an apology, but he had missed what I believe to be the point of the marathon. Or at least he was not aware of the way I had chosen to run the marathon that particular day. In a marathon, except at the elite level, you don't beat others, as you might in a mile or a 100-meter dash. Instead, you achieve a personal victory. If others finish in front of or behind you, it is only that their personal victories are more or less than yours. A person finishing behind you with less talent, or of a different age or sex, or various other limiting factors, may have achieved a far greater victory. And if the person's main goal in running the marathon was to raise money for charity, the amount of money collected may be a more important barometer of success than finishing time. As for who the "best" runner in any race might be, at the 1992 Boston Marathon, John A. Kelley, age 84, finished in a time of 5:58:32. The officials stopped timing at 5 hours, at which point 8,120 runners had crossed the line (not counting those running unofficially without numbers). It was the 61st and final time "Old John," a two-time winner of the race, would run Boston. He died in the fall of 2004 at the age of 97. None of the thousands finishing in front of Kelley could be said to have beaten him. He was a legend—like Pheidippides.

ONE BEAUTY OF THE MARATHON IS THAT THERE ARE MANY MORE WINNERS THAN THOSE WHO FINISH FIRST OVERALL OR IN THEIR AGE GROUPS.

One beauty of the marathon is that there are many more winners than those who finish first overall or in their age groups. "Everyone's a winner" is a dreadful cliché, but it happens to be true when the race involved is 26 miles and 385 yards long.

A LIFETIME OF MARATHONS

Reporters sometimes ask how many marathons I have run. For many years, I would respond, "About 100."

This amazed them: "You've run 100 marathons?"

I had to correct them because I didn't want to read in the newspaper the next morning that I had just run marathon number 101. "No," I would say. "I don't know how many marathons I've run. But it must be about 100."

Then in the spring of 1995, a year before the 100th Boston Marathon, I got curious about the exact number. (I now keep a daily training diary, but there were periods of my career when I did not.) Using the library at the Boston Athletic Association, I searched through old running magazines and newsletters for old marathon results. I was able to identify several races that I had little memory of running, including one in which I had finished first! But the actual total number of marathons I had run was fewer than what I had been telling reporters for years: It was only 90.

That was the bad news, but the good news was that with a little effort over the next 12 months, I would be able to run my 100th marathon at the 100th Boston. Thus, running a marathon a month became my goal for a year.

The 100th running of the Boston Marathon was one of the most difficult marathons of my career. That event coincided with publication of *Boston: A Century of Running*, my coffee-table book commemorating the 100 years of the race. I spent most of the week before the race doing media interviews and then 3 days at the Expo signing copies of the book and talking to runners—that plus a series of parties, including a Breakfast of Champions featuring most of those still living who had won the race. That included Canadian Johnny Miles, winner in 1925. It was a heady time, but by race day I was physically exhausted.

Rose and I had rented a house on Hopkinton Green within sight of the starting line. Rather than line up with the masses that morning, I watched the start from the house's front yard, then went in to view the race on TV. The lead runners had passed 3 miles before Rose suggested, "Don't you think it's time to go run?"

I joined the runners in the back of the pack. The atmosphere seemed electric, every runner realizing that they were part of a true, historic occasion. But by 8 miles, my battery was fully discharged. I hit the wall well before there should have been any wall to hit. The Newton hills were still another 8 miles down course, but my previously steady stride had been reduced to a stumbling shuffle. And although it had seemed relatively warm in Hopkinton, with a tailwind pushing the runners, as we got closer to the ocean, the wind switched, becoming a chilling headwind. Near the halfway point, I picked up a discarded long-sleeved shirt from the gutter. It was soaked with sweat, but it helped keep me warm to near the top of Heartbreak Hill, where I spotted a Mylar space blanket, also discarded. I wrapped it around myself as one more defense against the cold wind off the ocean.

In the last mile, I encountered Bill Wenmark, a coach from the Twin Cities, running with one of the runners he trained, Harvey Mackay, author of the best-selling book *Swim with the Sharks without Being Eaten Alive*. I knew Harvey, having written a profile article on him for *Runner's World*. Bill had provided valuable advice when I was writing the first edition of this book. Talk about having different priorities than finishing time. Bill ran with a belt to which were attached four silver helium balloons that hovered high over his head. The purpose of the balloons was so that runners he coached could spot him during the race. I figured that the three of us could finish together, but Bill and Harvey stopped just before the line to take pictures of each other. I continued running and finished the 100th Boston in an unmemorable 6 hours, including the half-hour or so it had taken me to cross the starting line after the gun sounded.

Did Moses Tannui and Uta Pippig, who crossed the line nearly 4 hours earlier, beat me? I don't think so. It was just one more example that all of us operate in our own spheres and define our own levels of victory.

One hundred being a round number, I probably should have called it a career, but I decided to lead pacing teams at the Chicago Marathon the next several years, then did the same at Honolulu. After running seven marathons in 7 months to celebrate my 70th birthday, I found myself with 111 marathons on my résumé: another number that sounded good when people asked how many I had run, a frequent question thrown at me, especially by first-timers.

At an appearance at a running store in Kalamazoo, Michigan, one young woman who asked that question seemed amazed. "Eleven marathons?" she asked. "Wow, that's a lot."

"No, not 11," I corrected her. "One hundred eleven marathons."

That truly dumbfounded the woman, but I am far from being the record holder when it comes to the number of marathons run. Sy Mah, a Toledo, Ohio, runner who often ran two and sometimes three marathons on a weekend, finished 524 races that were longer than 26 miles before his death from cancer at age 62 in 1988. Continually adding to the total was the focal point of Mah's running, so it was important that he kept precise records for each of his races. He was another legend. Mah usually finished in the high 3-hour range. I once told Sy that if he focused his attention for 6 months on a single race—training specifically for it, resisting the temptation to run other marathons so that he could taper and peak—he could probably improve his time by ½ hour, and maybe even break 3 hours, putting him near the top for his age group. Smiling, Sy conceded my point, but we both knew that was not what he was about. His joy was running as many marathons as possible and adding to his impressive string of numbers, which earned him an enviable spot in *The Guinness Book of World Records*. (In 1994, Norm Frank of Rochester, New York, broke Mah's record. Frank, who runs approximately 40 marathons a year, had pushed his record number to a devilishly difficult 870 by the end of 2004 and hoped to reach 1,000 within the next 3 years, when he would be age 76.)

In comparison, my own multiple marathon achievements

THE MARATHON NEVER CEASES TO BE A RACE OF JOY, A RACE OF WONDER.

were trivial, almost inconsequential. My lifetime total of 111, or whatever the number as you read this book, is merely a blip on the chart compared with the hundreds of marathons finished by Mah and Frank.

The marathon never ceases to be a race of joy, a race of wonder. Even when disaster strikes, when bad weather overwhelms you, when an intemperate pace results in a staggering finish, when nerves and anxiety stand in the way of giving your maximum effort, when your number one rival soundly thrashes you, when 18 weeks of training appear to have gone down the drain with little more than an ugly slurping sound, there remains something memorable about each marathon run.

I would have a hard time explaining that to the woman standing beside the course at the Twin Cities Marathon, who considered it odd that we had actually paid to "abuse" our bodies. But anyone who has crossed the finish line of a 26-mile, 385-yard race would understand. Sy Mah certainly knew. It's all part of the mystique of the marathon.

CHAPTER 2
LEARNING TO LOVE RUNNING

THE JOURNEY IS PART OF THE REWARD

How hard is it to train for a marathon? How difficult is it to push yourself out the door almost daily and run workouts up to 20 miles in length? Couldn't somebody invent a pill that would produce instant fitness and allow us to complete a race of 26 miles 385 yards without all that training, which must be both grueling and b-o-r-i-n-g, according to those who never have tried it?

Surprise! Most runners enjoy the training as much as, or more than, the marathon itself. In a poll I took among participants in my Inter*Active* Training Forums, I discovered that more than three out of every four respondents liked training as much as or more than the marathon. The percentage of those who liked training best was 28.6 percent, versus 22.4 percent who enjoyed the marathon most. The largest number (50 percent) claimed to like both equally. I included a fourth and largely negative option in my survey: "I enjoy neither and am just doing it because . . ." Not a single person chose that response!

So if you're starting one of my 18-week training programs and fear that running all that mileage may become a grind—particularly if your longest run up to now has been 2 or 3 miles—relax and enjoy. It might not seem so at the time, but looking back on your training after completing your first marathon, you might surprise yourself at how much fun it was, particularly if you trained with a like-minded group of individuals. Marathon running can be fun.

Typical of those responding to my survey was Lori Hauswirth, a clerk/treasurer from Merrill, Wisconsin. "The marathon is the reward, and the training is actually the harder of the two," claims Hauswirth. "But they are both equally enjoyable. Training does absorb a lot of time, but few everyday people can say they've ever been as dedicated to anything as those of us who train 18 weeks for a marathon. When spring comes after a fall marathon and a lazy winter, I find I missed the long runs in a strange sort of way."

Christine Currie, a school psychologist from Alexandria, Virginia, concurs. "Although I thoroughly enjoyed my first

EVERY WEEK WAS A HIGHLIGHT, WITH A NEW DISTANCE RECORD SET.

marathon, the training leading up to it was the most empowering thing I had ever done, at least physically," Currie says. "Every week was a highlight, with a new distance record set. I had that same excitement at mile 20 of the marathon, when I knew I was really going to finish it. But it was the journey that transformed me. The marathon was the reward."

John Grasser, a public affairs director from Chevy Chase, Maryland, says, "Immediately after my first marathon, I reflected on the previous 18 weeks and realized that while the race itself was the reward, it was really all that training over the 4½ months that made it fun and all worth it. I realized how much I looked forward to those long Sunday runs. And all that training put me in the best shape of my life. I was able to say I had accomplished something not many others had, having run 26.2 miles.

Paula McKinney of Georgia considers herself a stronger individual because of the challenges she faced during a 2-year buildup to her first marathon. "Whether it was adapting to rough weather conditions, overcoming mental obstacles, in either my running or personal life, the downtime caused by injuries, I discovered a new strength. Most of all, I never quit. Quitting would have been the easy route."

McKinney continues: "As for the marathon experience itself, the reward of crossing a finish line and having a volunteer remove my chip and hang a medal around my neck left me in awe of human fortitude and gave me an awareness that I could push past the merely the comfortable and enjoy even the excruciating moments. It allowed me to become the best Paula I could be—although I'm still working on it."

Mark Felipe, a defense analyst from Arlington, Virginia, found he enjoyed training on several levels: "Just the joy of lacing 'em up and going out speaks for itself. I like the peace of mind I get on long runs. I like the feeling of accomplishment after a tough run, and I like how my pants begin to fit better after about 6 weeks into a training cycle. But there's also a lot to be said for that rush you get from the crowd cheering you on while crossing the finish line. You can't separate the training from the marathon. They're part of the same parcel."

"The marathon is the destination," adds Martin Conlon, a small-business man from Wheeling, Illinois, "but getting there is what it's all about."

A GOAL AND FOCUS

Jim Fredericks, an emergency room nurse from South Milwaukee, has run three marathons, thus has experienced often the cycle of train, race, and relax. Fredericks looks forward to the challenge of each new week as the long runs keep getting longer and longer—and longer. "I count the runs and count the days," he says. "I am very aware of the surroundings on my running trail and watch as the environment goes from late spring through the summer and into early autumn. Working toward achieving a personal goal is fun and rewarding. The race itself is such a great experience. The atmosphere in the host city can be invigorating. I think both training and the race itself are equally rewarding. What I really notice is the sort of depression and feeling of emptiness I get a few days after the race. Working so hard for so long—and then it is all over—can be such a letdown. I guess that is one of the reasons I keep doing it. I start to plan my next race and training cycle almost as soon as I am finished with the last one."

"The marathon provides a goal, an incentive, and a focus," says Autumn Evans, a technical writer from Melbourne Beach, Florida. "Without the marathon, there is less reason to get out and train hard. Yes, one should exercise for one's health, but

THE MARATHON PROVIDES A GOAL, AN INCENTIVE, AND A FOCUS.

good health often is taken for granted; thus, we don't always do what we know we should.

"Completing a marathon, however, provides material rewards: a shirt, a medal, a certificate, and one's name in lights—or at least in the results booklet. In addition to the tangible benefits, the race itself provides entertainment, starting with the expo and ending with the finish line festivities. There's a feeling of camaraderie in the back-of-the-pack marathon that isn't present in many sports. Runners take care of each other, encourage each other, push each other. It's competition, but competition with oneself. Imaginative spectators post signs that bring smiles to the faces of weary runners. Venturesome athletes run in hilarious costumes. And before and during and after the event, race shirts or limping gaits or overheard discussions cause total strangers to strike up conversations."

Melissa Vetricek, a business analyst from Tampa, admits to having completed 15 marathons, yet has only begun to understand the event. "I'm still learning," she confesses, "but I consider the marathon itself more enjoyable than the training. Some training runs are fun, but other training runs—let's be honest—are not fun. You struggle through them because you see the carrot dangling before your eyes. The marathon is something I look forward to with eager anticipation and with each training run. It's hard not to when each run has a specific distance and effort level all with the purpose of preparing me to cover 26.2 miles as quickly as I can on race day. I guess I'm just such a goal-oriented person that only after I reach the goal am I able to relax and enjoy what I accomplished. Then it's time to set a new goal all over again!"

Cindy Southgate, a dressmaker from Kanata, Ontario, uses visual goals to motivate herself as she trains. "I love watching the days go by," says Southgate. "I have my schedule printed out and highlight each workout as it is completed. There's a great

> THERE'S A GREAT SENSE OF ACCOMPLISHMENT, SEEING THE WEEKS GO BY.

sense of accomplishment, seeing the weeks go by, as well as watching my progress."

The race remains central to the motivation of Cathy Wells, a medical student in Providence, Rhode Island, but she still feels there is nothing better than the training: "The confidence that comes after a great training run—where you feel invincible—is intoxicating. It makes you think that magic can happen in the marathon. And when you have a bad workout, it's such a relief to think 'at least this wasn't race day.' After a bad workout, there's always hope that the next one will be better. Having an off day at the marathon itself is so much more disappointing.

"The race is the 'proof' of the work you do in training, so I guess without the race, the training might be less fun and less meaningful. But ultimately, the training is why I run marathons."

Starrla Johnson, an animal technician from Somerville, Massachusetts, feels the opposite. To Johnson, the marathon is the end. "I wear myself out during training," she says, "and beat my body up week after week, and then I sort of let it heal itself every third week when I do step-back runs. Don't get me wrong. I love nailing a pace run and having a great 17-miler, but nothing is as exciting as race day. Lining up with thousands of other people with the only destination a painted line 26.2 miles down the road or trail, the surge of the crowd as the marathon starts, the chatter during the early miles, slippery water and Gatorade cups, the heavenly volunteers, the amazing people who cheer us along, the first step over 20 miles and knowing it all truly does start at that mile marker. Patting someone on the back if they're having a hard time, losing my mind between miles 22 and 23, the last water stop, and knowing the next time I walk I will have finished another marathon.

"All of these things make me love marathon day, but my favorite moment is searching for my parents at the finish line and finding them in the crowd."

Dave Dwyer, a clinical nurse manager from Madison, Wisconsin, states: "It is hard to beat the excitement, the actual physical thrill, and relief and joy and pride, when you see the finish line in your first marathon and can say, 'I'm a marathoner.' It is hard to beat the anticipation of the night before, the jumble of pleasure the morning of the event, and the thrill that rolls down your spine when you hear the starting gun. People haven't even begun to move forward, and already they're crying.

"The run itself kind of melts along with the other training runs, which have their moments, too. It is a journey, a long distance of revelation of self, of accomplishment and of failure, of goals met and those still ahead. After all of that, the medal is only icing on the cake. It is the inner warmth of the accomplishment that remains with you, medal or not."

CHAPTER 3
YOUR VERY FIRST STEPS

BEFORE RUNNING A MARATHON,
FIRST LEARN HOW TO RUN

What is the minimal level of fitness needed for someone to begin training for a marathon? I once thought I knew the answer to that question, although I'm less sure now. On my Web site, in the introduction to the 18-week training program for novice runners, I posted the following guidelines.

> People differ greatly in ability, but ideally before starting a marathon program, you should have been running about a year. You should be able to run distances between 3 and 6 miles. You should be training 3–5 days a week, averaging 15–25 miles a week. You should have run an occasional 5-K or 10-K race. It is possible to run a marathon with less of a training base (particularly if you come from another sport), but the higher your fitness level, the easier this 18-week program will be.

I still believe in those guidelines—particularly the final comment, that the higher your fitness level at the start of marathon training, the easier it will be to continue and complete that training—but I have come to modify my opinion of who should and shouldn't start training for a marathon. That's because I've seen too many people with a lesser training base suddenly decide, almost on a whim, to run a marathon, and they've succeeded! Whether their decision was wise or not, 18 weeks (or less) later, they cruised through 26 miles 385 yards with smiles on their faces.

Not everyone should approach a marathon without having run before, but if you're young and highly motivated (and maybe just a little foolish) or decide you want to complete a marathon to raise money for a charity, I'm not going to stand in your way. In a survey of people who participated in my Inter*Active* Forums, nearly half said that they had been running at least a year before they'd run their first marathons. But a quarter of those responding had started to run only 3 months before starting my 18-week program. Many others had begun to run only at the start of the program. Some started late and ran less. One individual queried our bulletin board 3 weeks before the marathon, wondering if it was too late to start. Everybody told him to wait until next year. We never did find out whether he heeded our advice or, if not, how he'd fared in the marathon with so little preparation.

The Web site guidelines were not designed to discourage people. I was just being realistic about what it takes to finish a marathon comfortably. Indeed, some people responding to my survey admitted being encouraged by them. Bill Rieske, a software engineer from Orem, Utah, felt that way. He wrote: "I was thinking a marathon was out of reach until I read your guidelines. The part that made me attempt one was 'It is possible to run a marathon with less of a training base.' I had run a 5-K and 10-K but wasn't averaging anything near 15–25 miles a week. Everything else I had read warned: 'Don't do a marathon until you've been running a year.' I trained as best as I could and slowly gained confidence that I could finish. I did that, but realized how much easier it would have been with a better training base. I kept running before my second marathon and finished feeling more comfortably." Rieske ran his first marathon in 4:15, his second in 3:35 on the same course.

Kousik Krishnan, MD, a cardiologist from Glenview, Illinois, had

TRAINING BASE

How much training did you do before your first marathon? This was the question I asked of runners who regularly visited my online Inter-*Active* training forums. Most of those answering were experienced marathoners with several 26-milers under their belts. But all had run a first marathon at one time or another, most of them using my 18-week program for novice runners. Here's how much they trained before marathon number one.

Training before marathon	Percentage
Less than 18 weeks	9.8%
Exactly 18 weeks	8.2%
3 months before 18-week program	26.2%
6 months before 18-week program	4.9%
12 months before 18-week program	3.3%
More than 1 year running	47.5%

According to this survey, how much running should people have done before starting a marathon training program? Apart from individuals whose training base extends more than a year, starting to run at least 3 months before embarking on a marathon training program seems about right. That allows you to test your legs, lose some weight, and determine whether or not you can follow a program that involves, in addition to weekend long runs, daily workouts 3 to 5 miles long.

run less than a year before doing his first marathon, but he felt he had a good fitness level. "I worked out three or four times a week with weights and biking. That made the transition easier." Krishnan finished his first marathon in 3:58.

Ed Carroll, a small-business owner from Tolland, Massachusetts, decided only 14 weeks before his first marathon to start training. "I felt I was well enough trained, but I blew it by going out way too fast." Carroll went through the first half in 2:05 but finished in 5:14.

"I had run on and off before training for a marathon," says Liz Reichman, a homemaker from Columbus, Ohio. "I was generally active: Spinning, stairclimbing, weight lifting, even aerobics, but not running. I approached the training knowing I was in great shape, but not great running shape." Reichman ran 4:14 in her first marathon.

Cathy Wells, a medical student from Providence, Rhode Island, had run 5 years before her first marathon but concedes she knew nothing about "training" before committing to a marathon. Wells recalls: "At the time, 9 miles was an intimidating distance, and I couldn't even conceive of running 26. A friend convinced me to train for the Philadelphia Marathon, and I haven't been the same since." Wells ran 3:46 in her first marathon and has done three more marathons since, with a PR of 3:16. "Running definitely has transformed my life," she says.

LEARNING TO RUN

In a related survey, I asked how many people had run the marathon as their first race of any distance. Based on conversations with many new runners, I expected that a large percentage would tell me that the marathon indeed was their first running race. I was surprised, then, to learn that 91 percent had at least run a 5-K or 10-K before stepping to the starting line of their first marathons. Admittedly, many had run that first race after beginning to train for a marathon to help in their preparations. This is something I encourage because at least you get the feel for the racing experience. You learn where to pin your number. (On the front, please.) You learn how to use an aid station. (Walking to drink works best.)

Judging from both surveys, I can see that the individual who never has taken a running step before committing to a first marathon may not exist. Even though individuals may not consider themselves "runners," they often have participated in other activities that provided at least some base of fitness before they began.

Running also is a basic activity, instinctive to our being. People need not be taught how to run. Children learn to run almost as soon as they learn to walk. Visit any elementary school playground, and you'll see kids sprinting all over the place. All children are born sprinters.

Children modify their behavior as they get older. Running starts to become a discipline rather than a natural form of exercise. An athlete who goes out for any sport in high school—football, basketball, tennis, or whatever—runs as part of the conditioning for that sport. High schoolers run either because their coach tells them to or because they know that getting in shape will help them make the team. Usually, young athletes run middle distance: a few laps on a track, then off to the main activity. It is only as adults that people forget to run and sometimes have to be retaught.

Let's talk about being a beginning runner. If you're an experienced runner who trains regularly and competes in 5-K races, you may be tempted to skip this chapter. With one or two exceptions, it probably won't teach you anything you don't already know. But hold on: In training runners for the LaSalle Banks Chicago Marathon, I often find I learn as much from novices as they learn from me. I enjoy talking to beginners and revisiting paths that I once may have trodden. Maybe you'd like to look over my shoulder as I talk to beginning runners and get them started on their first journeys.

Before you can hope to run long distances, you must start by running short distances—and running slowly. Some beginners (particularly if they're overweight) need to walk first, beginning with half an hour, 3 or 4 days a week. Then they start to jog a short distance until they get slightly out of breath, walk to recover, jog some more.

Jog, walk. Jog, walk. Jog, walk. After a while, they will be able to run a mile without stopping.

Before we move forward, there are some important kernels of information hidden in what I have just said. Even experienced runners can learn from it.

The pattern is this: Jog, walk. Jog, walk. Jog, walk. Expressed another way: Hard, easy. Hard, easy. Hard, easy. The most effective training programs—even at the basic level—mix bursts of difficult training with rest. Train, rest. Train, rest. Train, rest.

Rest. That may be the single most important word you will read in this book. (You'll encounter it again and again.) In a questionnaire I sent to coaches to gather information for the first edition

> *REST.* THAT MAY BE THE SINGLE MOST IMPORTANT WORD YOU WILL READ IN THIS BOOK.

of this book, one of the questions was "How important is rest in the training equation?"

The very first coach to return a completed questionnaire was Paul Goss of Foster City, California. His response was simple and direct: "More important than most runners know."

None of the other coaches who eventually responded improved on what Goss had to say.

STOP RESTING

With beginners the problem is not to get them to rest but to get them to stop resting. They have to get off the couch and away from the TV. They need to learn to become participants in sport, rather than spectators of sport. To those of us who accept running as a natural activity, that's not as easy as it might seem.

Beginners need motivation to begin—and to keep at it once they have begun. "The key factor in any beginner's training program is motivation," suggests Jack Daniels, PhD, an exercise physiologist and a coach at the State University of New York at Cortland. "If you're genetically gifted but not interested in training, you'll never develop."

Barring some medical problem, most people can run, but they aren't motivated to do so. Even if they want to start running, it takes courage to put on running shoes and step out on a sidewalk for the first time in front of friends and neighbors. A lot of potential runners never get moving, out of fear of looking foolish. They lack self-confidence. They fear failure.

It sometimes helps to join a class. Many running clubs offer classes for beginning runners. One advantage of a class situation is the group support you get from others of equal ability or lack of ability. The most important information any coach can offer beginners is not how to hold their arms or how far to jog without stopping but simply "You're looking good. You're doing great. Keep it up." Basic motivation. Once you start, natural running instincts, overlooked but not forgotten from childhood, will take over.

Joining a class can provide you with support, information, and good training routes, but in particular it can give you motivation as you train with others. If you are looking for a running class in your area, check with local health clubs, running clubs, sporting goods stores, or the organizers of major races. One good source of information is the Road Runners Club of America: RRCA, 8965 Guilford Road, Suite 150, Columbia, MD 21046; 410-290-3890; www.rrca.org. The RRCA has 670 member clubs, with 160,000 members. The organization's Web site lists clubs and contact information. The RRCA can point you in the right direction if you're looking to connect with other runners and runner support groups.

Many books have been written on beginning running as well. Jim Fixx's *The Complete Book of Running*, which sold nearly a million copies in the United States alone, got many people from the previous generation started running. I wrote a long article called "Beginning

Runner's Guide" for *Runner's World*, and it remains available in booklet form through my Web site. Most books and classes for beginners provide similar advice: Begin at an easy level; don't try to do too much too soon; don't get discouraged when your muscles ache.

Before beginning to think about running, much less running a marathon, there are some precautions you need to take.

CHECKING OUT THE SYSTEM

People older than 35 who want to start exercising should consider having a medical examination, including an exercise stress test. The American College of Sports Medicine recommends testing at age 40 for men and age 50 for women—if you're apparently healthy. But if you have any risk factor for coronary artery disease (high blood pressure, high cholesterol, smoking, diabetes, or a family history of heart problems), you should be tested prior to vigorous exercise at any age.

> IF YOU HAVE ANY RISK FACTOR FOR CORONARY ARTERY DISEASE (HIGH BLOOD PRESSURE, HIGH CHOLESTEROL, SMOKING, DIABETES, OR A FAMILY HISTORY OF HEART PROBLEMS), YOU SHOULD BE TESTED PRIOR TO VIGOROUS EXERCISE AT ANY AGE.

"This is particularly important if your family has a history of heart disease," states Jack H. Scaff Jr., MD, founder of the Honolulu Marathon, director of the highly successful Honolulu Marathon Clinic, and author of *My First Marathon*. "If you have been overweight or recently were a smoker, your risks also are high." Running is a relatively safe activity, but why take a chance?

The cardiology departments of many major medical centers provide exercise stress tests for $200 to $400, which are often covered by health insurance. The best type of test is "symptom-limited," in which you exercise until you attain your maximum tolerated exercise workload. If symptoms develop, the cardiologist may stop the test, but Paul D. Thompson, MD, director of preventive cardiology at Hartford Hospital in Connecticut, suggests that you avoid letting the cardiologist stop you when you reach your age-predicted maximum heart rate. "This 'maximum heart rate' varies a lot among individuals," says Dr. Thompson. "Using it as a stopping point can deny you a true maximal test."

A cardiologist uses an electrocardiograph (EKG) to monitor your heartbeat while you walk or jog on a treadmill. Or he or she may test you as you pedal an ergometer (exercise bicycle). The cardiologist will also record blood pressure. If your coronary arteries are even partially blocked, it should become apparent during stress. Changes in your heartbeat will appear on the EKG screen, and you will be asked to stop. This does not mean you cannot run, but you will need to begin under careful medical supervision. Doctors regularly prescribe exercise, including running, for patients who have suffered heart attacks. It is not uncommon for heart attack victims, even those who have had quadruple bypass operations, to finish marathons.

IF YOU'VE NEVER RUN BEFORE, FOCUS YOUR ATTENTION ON TIME, RATHER THAN DISTANCE OR PACE.

If no symptoms develop during your exam—and assuming there are no other medical problems—you will be cleared to start running.

Just because you pass an exercise stress test once, however, is no guarantee you will never suffer a heart attack, either while running or while engaged in other activities. Physicians now recommend that you have a physical every 2 to 3 years, more often as you get older or if your cardiologist determines you're in a high-risk category. Also, learn the heart attack symptoms. The classic symptoms include chest pain, but symptoms can include any generalized pain between the eyeballs and the belly button, even a toothache; often a woman will feel nausea and fatigue. "It's a myth that tingling, pain, and discomfort occur only in the left arm," says Dr. Scaff. "It can appear in the right arm, too." If such symptoms develop during a run, stop running immediately and seek medical advice. Even if the symptoms seem to diminish as you continue to run, that doesn't mean that you're safe.

HOW TO BEGIN

First, put on a pair of comfortable shoes. Although you will eventually need shoes specifically designed for running, for your first couple of short outings, you can start with whatever sports shoe you have.

Start to jog gently, on a smooth or soft surface if possible. Jog until you're somewhat out of breath; then begin to walk. Resume jogging when you feel comfortable, walking again if necessary. "Most people overestimate what they can do," says Stan James, MD, an orthopedist from Eugene, Oregon. When your tired muscles won't let you jog any farther, finish by walking.

If you've never run before, focus your attention on time rather than distance or pace. Set as your goal 15 minutes of combined jogging and walking. If you never have run before, are overweight, or have any health problems, that may be more than enough.

Record your time in a diary or simply on your calendar. Don't worry about distance and pace this early in your training.

Take the next day off. On the 3rd day, repeat the first day's workout, but again, don't worry about distance. If you go much farther or faster than the first day, you may be progressing too rapidly. Take the 4th day off.

On the 5th day, again repeat the basic workout, then rest the 6th and 7th days. Your training has followed the classic hard/easy pattern used by former University of Oregon track coach Bill Bowerman and countless other top coaches in training world-class runners. The pattern is the same; only the degree of difficulty is different.

WHEN TO RUN

Run at a time that is convenient for you. Here are the advantages and disadvantages of running at different times of the day.

Morning. Many runners run in the morning, before they eat breakfast. It's a good way to begin the day. Running can both wake you up and refresh you. If you run in the dark (particularly in winter), wear a reflective vest so motorists can see you. The one downside of training at this hour is that morning runners seem to get injured more often than afternoon runners do. That's probably because they're stiff after just getting out of bed. To combat this problem, start your morning run by walking or running very slowly; then stop to do some brief stretching exercises before continuing.

Midday. If you have an hour or more for lunch, you may be able to squeeze in a workout at this time. Some offices have health clubs with showers and encourage workers to exercise at midday. Learn to manage your time. Plan your lunch in advance so you can grab a quick cup of yogurt or bowl of soup before returning to work. Noon, when temperatures can be warmer, is a good time to run during the winter, but for that same reason it's a bad time during the dog days of summer.

The 2nd week, simply repeat the workouts you did during the 1st week. You may feel that you can run farther or go faster, but hold back. When Bowerman developed his championship athletes at the University of Oregon, he always felt it was better that they be somewhat undertrained than overtrained. Even though there was a chance the Oregon athletes might perform slightly below their potential while undertrained, their chances for injury were greatly reduced. If that conservative approach made sense for his highly talented athletes, why shouldn't it also work for you?

Evening. Stop for a workout on your way home from work. Or go for a quick run after returning home and before dinner. This may not work if *you* are the one who is expected to put food on the table or if there are kids waiting to be fed. If this is the case, negotiate days when you and your spouse can alternate training and homemaking. Late evening, after the kids go to bed, is another option, but this probably means running in the dark. You should always run in a safe area. There are some places where you do not want to run alone even in the daytime.

Weekend. On Saturdays and Sundays, most runners have more time for training. That being the case, you may want to plan your workout week so that you do most of your mileage on the weekends. Most runners (particularly those training for a marathon) do their long runs on the weekend.

Anytime. Who says that you need to run at the same time every day? There's a virtue in regularity, but you can also get caught in a rut. Once running becomes a regular part of your lifestyle, feel free to experiment with different training patterns.

The 2nd week is critical in any beginning running program. You may have been able to run through week 1 just from sheer beginner's enthusiasm. Even if your muscles were sore, if running seemed harder than you expected, and if you failed to see any improvement, you probably were able to keep going from the momentum generated by your decision to begin.

But now you're into your 2nd week. Maybe your muscles are still sore, you're getting bored with the same every-other-day routine, and it's dawned on you that you probably will never win an Olympic gold medal. You haven't yet experienced that "runner's high" one of your friends promised you. And it may feel as if running will never get any better.

Hang in there. It will.

CONTINUING TO RUN

Beginning with week 3, and continuing through weeks 4, 5, and 6, add 3 minutes to your workout each 7 days. During a 6-week beginner's training period, your daily and weekly (based on 3 workout days per week) training mileage should look like that in the table below.

> ## HOW FAST SHOULD YOU BE RUNNING? IT DOESN'T MATTER.

How fast should you be running? It doesn't matter. Again, you should be worrying about time, not distance or pace. You can record distance and pace, but if you try to increase either, you're more likely to get injured. Better to go too slow in the beginning than too fast.

At the end of this initial 6-week training period, treat yourself to a ½-hour run. When finished, consider what you have accomplished. In a period of 6 weeks, you have doubled your initial workout load. As you continue to run, there will be few times when you will be able to improve at this rate: 100 percent improvement in only 6 weeks! Improvement comes easily and suddenly when you're a beginner. It's more difficult for more experienced runners,

MILEAGE INCREASES

Week	Time per day (min)	Time per week (min)
1	15	45
2	15	45
3	18	54
4	21	63
5	24	72
6	27	81

and incredibly difficult for those at the top of the performance charts. But you should be able to continue to improve as a runner for many months, and perhaps years, to come, as long as you follow a sensible training program.

MOVING UP THE TRAINING LADDER

Almost all training designed to improve runners is based on moving from level to level. You work harder and improve, moving from a low level to a higher level. This is your body's progressive adaptation to increasing stress. The 18-week program of mine used by the CARA Marathon Training Class in Chicago features increases of approximately 1 mile a week for the weekend long runs. Over that time period, weekly mileage doubles. The changes in numbers are small; the changes in fitness and the body's capacity to adapt to stress are great.

Naturally, there are limits to how hard you can train and how much you can improve. Not everybody has a bulletproof body; not everybody is biomechanically sound. With beginning runners, a common problem is shin splints, more properly referred to by orthopedists as "medial tibial stress syndrome." Regardless of what the sports docs call the problem, it hurts. Your lower legs ache, and running becomes difficult. Anti-inflammatories, ice, and sometimes a new pair of shoes can help, but more often this is a problem that requires patience on the part of beginners. With better conditioning, shin splints disappear or become less of a problem for the beginning runner. Of course, once you have recovered and are at a point where you begin to do long runs as part of your marathon quest, other injuries threaten, a common one being to the iliotibial band (ITB), which connects the hip to the knee. "If it's not one thing, it's another," you may think.

Most runners survive shin splints, ITB pain, and other nagging injuries and go on to finish their first marathons, but the threat of any injury that might compromise or even end a runner's training haunts us all. Wise runners train to a point well below where they might get injured, but this is not easy to do. We all have points—or red lines—beyond which training hard enough to improve becomes impossible. For some of us, the point is higher than others.

On the Internet, I offer marathon training programs for novice, intermediate, and advanced runners. Not everybody can move from the first level in training programs through the second and then to the third. Moving to the second level may provide all the challenge you need. But even genetically gifted athletes need time to move from level to level to level. If you overtrain, you're likely to crash. Even if you don't injure yourself, you may discover that your competitive efforts deteriorate. You begin to run slower instead of faster. Sooner or later, this happens to almost all top athletes.

Top athletes are constantly pushing the envelope, trying to measure the limits of human performance. "There are two ways to learn about training," states Dr. James, the orthopedist from Oregon. "One is by having access to a very knowledgeable coach. The other is by trial and error." With a knowledgeable coach, you make errors less frequently.

If you are an athlete working without a coach, you may have difficulty recognizing how much and how fast to run. "Most people misestimate what they do," says Dr. James. "There is a difference between what the body perceives and what the mind perceives."

THE 5 PERCENT SOLUTION

How can you maximize your performance? How much can you improve?

When asked how much improvement runners might expect following a year's hard training, Dr. Daniels, the exercise physiologist and coach, initially suggests 5 percent as an upper limit. But it's a tough question. "There is no physiological basis for saying how much you can increase your workload," he finally admits. Runners differ enormously in both their capabilities and their capacities, he says. "Some people with little training background have tremendous potential for improvement. Others who have been running for many years may have improved as much as they can."

A new runner capable of running a 5-K in 30:00 may find it relatively easy to improve by 5 percent, which would mean cutting 1½ minutes to run a 28:30. A similar 5 percent improvement for a runner capable of running a 5-K in 15:00 would be somewhat less: 45 seconds, or a final time of 14:15. But few athletes improve that much at that level of performance without many years of increased training—and they may not improve even then.

So, if you can improve by 5 percent, you can be said to have outperformed the world's elite. That should be sufficient motivation to get you moving. Most reasonably talented runners, however, would settle for a 1 percent improvement, which would mean that runners who do a 5-K in 20:00 could get their time down to 19:48.

KEY PERFORMANCE FACTORS

Anyone can improve with practice, says Dr. Daniels. "Where you start, and whether or not you are genetically gifted, dictates where you finish—provided you optimize what you have," he says. "Optimizing what you have is the tricky part."

Dr. Daniels suggests four areas in which runners can improve in ability.

1. Oxygen delivery: When the heart muscle becomes stronger, your oxygen delivery system becomes more efficient.

2. Oxygen absorption: Training also results in increased blood-flow through the muscle fibers and improvement of the fibers themselves—all of which improve your ability to use oxygen.

3. Economy: You can learn to improve your technique and form in order to run faster while expending the same amount of energy.

4. Endurance: This means increasing how fast you can run before you hit your pain threshold. Basically, stronger muscles contract more effectively.

To improve to the highest level requires talent. But even people of average talent can rise above their abilities and achieve extremely high levels of success as runners. In perhaps no event is this truer than in the marathon.

CHAPTER 4
DIFFERENT VIEWS OF THE MARATHON

NONRUNNERS SAY THE FUNNIEST THINGS

"How many miles is this marathon?" That's a question that non-runners frequently ask those of us who run 26 miles 385 yards. And, yes, that is the exact distance of any running event that goes by the name "marathon."

We all know that—or should—but our nonrunning friends (and quite a few well-meaning mothers) often do not, so we answer politely and comfort ourselves with the fact that at least they cared enough to ask.

Runners stand out in our society. Once you are labeled as a "runner," curious people often ask what might most politely be described as uninformed questions about our sport. Nonrunners do say the funniest things. What are some of the strange comments that nonrunners have made about your running? Recently I asked a group of runners this question. The answers proved interesting.

Clinton James Adams, a paramedic from Charleston, South Carolina, was told by a coworker: "I haven't run in a while, but I used to run a mile somewhere around 3 minutes." However, Adams considers the funniest remark made to him by a nonrunner to be: "Oh, that's right. You're a runner. You probably don't eat carbs, do you?"

Mark Kramer, a finance manager from Lindenhurst, Illinois, had one friend tell him: "Twenty-six miles? I don't like to drive that far." Another said: "I don't want to run unless something is chasing me."

A parent at an open house asked Bob Winter, a math teacher

from New Lenox, Illinois, about his marathon running. The parent commented that in high school, he'd competed as a cross-country runner: "Back then, we would run a marathon twice a week." When Winter pointed out that high schools usually run only about 3 miles in their meets, the parent disagreed: "Not back then. We ran full marathons."

HOW MANY MILES IS THIS MARATHON?

Not all runners turn the other cheek. Gary Gagne, a project manager from Kitchener, Ontario, grumbled when a person asked: "Are you practicing for any races lately?" Gagne pointed out that it's called "training," not practice: "Practice is for hockey. I don't need to practice how to run. I already know how to do that."

Paula McKinney, of Georgia, is more polite. McKinney recalls a nurse (overweight and a smoker) who scolded her, "Don't you know running is bad for you?" McKinney responded, "I'd rather die smiling. And running makes me smile."

Stephanie Fritson, a school psychologist from Omaha, Nebraska, becomes particularly irritated when people ask her how far she runs a day. "I always feel compelled to go into this lengthy explanation of my training and why I run 20 miles on some days and 3 on others," says Fritson. "For some reason, the idea that I don't run a set number of miles every day really seems to confuse people."

Talk about confusion. Tosha Pearson, a gift shop owner from Goldwaithe, Texas, repeated to a nonrunning friend a conversation she'd had while running. The friend, shocked, interrupted her: "You mean you can talk while you run?"

NOT ONLY NONRUNNERS

But it's not only nonrunners who say funny things. Starrla Johnson, an animal technician from Somerville, Massachusetts, recalls watching the Providence Marathon with a running friend, who commented: "Doesn't that lady in first place know she can slow down? The second lady is way behind."

Tamara Paton, a management consultant from Toronto, reports that her boss once laughed at how long it took her to run a marathon. "Five hours?" he said. "I could walk a marathon faster than that." Paton's boss then did the math and decided she would be better off walking the race rather than running it. Paton later improved her marathon best to 4:35—running!

Nicole Long, a personal trainer from St. Louis, claims that people have asked her how many days she spends running a marathon: "And do you stop at some point to change shoes?"

Christine Currie, a school psychologist from Alexandria, Virginia, recalls a conversation about her time goals for the marathon. Her friend suggested: "Maybe instead of trying to beat your best time, you should just average the first two marathon times and shoot for that time." The friend also tried to talk her out of doing a fall marathon, not wanting Currie to become an "extremist."

DO YOU STOP AT SOME POINT TO CHANGE SHOES?

After mentioning to another friend that she had just finished a marathon with 20,000 other runners, the friend asked Currie, "What place did you take?"

Christina McMillan, a stay-at-home mom from McMinnville, Oregon, carried on a dialogue with her 6-year-old daughter, Audrey, about her first marathon. "She kept asking me if I was going to win. I kept telling her, 'No, but it would be so cool to finish.' My daughter got tired of hearing this; she wanted a winner! She finally said, 'In my eyes you'll be the winner.'"

Don White, a software support manager from Alpine, Utah, swears that someone once told him: "Did you have to buy any fancy equipment? I've got some old gym shoes I'm not using that you can borrow." Another person wondered whether or not running all those miles on a treadmill was boring.

Daiva Cooper, a stay-at-home mom from Colorado Springs, bought a shirt at the St. George Marathon that had "26.2" printed on the back. While Cooper was buying food at Disneyland, the vender looked at his shirt and asked: "What's 26.2? A new radio station?"

Ariel Parrish, 28, a software engineer from San Francisco, says that at work she gets two questions, one before and one after each weekend. On Friday the question is "You running any marathons this weekend?" On Monday, the question becomes "Did you run any marathons this weekend?"

Paula Sue Russell, a registered nurse from Findlay, Ohio, was asked by her dental hygienist, "Have you started having neck or shoulder trouble from your running?" Russell responded: "Not yet because I'm still using my legs and feet." Russell also attends Weight Watchers, where people ask why she would want to belong. "They have trouble believing that I can actually gain weight and run," says Russell. "They can't understand the calories consumed versus calories burned concept."

YOU HAVE *HOW* MANY PAIRS OF SNEAKERS?

Jon Skelly, an engineer from Dexter, Michigan, after admitting to an acquaintance that he was training for a marathon, was told, "Really? You don't look very fast."

In response to a person who had asked the length of a marathon, Andrew Smith, a mechanical engineer from Chicago, received the startled response "Did you say *miles*?"

Moms sometimes are the source of interesting comments. Jerry Wood, a teacher in Fort Smith, Arkansas, was told by his mother, "I wish they would televise your race so I could see you on TV." Gary Gagne, before the Around the Bay 30-K Race—which attracts 4,000 runners and an elite field—was told by his mother, "If you win, you'll get $3,000." After he finished 347th, nearly 45 minutes behind the leader, his mother told him, "Maybe if you trained harder, you'd win something."

Alastair Calder, a designer from Warren, Michigan, discussed his running with a coworker who couldn't imagine running a marathon because it would be too boring. "The same coworker then regaled me with a story about sitting in a tree for 9 hours with a bow and arrow, waiting to shoot a deer."

Steve Langley, a forecast manager from Beloit, Wisconsin, recalls running 15 miles with friends on a January morning with the temperature 5 degrees. Running through a park with a small lake, they passed several people sitting on buckets, ice-fishing. "Look at those idiots," said one of the fishermen. "They're going to freeze to death!" Langley admits thinking the same about them.

Steve Jones of Chatham, Illinois, who once placed fourth in a small marathon with 3:03:41, was asked by a nonrunning friend how he later did in the Boston Marathon. Jones said he placed 1,403rd. "I'm sorry," said the friend. "You must feel terrible."

Cathy Wells, a medical student from Providence, Rhode Island, frequently is asked, "What do you possibly think about when you run for 2 hours? Don't you get bored?" But her favorite reaction from a nonrunner was "You have *how* many pairs of sneakers?"

Despite what runners consider funny comments by nonrunners, things said by kids can be touching. Bob Langerveld, an air traffic controller from Oswego, Illinois, recalls limping past Buckingham Fountain after his first Chicago Marathon and seeing his family approaching. His 8-year-old son, Nick, asked: "Did you win?"

Langerveld confessed he had not and was told, "Well, you'll win next year."

We all do, each time we finish a marathon.

CHAPTER 5

YOUR FIRST 26-MILER

THE FIRST TIME IS ALWAYS VERY, VERY SPECIAL

When I wrote a profile of Gale Williams for *Runner's World* some years ago, it was more because of her celebrity status as a horn player with the Chicago Symphony Orchestra (CSO) than because of her ability as a runner. Williams ran mainly for fitness. Three or 4 days a week, she jogged the several miles from her Evanston, Illinois, home to the lake and back. When the CSO played at Ravinia during the summers, she biked 11 miles to rehearsals. Williams told me at that time that someday she'd like to run a marathon to celebrate her coming 40th birthday.

Half a dozen years later, she still hadn't run one.

Then Williams learned that the daughter of one of the CSO bass players had leukemia. Williams earlier had received a mailing from the Leukemia Society of America about its Team in Training program, in which marathon runners raise money to help cure leukemia.

"That provided the push I needed," said Williams. She finished the 1997 Chicago Marathon in 4:41:46 and enjoyed the experience so much she made almost immediate plans to run the race again the following year, which she did.

Williams eventually shifted her training goals, lifting weights so she could do a technical climb of the Grand Teton in Jackson Hole, Wyoming, to celebrate her 50th birthday. (A painful foot condition called plantar fasciitis had sidelined her temporarily as a runner.) "Running is easier than hiking with a pack," Williams tells me. She's already begun to consider doing her next marathon with a friend from Germany.

People decide to run marathons for different reasons. Consider one runner in his fifties, who joined the Chicago Area Running Association (CARA) Marathon Training Class to prepare for his first marathon. For the approximately 2,000 runners who join its class each year, CARA offers a series of evening clinics plus weekend workouts in a dozen different locations, one of them being the Prairie Path, west of the city. I lecture at the clinics and try to attend as many of the workouts as possible. I particularly enjoy running with the class on the Prairie Path because of its forgiving gravel surface and the surrounding trees that shade runners from the sun. During one such visit, the runner in his fifties fell into step with me. He said that in addition to playing tennis, he had been running for nearly 30 years. Yet here he was, training for his first marathon!

I asked him why it had taken him so long to get around to running a marathon. He shrugged and smiled as though to suggest there was no answer: "It seemed like the right time." That might be the runner's equivalent to the mountain climber's "because it's there," explaining why anybody would want to climb Mount Everest. The following year, I encountered the runner again on the Prairie Path, training with the class for his third marathon. Between the two runs in Chicago, he had sandwiched in Grandma's Marathon, in Duluth, Minnesota.

Olympic gold medalist Kerri Strug ran her first marathon in 1999. Strug didn't win her Olympic medal as a runner. She won it as a gymnast. Is there anybody who watched the telecast of the 1996 Olympic Games from Atlanta who missed the image of Strug's coach, Bela Karolyi, carrying the gymnast off the floor after she injured her ankle in the vault? Yet here was this Olympic champion, finishing the 1999 Houston Marathon in 4:12:06. That's a time countless recreational runners better each year. That's a time even you might be able to match with a bit of training.

Retired as a competitive gymnast, and at age 21 a student at Stanford University, Strug decided she wanted to run a marathon in her hometown. I loved her explanation, which was quoted in an article in the *Houston Chronicle*: "I spent my entire life focused on only one thing: gymnastics. All I wanted was to compete and win. Everything I did, every moment of my life, was dedicated to only one goal. And I wouldn't change anything about that part of my life.

"But I've learned there are different phases in a person's life. Now I know there are a lot of things out there, and I want to experience as many of them as I can. I'm sick of doing serious stuff. I want to do cool stuff. I want to accomplish neat things, personal things. The greatest thing in my life was winning the gold medal, but I realize I don't have to win to be happy."

> "I WANT TO DO COOL STUFF. I WANT TO ACCOMPLISH NEAT THINGS, PERSONAL THINGS."
> —OLYMPIC GYMNASTICS GOLD MEDALIST KERRI STRUG ON WHY SHE DECIDED TO RUN A MARATHON.

Strug didn't stop with that one marathon. She ran Houston again 2 years later, did Boston, and was training for her fourth when I contacted her while working on this book.

Bob Winter, a teacher from New Lenox, Illinois, ran his first marathon because his friends doubted he could do even one. "That became a huge motivator for me on those days when I didn't want to go out and run," Winter recalls. "After that, I was hooked, and now I do marathons because I love setting goals and working hard to reach them."

Lori Hauswirth, a clerk/treasurer from Merrill, Wisconsin, ran her first marathon for a similar reason. After completing a half marathon one summer, she mentioned to her husband that she was

(continued on page 56)

WHY FIRST TIMERS DID IT

People decide to run their first marathons for a number of reasons. Here's a sampling of runners and what got them going.

Nels Nelson, Plainfield, Illinois: "I had been running 35 miles a week for a year and a half and thought, 'I think I'll try a marathon this year.' No specific training until then. No long runs. No clue."

Gordon Booth, Bloomfield Hills, Michigan: "The thought of trying something that seemed impossible appealed to me. You had to work hard and do your best to succeed. That fit my outlook on life."

David Kleeman, Chicago: "Nearing 40, I was unhappy with my sedentary lifestyle and started cycling. Surprisingly, I found I responded well to the physical challenge and soon began running when weather prevented cycling. One day a short run turned into a long run, and I realized I could become a marathoner."

Alan Ford, Loganville, Georgia: "I began running when I started a new job and most of my coworkers were runners. I started running with them at lunch, and a 5-K race led to a 10-K race, and that led to a half marathon. I was hooked, and you know what happened after that."

Joseph Parise, Glen Carbon, Illinois: "I resumed running during a most difficult period of my life, a time when I was trying to extract myself from a failed marriage. After all the accusations and anger during divorce mediation, running thus became a place of solace. The marathon came as a first step across the threshold into a post-married world."

Jorge Villegas, Miramar, Florida: "My legs were too old for soccer, and I was spending too much money on golf balls. But mostly it was because my kids could tell their friends, 'My dad runs marathons. What about yours?'"

Julie Koehler, Chicago: "I was very moved by watching the New York City Marathon on TV soon after September 11, 2001. All those people coming together for a mutual goal: It seemed so pure. The next year I signed up for Chicago, never having run before, and spent race day feeling good about myself and fellow runners. Marathons inspire people."

Patti Sandison-Cattell, Canada: "As a fitness instructor, I was looking for a way to put my passion into setting a personal goal. That was seven marathons ago."

Jon Trott, Chicago: "Weighing in at a flabby 265 pounds, I started lifting weights and dieting, then discovered I had high cholesterol. A doctor told me bluntly: 'Start walking instead of lifting!' One day without any real forethought and dressed in jeans, I began running. That led to my first marathon."

Paula Sue Russell, Findlay, Ohio: "I quit a 25-year smoking habit and took up running to clean out my lungs. I ran a 10-K that also had a marathon and stood at the finish line, watching the marathon participants finishing. I was so impressed that I made a vow to do the same."

Rob Marks, Bethesda, Maryland: "My mom died of cancer. My brothers and I had not done any fund-raising over the years as children and careers absorbed our time. But after a physical exam revealed that I was overweight and had too-high cholesterol, this provided the motivation to run a marathon and remember my mom at the same time. I raised more than $10,000 in her name preparing for my first marathon, and I can't remember anything I had done before or expect to do in the future being more meaningful."

Steve Belay, Decorah, Iowa: "A client who was severely handicapped used a walker, rather than a wheelchair. When I asked her one day why she didn't take the easier route, she looked at me and said, 'It is important to me to celebrate my mobility.' Later, when I decided to run a marathon, thinking of her kept me moving."

Doug Branscombe, South Windsor, Connecticut: "My brother and I had discussed running a marathon. I waffled between 'I'd like to do that' and 'Why would anyone want to do that?' One day while driving the expressway, I got a call from my brother, asking how serious I was about running a marathon. I replied, 'How serious do you want to be?' We decided it was something we wanted to do together."

Colleen Gibbs, Carlsbad, California: "As the youngest girl in a family of six, I was considered the one who had the most potential, but never lived up to it. At age 40, I was in good shape, due to many outdoor pursuits, but had stopped running after my first baby. One day my oldest sister, not particularly athletic, called to say she had just finished a half marathon. I was so impressed that the next day I joined a running group."

Dave Russ, Milwaukee: "I used to laugh at marathoners when I lived in Texas. Then, after getting a job with a company whose offices overlooked the finish line of the Boston Marathon, I witnessed the joy of people finishing 26 miles. I said to myself, 'Maybe they know something I don't know.'"

Jim Tritz, Sioux City, Iowa: "I have an unwritten list of things I want to accomplish in my lifetime. Unwritten because it changes with time. When I hit 35, I decided it was time to run a marathon. Crossing the finish line, I said to myself, 'I can cross that one off the list.' A couple of days later, I decided I could have run faster, and now my goal is to qualify for Boston by age 40."

considering doing a marathon next. His reaction: "Yeah, right." For Hauswirth, that was all the motivation she needed to commit to double her distance. "It was a dare, so to speak," she says. Six years later, she completed her eighth marathon and prepared to run her ninth at Boston, after qualifying for that race.

Tracy Eaves, a chief financial officer from Schnecksville, Pennsylvania, states that she was in the midst of maintaining a full-time-plus career: managing a household and raising two toddlers. "I was beginning to feel a little out of control," Eaves recalls. "I needed an interest that was all mine."

Eaves had run in high school, but for 15 years her training had become what she described as "on and off the treadmill." She decided to start running regularly again. One week after making that decision, she signed up for the 2003 Chicago Marathon to motivate herself to continue. Says Eaves: "At the time, I wasn't sure what I was thinking, but eventually I realized that completing a marathon could become the ultimate statement that I hadn't given my life over to everyone else."

One year later, she was training for marathon number two. Eaves reflected on what had become a significant change of life focus. "I'm more together now. My kids recognize the value of exercise, my husband helps more around the house, and we all are happier, due in large part to my decision to get out and run."

Starrla Johnson, an animal technician from Somerville, Massachusetts, had run track and cross-country in high school but never considered running a marathon until she visited a friend who worked at a hotel near the finish line of the Boston Marathon. Johnson recalls: "On the day of the marathon I sat on a newspaper box for 3 hours, totally entranced, watching runners stream across a yellow line painted on the street. I laced up my running shoes that evening. My first run took me 2 miles."

A year and a half later, Johnson finished her first marathon, running 4:05 at the Baystate Marathon, in Lowell, Massachusetts. "I loved calling my high school coach and telling him I just ran a marathon," says Johnson. "I loved even more calling him three marathons later and telling him I qualified for Boston."

DIFFERING GOALS

There are three goals in marathon running: (1) to finish, (2) to improve, and (3) to win. Which goal you strive for depends on what level of running you're at.

Finishing

To finish is important to the beginning or novice marathoner. More and more runners are running their first marathons these days. At some marathons, nearly 40 percent of the field may consist of first timers. For them, covering 26 miles and 385 yards equals victory. Regardless of time, regardless of place, the prime goal is to get to the finish line standing up and in reasonably good shape. Friends and relatives don't want to hear about your time—don't even understand what the numbers mean—they just want to hear that you finished. Finishing should be your first goal, maybe your only goal.

> REGARDLESS OF TIME, REGARDLESS OF PLACE, THE PRIME GOAL FOR FIRST TIMERS IS TO GET TO THE FINISH LINE STANDING UP AND IN REASONABLY GOOD SHAPE.

Finish with a smile on your face. Finish knowing you might have done better if you had trained a bit harder or pushed the pace earlier. Notice careful use in the previous sentence of the word "might." You might not finish, or even start the race, if you make a mistake in training or in the race itself. Run and train conservatively for your first marathon.

Time goals are important only for experienced runners. Worry about time goals only if you run a second or third marathon. Set as your primary goal enjoying the experience, like Kerri Strug did. Regardless of how fast or slow you run—unless you set your goal too high—you will look back on that first completed marathon as a significant experience, a portentous point in your life.

Whether or not you enjoy the experience as a first-time marathoner enough to become a next-time marathoner may be irrelevant. For most beginners, to finish is to win. And for many, once is enough.

Improving

To improve is the goal of the seasoned runner. Seasoned could describe anybody who has run for several years, who has finished a first marathon—or two or three—and wants to run faster. For these runners, improving from 6 hours to 5, from 5 hours to 4, from 4 hours to 3, or various gradients within those hour blocks is akin to victory. Setting personal records is the name of the game for many of us. It doesn't matter if the PR is for your career, your current age group, the year, or the month of June. Take your victories where you can find them.

Improvement doesn't come easily. You have to work at it. On my Web site, I offer five separate programs for runners at various levels: Novice, Intermediate-I, Intermediate-II, Advanced-I, and Advanced-II. Each program provides a slight step upward in difficulty. If you finished your first marathon by following the Novice schedule, peaking at 40 miles a week, you may need to move to one of the Intermediate programs and increase your mileage to 45 or 55, or more, to improve in future marathons. Eventually, you may need to take another step upward to one of the Advanced programs, adding speedwork and other means of fine-tuning your skills (or compensating for lack of skills). You may need to add supplemental exercises, lift weights, and learn to stretch properly to get better. You also may need to pay attention to diet. Prerace diet is particularly important for endurance events lasting over 2 hours, as is fluid intake, but your day-by-day diet is equally important, maybe more so.

If you run many marathons, at some point in your life it becomes increasingly difficult to snip seconds off your PR. And inevitably, if you stay in marathoning long enough, improvement may become impossible—at least as measured on the clock. I certainly never expect to see the underside of 3 hours again despite my marathon PR of 2:21:55.

Nevertheless, each move to a new (5-year) age group provides an opportunity for improvement within that age group. And as an aging runner's career ascends peaks and drops into valleys, it becomes possible to allow yourself to sink to new lows (by backing off training) so that you can establish new highs (by increasing that training). For some runners, every marathon is like their first, each one is a new

> **DEPENDING ON HOW YOU VIEW THE SPORT, YOU CAN CONTINUE TO IMPROVE AS A MARATHONER FOREVER.**

adventure. Even after 111 marathons, I certainly feel that way, and I don't consider myself unique. Depending on how you view the sport, you can continue to improve as a marathoner forever.

Winning

To win is the goal of the elite runner, but "winning" (in its narrow definition of crossing the finish line first) is a goal only a small percentage of runners will ever achieve. In my long career I've won four marathons overall: Windy City in Chicago in 1964; the Cayuga Marathon in Indiana in 1966; Heart of America in Columbus, Missouri, in 1968; and Longest Day in Brookings, South Dakota, in 1972. I've won my age group on numerous occasions, including a TAC (the Athletics Congress) national championship. I also won my age group (M45) and a gold medal at the 1981 World Masters Championships, although I was beaten by runners in the youngest (M40) age group.

My early wins came relatively easily. Decades ago in the United

States, the typical road race attracted at best a few dozen runners. If you were a reasonably competent runner, the odds were decent that you might cross the finish line in first place sometime if you trained properly and chose the right race. My four victories were with times slower than 2:30, pedestrian by today's standards. Several of my training companions scored marathon victories with times in the 2:45 range.

In today's marathon scene, with race fields as large as 40,000 and first-place cash prizes of $100,000 or more, the odds of crossing the line first have diminished considerably. A tiny percentage of those running have a chance of doing so. A still-small percentage might earn an award for finishing high in their age group. Most people return from a completed marathon with no more than a race T-shirt and a medal or certificate that is given to all finishers.

Nevertheless, the training secrets that work for the running elite—the athletes whose pictures appear on the cover of *Runner's World*, if not *Rolling Stone*—can help the less gifted to improve and maximize their potential. And this in itself may be a more significant victory than merely crossing the finish line first.

BOSTON: A FAVORITE GOAL

One standard of achievement is running fast enough to qualify for the Boston Athletic Association Marathon, the granddaddy of American marathons. When I first ran Boston, in 1959, anyone could enter—and there wasn't even an entry fee! Fewer than 200 of us appeared that year on Patriots' Day, a holiday in New England. Within the decade, however, the Boston race had become so popular that organizers imposed a qualifying time of 4 hours to limit the field.

That requirement merely spurred runners to train harder. Boston became the standard for marathon excellence. By qualifying for the Boston Marathon, runners achieved status among their peers. It earned you bragging rights to be able to say nonchalantly that you had "qualified for Boston." Boston's numbers continued to increase

QUALIFYING FOR BOSTON

In order to participate in the Boston Athletic Association Marathon, you must qualify by running a relatively fast time in another marathon, one certified as having an accurately measured 26-mile-385-yard course. The qualifying period usually stretches a year and a half before the Boston Marathon you want to run, and your qualifying time is based on your age on the date of that marathon.

The following times were to qualify for the 2005 Boston Athletic Association Marathon. If planning to run in a later year, check the Boston Athletic Association Web site (www.bostonmarathon.org) for current standards:

Age group	Men	Women
18–34	3:10	3:40
35–39	3:15	3:45
40–44	3:20	3:50
45–49	3:30	4:00
50–54	3:35	4:05
55–59	3:45	4:15
60–64	4:00	4:30
65–69	4:15	4:45
70–74	4:30	5:00
75–79	4:45	5:15
80 and over	5:00	5:30

You don't need to run precisely as fast as the times listed. The BAA gives you the benefit of the doubt if you are within 59 seconds. Thus, 3:10:59 will suffice for a male in the youngest age group, the same leeway allowed to all runners. But if the clock clicks over to 3:11:00 or the equivalent in your age group, you need to try, try again. In marathons timed with chips and electronic mats, "chip time" (begun the minute you cross the starting line) is used for Boston qualifying.

because once a runner qualified, it seemed almost obligatory to go to Boston to run. So the organizers of the marathon lowered the standard from 4:00 to 3:30 to 3:00, until by the mid-1980s if you were a male under 40, you had to run 2:50 to qualify.

That standard was too tough. Four hours is a reasonable time for a runner of average ability who is willing to train hard, but to run the course more than an hour faster requires a certain natural ability. To get into the Boston Marathon, you needed to combine talent and training.

Eventually, Boston relaxed its standards to 3:10 for the fastest age group (18–34), with a sliding scale of slower times in other categories depending on age and sex. In recent years, to qualify you had to run that time on a certified course if you were a male younger than 35. If you were older, the qualifying time grew progressively slower for each 5-year age group, tipping upward by increasingly kinder increments to 5:00 for those over the age of 80. The base standard for females became 3:40, with a similar upward-sliding scale to 5:30.

Partly because of the graduated qualifying standards that reward older runners for their perseverance, Boston attracts a larger percentage of masters runners (over age 40) than any marathon other than those limited to runners over that age, such as the World Masters Championships. In 2004, 54 percent of the field at Boston were over the age of 40.

SLOW RUNNERS DESERVE RESPECT, TOO

The first rule for anyone starting his or her first marathon, unless you are already among the running elite, is to make your goal merely finishing the race. Select a pace and shoot for a time much slower than you think possible, just to get a finish under your belt. After achieving the "victory" of a finish, then—and only then— should you contemplate training harder to finish with faster times.

Almost anyone can finish a marathon. The distance of 26 miles and 385 yards is not that far when you think about it. By walking at a comfortable pace of 3 mph, you could cover the distance in about 9 hours. Not many people would be waiting around to greet you, but you could finish. More and more people, particularly those in the various charity training programs where the principle goal is raising money rather than finishing fast, choose to walk rather than run. Some marathons provide early starting times for walkers and slower runners. The Bermuda Marathon, one of my favorites, offers slow runners a 2-hour lead.

Other early-start marathons include Avenue of the Giants, in Bayside, California, and Flying Pig, in Cincinnati, where walkers get a 1-hour lead. (Racewalkers, who can maintain faster than a 15:00 pace, are invited to start with the runners.) Many other marathons allow recreational walkers to sneak onto the course early without publicizing it.

Starting early offers mixed blessings. One problem is that there may be few volunteers on the course to assist you before the main race begins. But that still beats being stuck on the course long after everybody has headed home. Toward the end of the marathon in Chicago, policemen in squad cars move relentlessly past the slowest runners, requesting that they move to the sidewalk. Given the necessity of returning city streets to the citizens of any big city, it's a reasonable request to make of those whose splits indicate they will miss the 7-hour time when the Chicago course officially closes. Reasonable unless you are one of those being passed by the squad cars, since going up and down curbs each block can be painful and inconvenient. Nevertheless, in Chicago at least a few officials hang around to welcome late finishers, whose 8- and 9-hour times somehow make it into the results booklet. Some marathons close their courses earlier; a few stay open until everyone finishes. If you're worried about finishing within a specific time period in your chosen marathon, check to determine race policy, which usually is stated on the entry blank and/or on the race Web site.

While trying to do enough races so I could run my 100th marathon at the 100th Boston, I chose early starts in my 98th and 99th races at Bermuda and at the Trail's End Marathon, in Seaside, Oregon. In Bermuda, despite a gentle beginning, I found myself "leading" the race after a half-dozen miles, several other runners tucked in behind as we moved along the oceanfront.

Unfortunately, organizers had provided no lead vehicle to guide early starters. Although I had raced in Bermuda before, I took a wrong turn inland, following a line on the road meant for drivers, not runners. I realized my mistake a half-mile or so later but didn't want to make a U-turn to get back to the course, since that would have meant running 27 or 28 miles that day. We weren't in a race for prizes, so I told those accompanying me that they could either turn back or continue to follow, since I thought I knew a shortcut back to the course. Some turned back; some followed. After twisting through the interior of the island, I finally found my way back onto the main route.

I might have been tempted to congratulate myself for my navigating skills, but after several more minutes of running, I came to a mile marker and realized I was now running the course backward! I eventually got myself turned around and finished third in my age group. I debated disqualifying myself, but the next runner in line to receive the award had a time a half-hour slower. I have no idea how far I actually ran that day, but I still count Bermuda as one of the 99 marathons run en route to the 100th Boston.

Slow runners are accommodated better today than they were when I ran my first marathon at Boston, in 1959. The last finishers in the Honolulu Marathon, one of the few races in which the officials wait for everybody, usually come in at around 8 or 9 hours. That's a walking pace. By jogging as well as walking, you should be able to move at a speed of 4 mph. That pace will get you to the finish line in under 7 hours.

In 1983, my wife, Rose, took a year's sabbatical from her work as a teacher to research her family history. I was leading a tour of runners to the Honolulu Marathon and said that I'd take her—but only if she ran the race. That could be classified as spousal abuse, but she said okay, trained a bit in addition to her usual exercise of tennis, biking, and other activities, and finished the marathon in 6½ hours, walking a good portion of the second half of the course. I bought her a special plaque commemorating what she still considers a special achievement, although she has no plans to run another marathon.

Several years later, our daughter Laura trained hard enough to knock an hour off the family female time at the Chicago Marathon. I ran with Laura, who walked a lot in the closing stages and finished in better shape than I did. Slow running is not necessarily easier than fast running. For one thing, you're out in the sun longer. Four-time Boston and New York City Marathon champion Bill Rodgers once said respectfully about those in the back of the pack, "I can't even imagine what it's like to run for 5 or 6 hours."

> BOSTON MARATHON CHAMPION BILL RODGERS ONCE SAID RESPECTFULLY ABOUT THOSE IN THE BACK OF THE PACK, "I CAN'T EVEN IMAGINE WHAT IT'S LIKE TO RUN FOR 5 OR 6 HOURS."

With a little more conditioning and determination, you can run at a pace of 12 minutes per mile, or 5 mph. At this rate you could complete the marathon distance in close to 5 hours, which is a reasonable goal for a "fitness jogger" who only wants to finish. In taking its pacing teams to different marathons, *Runner's World* offered 5 hours as its slowest pace group. In 1998 I led the 5-hour group at Chicago for the magazine and had a lot of fun doing so, interacting with the several hundred people following me. The following year, when *Runner's World*, as planned, shifted to a different marathon, I prevailed on the organizers of the Chicago Marathon to form their own pacing teams. Chicago now offers more than two dozen pacing teams, from 2:50 to 6:00, with nearly 100 team leaders, who for the 2004 race could boast 1,521 marathons, according to team leader Dennis Linehan Jr.

In Chicago in 1998, at least I didn't get anybody lost, but I had help from two other leaders: Mary Burke and Fred Hoehn. Mary kept us relaxed by leading group chants:

"Who are we?"

"Five hours!"

"What are we?"

"Best looking!"

Midway through the run, another runner turned to me and said, "I've run 11 marathons and never had this much fun before." In most of the big marathons today, many people cross the line at around 5 hours, smiling proudly, looking and feeling better than many of those who preceded them in half that time.

Moving into the 4-hour or 3-hour bracket requires more training, and getting into the 2-hour bracket requires both training and talent. The world record for men, as I write this, is 2:04:55, the time Paul Tergat of Kenya ran to win the 2003 Berlin Marathon. Given the short shelf time for world records these days, that record may have been bettered by the time you read these words, although we may be years away from seeing a runner break 2 hours and move into the 1-hour bracket. Some pundits believe we will never see that day—although I can remember when the world record was in the mid-2:20s. Great Britain's Jim Peters, once described as the greatest marathoner ever, improved the world record from 2:26:07 to 2:17:39 between 1952 and 1954.

In that era, less than a half century ago, many considered a sub-2:20 marathon nearly impossible, but we have been required to revise our thinking about the limits of human achievement. As I revise this book for its third edition, the women's marathon record is 2:15:25, run by Paula Radcliffe of Great Britain at the 2003 London Marathon. Records improve rapidly. In the second edition of this book, I listed the women's world record as 2:20:47. That record was reduced by more than 5 minutes in only 5 years! I commented in that edition: "It is quite possible that by the time you read these words, some woman will have run faster than 2:20." Okay, I got that right. Would everybody reading this paragraph please pencil in the time "2:10" as the next major goal for women runners? Yet, as recently as the early 1970s, female runners were restricted to races of a few miles because male officials believed women were incapable of going much farther.

Impossible goals sometimes prove possible. Most people, of course, never come close to achieving the times of the running elite. As marathons increase in size and more and more people of different abilities realize that lack of speed is no impediment to participation, median times decline. The slowest marathon recorded may have come one year at Honolulu, where one

ALTHOUGH STATISTICIANS FIND IT CONVENIENT TO TALK ABOUT MEDIAN OR AVERAGE TIMES, I LIKE TO BELIEVE THAT THERE ARE NO AVERAGE RUNNERS.

man took more than 29 hours! (He fell, was injured, went to the hospital, and returned the following day to finish.)

Although statisticians find it convenient to talk about median or average times, I like to believe that there are no average runners. I consider us all above average—at least as individuals. When you even begin to consider the possibility of finishing your first marathon, you move well beyond anything that might be described as "average."

Time as a goal becomes irrelevant for someone attempting a marathon. The only goal worth considering for first-time marathoners is the finish line.

NO REASON TO BE LONELY

Selecting your first marathon may be a critical decision. Unless you decide to run a small local marathon because it is near home (a logical reason), you will probably be best served by entering one of the big-city marathons. With more people in the field, you will feel less lonely running back in the pack, and there usually is more crowd support. If you have never felt loved before, you should try running one of the big-city marathons with spectators lining the course from start to finish, cheering everyone on, slow or fast.

In fact, the back-of-the-packers get most of the cheers. Because they're moving slower, they take a longer time to pass those who are applauding. Often the leaders dart by so quickly, spectators just stare in awe. It is a sad commentary on the popularity of running that most spectators know little about who is leading the race.

Don Kardong, a senior writer for *Runner's World*, once covered the Boston Marathon from his hotel room. The day before the race, he had scouted the course to write down the telephone numbers of pay phones at various intervals along the way. On race day he called each booth at the proper moment and asked whoever answered for a report. "Who's leading?" he asked one person who answered.

"Just a minute," said the respondent, noting that the lead pack had not yet passed the booth. When he returned to the booth, the man announced, "Some cop on a motorcycle."

At the Chicago Marathon in 2002, I finagled a ride in the press van that would follow the lead women, offering me an up-close-and-personal view of Paula Radcliffe in her attempt to break the world record. (Radcliffe succeeded, running 2:17:18 that day.) But I was surprised at what seemed like relatively few spectators on the course, particularly in the first few miles as it wound through downtown Chicago. Later, when I talked to friends who had finished several hours behind Radcliffe, they described large numbers of spectators for the entire length of their 26-mile journey. I realized then that many Chicagoans living in high-rise buildings near the course probably had watched the elite runners on TV, then rushed downstairs to cheer the slower runners passing.

Thus, no one should feel embarrassed at running far in the rear. Another advantage of a big field is that if you stand in the back row, it may take you 10 minutes or more to even cross the starting line, relieving you of any latent desire for a fast time. With any luck, the field will be so big that the beginners will also be forced to cover the first several miles at a pace somewhat slower than average, thus storing energy for the last few miles. You may think you're losing time by starting slow, but actually you're gaining.

At the Motor City Marathon in Detroit in 1991, I decided to

> **YOU MAY THINK YOU'RE LOSING TIME BY STARTING SLOW, BUT ACTUALLY YOU'RE GAINING.**

do just that. With a field of about 2,000 and a wide starting area, it took me about a minute to reach and cross the starting line. I was last among the starting group across the line, although several runners who must have arrived late soon passed me. I walked most of the first mile before eventually breaking into a gentle jog, but I ran the second half of the race faster than the first and finished comfortably—or at least as comfortable as one can be when finishing a 26-mile race. Starting slow is an intelligent approach to running the marathon—one, I admit, that I haven't always taken.

The dynamics of race starts began to change toward the end of the 1990s, with the arrival of the ChampionChip, a small device that runners attached to one of their shoes. As you cross an electronic carpet at the starting line, your exact start time is automatically recorded. Additional carpets along the course record when you pass set points (and help catch cheaters who don't go the full distance). Finally, as you cross the finish line, your exact time on the course is recorded. This device has been a godsend for runners qualifying for Boston, since all starting delays become irrelevant.

Another reason to run big marathons, at least your first time, is that these events often are better financed, with better support systems and more volunteers, resulting in more aid stations and everything else you need to make your race more enjoyable. Not to be overlooked are the glitz and glamour that surround many big-city events. Bands playing and balloons in the air may not make you run faster, but these diversions may make you feel better.

One question frequently asked on the online bulletin board I manage is whether runners who train alone, listening to music to help them through the tough miles, should also run the marathon listening to their records and radios. Most experienced marathoners say no. "I don't like doing any training run without music, even if only 3 miles," says David Russ, a beer executive from Milwaukee. "But for marathons, I leave the music at home. There's usually too much happening out on the course to miss. Wearing a music player really does take away from the racing experience."

But many marathoners probably could learn a lesson from beginners. Having completed one or two marathons comfortably, though relatively untrained, beginners often get caught in the trap of thinking that speedier is better, that they have to run each race progressively faster to justify the time they have spent in training. They forget the first marathoner's joy. But sometimes you have to return to your roots by running slower than your potential. Realistically speaking, few of your nonrunning friends will know or care whether you fail to run a PR. All they want to hear is that you finished.

As with other endeavors, it is a basic tenet of marathon running that rewards come to those who persevere. We all begin with various levels of talent, but we improve in relation to the amount of effort we expend and how we maximize that talent.

CHAPTER 6
LEARNING TO TRAIN RIGHT

EVOLUTION OF THE CHICAGO MARATHON TRAINING PLAN

Bill Fitzgerald remembers his attitude about people he saw running in the park in the years before he became a runner: "I thought, 'Why would anyone waste their time doing that? It can't be fun.' I didn't see any smiles on their faces."

The year was 1986. Fitzgerald was 36. He comments: "That's an age when males frequently encounter their own mortality." Though he had played some sports growing up in suburban Oak Park, Illinois—football, basketball, softball, hockey—Fitzgerald was never quite good enough to make a team. He lived a somewhat sedentary life as a security administrator for Chicago's Water Reclamation District. He had begun to gain weight. "I decided, let's try this thing called jogging," he says.

Fitzgerald went to Portage Park, near his apartment, and started to jog. A sidewalk wound through the park, covering a distance of about a mile. He planned to go one lap—but failed! "I got mad at myself," he recalls. "I vowed to finish that lap. I returned each day and ran just a little bit farther. Seeing my improvement gave me a sense of accomplishment." When Fitzgerald finally finished a 1-mile lap, he felt like he had "won the Boston Marathon."

Fitzgerald continued to run and eventually completed a 5-K race. Friends suggested he run the Shamrock Shuffle, a popular Chicago

8-K held each spring. Uncertain how to train for this longer event, Fitzgerald unwisely doubled his training mileage, got shin splints (a general term for soreness in the front lower leg), and had to miss the race. By the spring of 1989, he had met an experienced runner named C. C. Becker at a local health club. With Becker serving as his mentor, Fitzgerald finished the Shuffle as well as a half marathon in April. At that point he figured he was ready to attempt a full marathon. Becker suggested that Fitzgerald join the Lincoln Park Pacers. The club met Saturday mornings at the Chicago Area Runners Association (CARA) message board beside the jogging path in Lincoln Park. The Pacers would run 5 to 10 miles, then adjourn to a nearby café for breakfast.

After one workout, a woman runner told Fitzgerald, "Some guy's starting a class next week to prepare people for the Chicago Marathon." Fitzgerald and the woman attended the first meeting of the class in July. About 35 runners appeared. The meeting was at O'Sullivan's Public House, "a real Irish shot-and-a-beer joint," recalls Fitzgerald. That "some guy" turned out to be Brian Piper, a computer systems analyst and member of the CARA board of directors. Piper outlined a 15-week training program that included a gradual mileage buildup approaching the marathon. The class also featured a series of clinics with speakers offering nutritional and medical advice. Chicago Marathon race director Carey Pinkowski (a top-notch runner in his competitive days, including a college career at Villanova) also appeared, to encourage class members.

PIPER BEGAN TO THINK THAT THERE OUGHT TO BE SOME WAY TO HELP FIRST-TIME MARATHONERS AVOID ALL THE MISTAKES HE HAD MADE.

Piper, like Fitzgerald, was typical of the new breed of runner attracted to running for its fitness benefits. Piper had swum competitively in high school and as a freshman at the University of Iowa.

But he quit college swimming because it was too time-consuming, and instead he began to do some running with members of the track team who lived in his dormitory. "I had to struggle to keep up," he says, "but it established running as an alternative activity for staying in shape."

Nevertheless, a year out of college and working for the Regional Transportation Authority in Chicago, Piper found himself 25 pounds overweight. His motivation was the same as Fitzgerald's: to lose weight and get fit. Piper selected the 1981 Chicago Marathon as his goal, then made all the common beginner's mistakes while training and in the race: "I didn't do enough long runs. I ran everything at the same pace. I failed to take enough water. I wore cotton shorts, which resulted in bad chafing. Everything was strictly trial and error. Other than what you read in *Runner's World*, it was hard to get good training advice." Piper finished his first marathon in 3:54, but he was forced to walk a lot. "There were a lot of 7:00 miles in the beginning, and a lot of 10:00 miles near the end," Piper admits.

Undeterred, Piper set as his next goal qualifying for the Boston Marathon. It took 5 years, but in 1986 he finally ran a 2:58:25 at the Twin Cities Marathon and was Boston-bound. He was then 32 years old. "I began to think that there ought to be some way to help first-time marathoners avoid all the mistakes I had made."

At a CARA meeting in the spring of 1989, Piper suggested to executive director Matt Mimlitz that the organization sponsor a marathon training class. That brought Piper and Fitzgerald together at O'Sullivan's Pub: one the teacher, one the pupil. It would be an encounter from which many runners—both in Chicago and elsewhere—would benefit greatly.

THE ST. LOUIS SYSTEM

Piper brought with him to Chicago a 15-week training program borrowed from the St. Louis Track Club, which sponsored its own marathon class. The club offered training schedules for runners whose base mileage (the number of miles they usually ran weekly) was 30 (novice), 40 (intermediate), or 50 (advanced) miles. The program followed a hard/easy approach, featuring 2 or 3 hard days a week and 2 or 3 hard weeks a month. Runners did long runs on Tuesdays, Thursdays, and Sundays (the Sunday runs were the longest). Wednesdays and Saturdays, they ran easy. Mondays and Fridays were rest days. The pattern went like this:

Monday: No running most weeks for novice runners. Intermediate and advanced runners ran 4 to 5 miles.

Tuesday: Long runs between 6 to 10 miles, with the peak coming in the 10th and 12th weeks. Intermediate and advanced runners ran somewhat more mileage.

Wednesday: An easy run of 4 to 5 miles for novices, with intermediate and advanced runners doing a mile or two more.

Thursday: The second-longest run of the week. The novice buildup went from 7 to 12 miles. Intermediate and advanced runners did more runs at peak distances of 12 and 13 miles.

Friday: No running for novice and intermediate runners. Advanced runners ran 6 miles this day.

Saturday: An easy run of 4 to 5 miles for each category of runners.

Sunday: The weekend long run. Novices began at 9 miles and reached 21 in the 12th week. Intermediates went from 11 to 22 miles, with three runs over 20. Advanced runners went from 13 to 23 miles, with five runs over 20.

The unique feature of the St. Louis program was its step-up, step-back approach in the mileage buildup. Miles did not increase in a continuous ascending line (9, 10, 11, 12, and so forth) but rather in a series of waves: step up to one level, then step back for recovery, then up to a higher level.

This was the schedule that Fitzgerald and the other 34 members of CARA's Chicago Marathon training class followed in the first year. In many respects, the approach was similar to what Fitzgerald

ST. LOUIS TRACK CLUB MILEAGE PROGRESSION

Week	Longest runs			Weekly mileage		
	Novice	Intermediate	Advanced	Novice	Intermediate	Advanced
1	9	11	13	30	40	50
2	11	13	16	34	44	55
3	10	12	14	36	45	55
4	13	15	18	40	50	61
5	15	16	20	44	53	64
6	10	13	15	36	47	57
7	16	18	21	46	55	65
8	18	20	22	52	59	66
9	13	15	17	41	51	60
10	20	21	22	56	61	67
11	14	16	18	42	52	62
12	21	22	23	57	62	69
13	16	17	17	49	53	61
14	14	14	15	42	47	58
15	26.2	26.2	26.2	44	50	52

had done instinctively when he'd first started to jog in Portage Park. He had gone a little bit farther each day and grown stronger day by day until finally he could finish a mile. In the CARA class, he went farther every week until finally he could finish a marathon. All marathon training programs are built on similar progressions.

Fitzgerald finished his first marathon in 3:54, coincidentally the same time that his mentor, Piper, had achieved in his first marathon 8 years before. "I finished feeling a lot better than Brian," boasts Fitzgerald. "I had better coaching."

Fitzgerald would eventually qualify for Boston by running 3:20:54 in the 1992 Chicago Marathon. By that time, the marathon training class had expanded to several hundred runners annually. Fitzgerald began to share leadership duties with Piper, becoming codirector. In the Chicago Marathon training class's 10th anniversary year of 1998, nearly 1,000 runners participated, and within a few years, the number of entrants more than doubled. Tom Moran, later to serve as CARA president, assumed leadership from Piper

> FITZGERALD HAD GONE A LITTLE BIT FARTHER EACH DAY, AND GROWN STRONGER DAY BY DAY. ALL MARATHON TRAINING PROGRAMS ARE BUILT ON SIMILAR PROGRESSIONS.

and Fitzgerald. CARA executive director David Patt also assigned that organization's program director, Beth Onines, to spend more time supervising details. "The program became too big for volunteer coordinators," says Patt.

To meet demand, the class expanded its midweek clinics to serve four areas of the city: central, north, west, and south. The class featured weekend long runs for each area class on Saturdays. The central and west classes also offered Sunday runs. Drive through Chicago's Lincoln Park on a weekend morning during the summer months and you'll see runners swarming like bees on the jogging paths. Many, if not most, of them are training for the marathon.

A key feature of the Chicago Marathon training class is its volunteer group leaders, approximately 100 of them, who pace runners during their long training runs. Regardless of whether you want to run a 7:00 pace or a 12:00 pace, someone is there to guide you—and offer midworkout training suggestions. "Our volunteers are the strength of our program," says Piper. "If you have a question, you can get it answered midstride."

Another reason for the popularity of the class is its social aspect: runners meeting runners. "It's easier to run in a group, and it's a lot more fun," says Piper. While running in the 1970s and 1980s may have been the province of baby boomers seeking to delay aging, running in the 1990s became the province of Generation X, whose plan is never to grow old.

And as the class continued into a new millennium, another subtle shift in demographics occurred. Increasing numbers of female runners, daughters of the baby boomers, began to embrace the marathon. In many marathons today, such as the Rock 'n' Roll Marathon in San Diego and other theme-music marathons organized by Elite Racing, female runners outnumber male marathon runners. Not only do women outnumber men at the Walt Disney World Marathon, but they outnumber them by a ratio of two to one in the consecutively run half marathon! More males than females run the Chicago Marathon, but women have the edge among under-30 entrants.

"We've got the best dating service in town," hints Fitzgerald. "Where would you rather meet your future spouse: Friday night in some smoky bar or Saturday morning on the jogging path?"

And although enrollees may begin the class and still stay out late on Friday nights, after several weeks they realize that if they expect to run well early the next morning, they need to head home long before their carriage turns into a pumpkin. Usually this message sinks in by the 4th and 5th weeks, at which point the weekend long runs reach 9 and 10 miles.

Although the step-up, step-back pattern remains the same, the Chicago mileage buildup now differs from that of the original St. Louis program. It has been a gradual evolution, not a sudden change. After the Chicago class's first marathon in 1989, Piper invited me to speak at its awards banquet. Several years later, with the number of participants in both the Chicago Marathon and the class increasing, I became a training consultant for the class.

MONDAY NIGHT CLASS

This was not my first experience coaching marathoners. A dozen years earlier, I had worked with Ron Gunn, dean of sports education at Southwestern Michigan College in Dowagiac, to teach adults how to finish a marathon. Dubbed "Monday Night Class," this was one of the first classes designed for adult runners, as opposed to student athletes.

Gunn coached track and cross-country at SMC, winning several national junior college championships. My son Kevin ran on one of those championship teams in 1978. Dowagiac was a small town of 6,583 located in a Michigan county (Cass) that had the distinction of having more pig farms than any other county in the United States. The nickname for the college's sports teams was "Roadrunners," and Gunn maintained a close relationship with townspeople, who often came to meets to cheer his teams. The teams did their part by helping with local charitable projects.

Gunn also belonged to the Rotary Club, as did lumberyard operator Dick Judd, who told Gunn one evening: "You keep preaching how running is good for you. When are you going to teach us how to do it?"

At first, Gunn was not enthusiastic about organizing a jogging class. First, he was busy enough coaching his teams and supervising the athletic department. Second, he suspected that most of those who said they might join a jogging class would soon lose interest and move on to something else. He purposely scheduled the class on Monday night in competition with ABC's *Monday Night Football*, figuring that would hasten the class's demise.

Gunn underestimated his own ability to motivate adults as well as college students. The fact that Dowagiac was a small town where many in the class already knew one another from churches or clubs undoubtedly contributed to the easy sociability that developed. The class was divided roughly evenly between men and women, many of them couples. Many of the men belonged to Rotary. Many of the women were members of the Junior Arts Club. A large number attended First Methodist Church.

Several members of his class lost as much as 100 pounds. Others were able to stop smoking. They discovered that while running was never easy, it was more fun than they'd thought. Class members often ended runs at one another's house, sticking around to chat and drink a beer or two. "Sociability became the key to maintaining interest," said Gunn. When the class finished one run at a local bar, the owner and his wife decided that the group was having so much fun, they too would enroll. A year later and 30 pounds lighter, the bar owners finished their first marathon.

That was when I got involved, working with Gunn to design a training program that would prepare a group of middle-aged men and women to complete a marathon. From my own successful distance-running career, I knew the type of training necessary for runners at the front of the pack to run fast times. I was not yet certain how you trained people to finish in the middle or even the back of the pack, particularly when those people had started running only a few weeks before. I would soon learn. Ron Gunn and I led a group of 35 runners to the Honolulu Marathon, and each one of them finished—and finished with smiles on their faces.

In retrospect, the training program I designed for that first Monday Night Class was much harsher, with much more mileage than I now feel is necessary for first-time marathoners, but it proved a beginning for me as a marathon coach. Like many teachers, I feel I learn as much from my students as they from me. The Monday Night Class continues to this day, and I recently appeared at its 25th-anniversary celebration. Not everybody still runs marathons, or even runs, because many of the class's original members, now in their sixties and seventies, have switched from running to walking. In the fall of 2004, Gunn led a group of Monday-Nighters on a hike through the Grand Canyon, 42 of them going from one rim to the other.

Several years after training the Monday Night Class, I began coaching my son Kevin, who after 2 years at SMC transferred to Indiana University, graduating in 1982. Kevin wanted to qualify for the 1984 Olympic Trials in the marathon. To do so, he would need to match the Trials standard of 2:19:05, no easy task for someone who had a full-time job for an accounting firm, Peat Marwick & Mitchell. To most efficiently utilize Kevin's time, I designed a training program that crammed most of the hard work—including a weekly long run—into the weekend, when he had more hours not only to train but also to rest from that hard training. I bracketed weekends of hard training, including long runs, with rest on Fridays and Mondays. Kevin eventually did achieve that Trials qualifying time (2:18:50) at the 1983 Lake County Marathon, in the northern suburbs of Chicago.

> TO MOST EFFICIENTLY UTILIZE KEVIN'S TIME, I DESIGNED A TRAINING PROGRAM THAT CRAMMED MOST OF THE HARD WORK INTO THE WEEKEND.

THE CHICAGO APPROACH

Thus, when Brian Piper asked me to help train runners in the Chicago Marathon Training Class, I was able to draw on my experience coaching both the Monday Night Class and my son Kevin. Over a period of time, Piper and I modified the training approach, expanding the time period from 15 to 18 weeks and also cutting back on the mileage in recognition that not everybody joins the class with a 30- to 50-mile-a-week base. (That was something I had learned working with the Monday Night Class.)

Blessed with youthful enthusiasm, many of today's runners choose the marathon as their first race, never having seen the starting line of a 5-K. They also have busy lives, so they don't always have time for midweek runs that last more than an hour—but they do have this time on the weekends. (That was something I had learned working with Kevin.)

But perhaps an equally important key to the Chicago approach was the "step-back" concept, which Piper had borrowed from the

St. Louis Track Club. Cutting the long run mileage back every 3rd week, we deduced, would allow runners to recover both physically and psychologically for the next step upward in mileage. Toward the end of the program,

KEY TO THE CHICAGO APPROACH WAS THE "STEP-BACK" CONCEPT.

when long-run mileage approached its peak of 20 miles, we inserted step-back weeks every other week. By stretching less mileage over a longer period, we found that we could reduce runners' risk of injury and increase their chance of success. At the same time, we also offered intermediate and advanced programs for runners seeking to improve their previous marathon times. The intermediate programs offered more mileage; the advanced programs introduced speedwork.

The Chicago Marathon training class follows this approach with its novice runners.

Monday: No running. It's important to rest after the weekend long runs.

Tuesday: Easy runs building from 3 to a maximum of 5 miles by the 14th week of the 18-week program. (This is in contrast to the St. Louis approach, with its peak of 10 miles on Tuesdays.)

Wednesday: The second-longest run of the week: 3 miles, building to 10 by the 15th week.

Thursday: The same as Tuesday: an easy run from 3 to 5 miles.

Friday: No running. It's also important to rest before the weekend long runs.

Saturday: The key to the marathon program: a long run that builds from 6 miles in the 1st week to 20 in the 15th week, but with step-backs every 3rd week to permit runners to gather energy for the next push upward.

Sunday: Cross-training of about an hour for recovery. This could be cycling, swimming, walking, or even some light jogging. Runners who do their long runs on Sundays cross-train on Saturdays.

The maximum weekly mileage for the Chicago program is 40 miles in the 15th week, when we do our 20-miler. In general, runners cover about as many miles during the rest of the week as they run in their long weekend run. (For instance, in week 11 the long run is 16 miles; the total mileage that week is 32.) Of course, intermediate and advanced runners do somewhat more mileage as they strive for improved times.

The Chicago program follows a very simple schedule, but it works, as thousands of runners have now proved. In fact, tens of thousands, perhaps hundreds of thousands, of runners follow this same schedule, which is posted on my Web site and also is available

THE CHICAGO PROGRAM

Week	Mon	Tue	Wed	Thu	Fri	Sat	Sun
1	rest	3-mi run	3-mi run	3-min run	rest	6	cross
2	rest	3-mi run	3-mi run	3-min run	rest	7	cross
3	rest	3-mi run	4-mi run	3-min run	rest	5	cross
4	rest	3-mi run	4-mi run	3-min run	rest	9	cross
5	rest	3-mi run	5-mi run	3-min run	rest	10	cross
6	rest	3-mi run	5-mi run	3-min run	rest	7	cross
7	rest	3-mi run	6-mi run	3-min run	rest	12	cross
8	rest	3-mi run	6-mi run	3-min run	rest	13	cross
9	rest	3-mi run	7-mi run	4-mi run	rest	10	cross
10	rest	3-mi run	7-mi run	4-mi run	rest	15	cross
11	rest	4-mi run	8-mi run	4-mi run	rest	16	cross
12	rest	4-mi run	8-mi run	5-mi run	rest	12	cross
13	rest	4-mi run	9-mi run	5-mi run	rest	18	cross
14	rest	5-mi run	9-mi run	5-mi run	rest	14	cross
15	rest	5-mi run	10-mi run	5-mi run	rest	20	cross
16	rest	5-mi run	8-mi run	4-mi run	rest	12	cross
17	rest	4-mi run	6-mi run	3-mi run	rest	8	cross
18	rest	3-mi run	4-mi run	2-mi run	rest	rest	**race**

in an interactive format. Before the 2004 Chicago Marathon, 5,498 runners, or approximately 14 percent of the field, signed up to receive daily e-mail messages from me, telling them how to train. The Hong Kong Marathon recently began using my programs for its runners. In the period since I first started working with Brian Piper's class, the technology that transmits information to runners all over the world has increased exponentially, more than any of us could have anticipated.

Nevertheless, Piper warns: "Running a marathon never will be easy. If it were easy, the challenge would be gone. But learning to train right can increase your enjoyment in both training for and running the race."

CHAPTER 7

10 TRUTHS ABOUT MARATHON ACHIEVEMENT

LEARN TO DO IT RIGHT BY FOLLOWING THIS ADVICE

Despite their apparent lack of coaching credentials, Brian Piper and Bill Fitzgerald succeeded in Chicago by borrowing the best ideas from other marathon coaches from New York to Dallas to Honolulu. I've done the same; plus, I've learned a lot from runners I have advised and coached both in person and on the Internet. Here are 10 truths that can help you achieve success in your next marathon.

Truth Number 1: Progressively longer runs will get you to the finish line.

Runners in Chicago using my programs begin 18 weeks before the race, with 6 miles for novices, 8 miles for intermediates, and 10 miles for advanced runners. The maximum long run is 20 miles 3 weeks before the race, with novices running this distance once, intermediates twice, and advanced runners three times.

Although the end point may be slightly different, most training programs center on similar, progressive buildups. Bill Wenmark, who prepares runners for the Twin Cities and Grandma's Marathons, sometimes lets his most experienced runners (those who have run 10 marathons) go as far as 30 miles for their longest runs. Jeff Galloway of Atlanta pushes his groups to 26 to 28 miles. On the short side, Jack H. Scaff Jr., MD, founder of the Honolulu Marathon, director of the highly successful Honolulu Marathon Clinic, and author of *My First Marathon*, considers 15 miles sufficiently far in terms of the long run for first timers—provided their goal is only to finish. Runners in Dr. Scaff's Honolulu Marathon clinic begin in March and prepare 9 months for the December race, so they have a broader base than runners in many other programs. Bob Williams of Portland, Oregon, has runners go 20 to 23 miles on their last long run but suggests that experienced runners get in six runs of 18 miles or more in the last 2 months. Robert Vaughan in Dallas favors running for a certain number of minutes, as opposed to counting miles; his end goal for a long run is 3 hours 30 minutes. Benji Durden (a former world-class marathoner turned coach) of Boulder, Colorado, feels the same. If I were training runners outside the United States, where distances more often are measured in kilometers rather than miles, I probably would pick 30 kilometers (18.6 miles) as my maximum long run distance because it is a handy round number.

Numbers aside, what all programs have in common—other than a loving, hands-on approach—is the progression. "It's the same in any sport," explains Piper. "If you were weight training, you'd begin with low weights and few reps. Progressively longer training runs are specific to the sport of marathon running."

Piper considers the psychological reasons for the buildup in weekly long runs to be equal to the physiological reasons, and I certainly agree. "You need to prepare yourself mentally," he says. "Riding 4 hours or more in a car can be very boring. You need to develop psychological strategies for combating that same boredom while running 26 miles."

During the months-long buildup for any marathon, weekly mileage increases along with the length of the long run. Novices in my program more than double their weekly mileage from 15 miles

TOO LONG OR TOO SHORT?

A frequently asked question relates to the fact that the maximum long-run distance in all my training programs is 20 miles. First timers particularly wonder how they can cover 26 miles in a race when they never go that far in practice.

My response is that the distance between 20 and 26 miles is sacred territory: You should be allowed to enter that ground only when wearing a number on your chest. More to the point, running longer than 20 miles in training increases exponentially your risk of injury. During my elite years, I experimented with runs up to 50 kilometers (31 miles) but felt all this did was break me down.

Coach Bill Wenmark, however, does recommend runs that far—but only for experienced runners, those who have run nearly 10 marathons. "The overdistance works well if you want to improve your time," suggests Wenmark. "Runners pass 26.2 miles still running, and the mental and physical experience builds confidence for the closing miles of the race. Nevertheless, I don't advise running this far in the period 6 weeks from the marathon."

to 40 miles. For more advanced runners already training 40 miles weekly, an increase of 50 percent to near 60 miles is common. Where you end in weekly mileage depends partly on where you begin.

Truth Number 2: Scheduling rest days is the key to staying healthy.

Mileage buildups of the magnitude required to finish a marathon create stress. A certain amount of stress is acceptable and good, since stress creates strength. Too much stress, however, is bad. Many runners have conditioned themselves mentally and physically to run every day, with few days off to rest. This may be all right if you run easy, training for health and enjoyment with an occasional 5-K thrown in for spice. If you are peaking for a marathon, however, failure to take rest days is a ticket to injury, suggests Dr. Scaff. This is particularly true for first timers. Says Dr. Scaff: "Any person who runs more than 5 days a week in the first year will have a 100 percent chance of injury!"

Vaughan echoes Dr. Scaff's advice: "We tell our class it's better to show up at the starting line undertrained, rather than to be injured and not get there." I couldn't agree more, and I frequently use those same words in counseling runners online. Anybody who logs onto my bulletin boards becomes used to me saying over and over again to runners troubled with fatigue, nagging injuries, or repeated colds: "Less is often best!"

Runners planning to run Chicago start my 18-week training program in early June to prepare for that October race. My Inter*Active* bulletin boards feature a half dozen forums. One of them, titled "Body Shop," deals with issues related to health, diet,

> **IT'S BETTER TO SHOW UP AT THE STARTING LINE UNDERTRAINED THAN NOT GET THERE.**

and injuries. That forum gets less traffic than several of the others through most of the year, but each August it overflows with questions from limping runners who want help diagnosing their injuries, which occurred inevitably as they reached the high-mileage phase of their training. That's when proper rest becomes even more essential.

Dr. Scaff notes that the musculoskeletal system generally requires 48 hours to recover after hard work. "The whole purpose of training is to break the body down so it will rebuild itself stronger than before. It's when you fail to allow time for the rebuilding phase that problems occur." Overtraining can result in muscle injuries and stress fractures that halt training or in upper-respiratory illnesses and frequent bouts of fatigue that limit performance. Research by David C. Nieman, DrPH, director of the human performance laboratory at Appalachian State University in Boone, North Carolina, suggests that runners at peak training depress their immune systems and so become easy flu victims. This is particularly true for the weeks immediately before and after a marathon.

To avoid the stress that comes with overtraining, bracket the hardest workouts of the week (specifically the long runs) with easy days and/or days of total rest. Dr. Scaff also promotes cross-training (walking, swimming, cycling) another way to reduce the stress of the marathon buildup.

Truth Number 3: Taking one step back allows you to take two steps forward.

Taking rest days is not enough to guard against the dangers of overtraining; most successful marathon programs also include rest weeks in which runners both cut mileage and eliminate the weekend long run. The late Chuck Cornett of Orange Park, Florida, promoted a marathon training program in which every 4th or 5th week featured a 50 percent drop in mileage. Our class in Chicago moderates the long run every 3rd week. Portland's Bob Williams suggests a 25 percent mileage drop every other week, particularly as mileage mounts toward the end of the program.

Williams explains the rationale behind this step-back approach: "When you get up beyond 15 miles for your long run, or 40 miles for your weekly mileage, some people can handle that level of stress, but many cannot. It becomes a grind. The intensity of effort required to cover that many miles can be daunting to some people."

Williams believes psychological recovery is as important as physiological recovery. "Running 20 miles in a workout the first time may be euphoric, but it's also emotionally draining," he says. "You can slow down to go the distance, but you're still spending a lot of time on your feet. Just focusing your mind for several hours of time can be exhausting."

Regularly scheduled step-back weeks make it possible to survive the stress load that is part and parcel of the high mileage necessary for successful marathon training. You relax, knowing that you can store strength to push ahead to the next level of achievement.

Truth Number 4: Speed training can be a double-edged sword.

San Diego's Thom Hunt benefited from speed training when he prepared for the 2:12:14 PR he achieved in the 1986 New Jersey Waterfront Marathon, but as a coach of other runners, he knows that methods and goals are different for first timers. "They don't need sophisticated training methods," says Hunt. "Their main goal is to finish. Speed training gets in the way. It can unnecessarily raise the risk of injury."

One reason that it is not a good idea to add the stress of trying to run fast to the stress of trying to run progressively farther is that it is one stress too many—even for experienced runners. Danny Perez, a coach from Norwalk, California, offers another reason: "Elite runners often spend 20 minutes a day working on the flexibility it requires to run fast. Beginners don't have time for that. You put them on a track, and they'll explode."

Nevertheless, once you have finished that first marathon, and finished several more in faster times, you may reach a plateau in performance that can be frustrating if you are one of those people who are motivated by improvement. When this happens, speed training can be that "something extra" that offers you the hope of a breakthrough.

"That's when improving the quality of training can help," admits Hunt. "Then you might consider fartlek (instinctive running at various paces), intervals, hills, and the other tricks of the speed trade." Even then, runners should consider reserving speed training for other times of the year, and not try to do it as part of their high-mileage marathon buildup.

"You want to run fast," warns Hunt, "but you don't want to run hurt."

Not only speed training but also other forms of exercise can cause injuries. Many first-time marathoners come to the sport of running from complementary sports, such as soccer or volleyball, or they participate in aerobic classes. Some have heard that strength training can make you a better runner. Yes, but you don't want to start anything new during your marathon buildup, and some activities need to be eliminated until the marathon is over. Doing a long run in the morning and attending a Spinning class (or even a yoga class) in the afternoon is not a good idea.

Truth Number 5: Learning pace and learning to race are the two most critical skills.

"Anybody can run 26 miles if they run the right pace," advises Vaughan. "If they try to run too fast, they'll crash. If they run slowly enough at the start, they'll make it." That strategy works well for beginners, but more

ANYBODY CAN RUN 26 MILES IF THEY RUN THE RIGHT PACE.

experienced runners must fine-tune their paces if they hope to achieve peak performance. The goal for many experienced runners is to achieve "negative splits," where they run the first half slightly slower than the second half. In other words, someone hoping to finish in 4 hours would go through the first 13.1 miles in 2:00:01 or slower and hope to do the second 13.1 in 1:59:59 or faster. It's not easy because the course profile and weather conditions can have an immeasurable effect on your pace. The Boston Marathon is a race with its tougher hills in the second half of the race. Running a fast first half might get you to the finish line faster on certain occasions (some runners like a time cushion), but that strategy entails some risk, since even a slight miscalculation can result in failure.

The pacing teams that have become popular in many marathons, including Chicago, take a lot of the guesswork out of staying on pace during a race. One way to fine-tune your pace is to include some training at race pace during your buildup. Whether your pace is 6:00 miles (2:37 at the finish) or 12:00 miles (5:15 finish), you need to know how it feels to achieve that pace. My intermediate and advanced training programs include pace runs on Saturdays before the long runs on Sundays.

Most novice runners, however, don't know their marathon pace because they never have tested it in a marathon, and many have not run races at shorter distances. Running occasional races will help you test your limits and determine your approximate marathon pace.

Like most coaches, Vaughan warns against racing too often during the marathon buildup period. "Once every 3rd or 4th week seems to be the limit," he suggests. "Otherwise you risk tearing yourself down." Prudence also suggests cutting back overall mileage and skipping the long run during weeks that include a test race. I usually advise runners who want to run a specific race to schedule it at the end of a step-back week, even though they may need to juggle weeks in their planned schedule to do so.

Truth Number 6: Consistency, rather than spectacular workouts, is what counts in the long run.

One popular workout used by runners seeking to improve their marathon times is "Yasso Repeats," recommended by Bart Yasso, promotions director for *Runner's World*. Yasso theorized that if you could run the marathon in 3 hours, you should be able to run 10 × 800 meters in an average time of 3 minutes for each repeat. If you're a 3:30 marathoner, you could do your 800 repeats in 3:30. Four-hour marathoners, 4:00 repeats, and so forth. That might be considered an athletic *tromp l'oeil*, a trick to deceive the eye, although I admit Yasso came up with an interesting way to both quantify speed training and motivate runners to select an achievable

WHAT THEY LEARNED TRAINING

When I asked runners participating in my online bulletin board what lessons they learned training for a marathon, I got these responses.

Kateri Paeglow, DeKalb, Illinois: picked a training program and followed it precisely: "If you are training alone and new to the sport, having a definite schedule keeps you honest. It got me to the start healthy."

Juli Bobman, Florida: discovered that training for a marathon is not spontaneous: "I realized I must research it, study it, and truly understand it so I don't get hurt. I learned the difference between life happening around you and making life happen."

Brent Sinclair, Grayslake, Illinois: tried not to look too far ahead: "In the first week, that 20-miler near the end seems incomprehensible. But it doesn't seem that bad 2 weeks after you've run 18. What's another 2 more miles, right?"

Kousik Krishnan, Glenview, Illinois: learned not to push hard early in the program: "Every long run could be run further. Every speed workout could be run faster. However, overly ambitious running can lead to overuse injuries and fatigue."

Liz Reichman, Columbus, Ohio: learned what to wear—and what not to wear: "I bought all this snazzy winter running gear: tights,

goal. I recommend Yasso Repeats for runners using my Advanced programs. Unfortunately, some runners get it backward and feel that if they can run a workout that hard, they can achieve their goal marathon times. "It's not that simple," concedes Yasso. "If you have to bust your gut to achieve that workout goal, you're not going to make it in the marathon."

Extra-long runs, including those 30-mile long runs mentioned earlier, don't always work. Or at least they don't work if you haven't

gloves, hat. On my first, cold long run, I cooked! I experimented with temperature control, and by the marathon had figured it out."

Jim Fredericks, South Milwaukee: learned from his mistakes: "Training and running marathons is an evolving process. It's trial and error. Every one of my mistakes made me a better runner."

Rhonda Wagner, Osceola, Indiana: encountered good days and bad days: "Some days, I could not wait to put on my running shoes. Other days, I had to drag myself out the door. I learned as much from the bad days. I discovered my inner power."

Don Pockock, Winston-Salem, North Carolina: realized the benefits of perseverance: "You can run farther and faster than you realize as long as you make a plan and stick with it."

Jack Kester, Lemont, Illinois: found that each step upward in distance marked an achievement: "I enjoyed knowing each week that I had run further than ever before in my life. That really motivated me to continue the training."

Jon Trott, Chicago: learned he loved the training as much as the race itself: "Those lonely runs along the lakefront became the glue to my day. The marathon merely served as the impetus to get me out there."

nudged your mileage up over a period of months and even years so such pinnacle workouts can be handled without excessive strain. In all training matters, it is consistency that counts. "Consistency with a purpose is critical to success in the marathon," Wenmark insists. It is the gradual buildup of a lot of miles that turns a 5-K runner into a marathoner. In my Novice program, Tuesdays and Thursdays are easy days, when runners go only 3 to 5 miles, most often running at a conversational pace.

This sounds like a "throwaway" workout, one you could eliminate from your schedule without damaging your fitness much. But you can't. Every workout is important. Even running 3 miles at an easy pace, you're burning close to 300 calories, checking out your system, loosening your legs to ready yourself for the next hard day's training. From messages posted to my online bulletin boards, I know that many runners take pride in following my training schedules precisely as they are written, day after day, week after week, month after month. If they miss even a single day, they wonder if they have compromised their training. Have a wedding scheduled one weekend? They ask my permission to do the long run the weekend before or the weekend after. One runner from Salt Lake City even wondered if he could do his Saturday long runs on Mondays, when he had the day off. Sure, I said. And it's okay to flip-flop workouts and weeks, just as long as you don't lose too many pieces from the puzzle.

Is this anal behavior? I guess so, but consistency in training always worked for me, and it should work for you, too.

Truth Number 7: Nutrition is an oft-overlooked factor in marathon success.

Yes, everybody knows that runners are supposed to eat pasta the night before the marathon to maximize glycogen storage in their muscles, but if you pay attention to what you eat only that one meal, you never will have success as a runner. You need to eat right before your long runs in training, too. And every other day of the week. Eating intelligently is a key to marathon success. If you make poor food choices, you compromise your ability to train hard—or even to train easy. You also miss the opportunity to train your intestinal tract to comfortably manage food and fluids while running. Consistency works in training, and consistency works in nutrition, too.

That doesn't mean you can't have an occasional burger with chips and wash them down with a mug of beer, but the most successful marathoners follow diets that contain near 55 percent carbohydrates, 30 percent fats, and 15 percent protein. That ratio works for good health, too. Forget what you read about low-carb diets, whether designed by Dr. Atkins or anyone else. Low-carb diets may offer some short-term weight-loss benefits, but they simply don't work for endurance athletes, for whom carbohydrates serve as the preferred fuel for all their workouts.

That doesn't mean spaghetti 7 nights a week. Other good sources of carbohydrate, according to Nancy Clark, RD, a sports dietitian in private practice in the Boston area and author of *Nancy Clark's Sports Nutrition Guidebook* (www.nancyclark.com), are cereals, fruits, juices, breads, rice, plain baked potatoes, peas, corn, fruit, yogurt, and frozen yogurt. But not ice cream, cheesy lasagna, and pepperoni pizza. Those foods often get confused with carbohydrates but actually contribute more fat than needed to your diet. "Carbo-loading should being months before the race, not the night before," advises Clark.

Truth Number 8: Practice everything connected with the marathon, not just the running of it.

The purpose of the long runs is to get your legs in shape but also to get the systems around those legs in shape. A critical item for running success is learning to drink on the run and finding the proper combination of water and replacement drink that works best for you. And if your marathon of choice has a specific replacement drink, you'd better practice drinking that, too. You don't want to get to the first aid station only to discover you don't like the taste of the drink. There is also no exact formula for how much of what to drink, since that depends not only on individual runners' preferences but also on weather conditions.

You definitely need to learn what foods the night before or the morning before may upset your stomach, and avoid them race day.

That's another reason that some racing is necessary during the marathon buildup. "Some newcomers are afraid of racing," says Vaughan. "But running occasional races will help you get used to the race experience: how to warm up, where to pin your number, what it feels like running in a crowd, whether or not your shoes will cause blisters. It's always best to make your mistakes in unimportant races, so that you can make corrections for marathon day."

Once you decide on your race day strategy, stick with it. Don't make sudden changes. Bill Fitzgerald recalls going to the Honolulu Marathon in 1989 on a tour led by Ron Gunn and me. Fitzgerald recalls asking Gunn the night before the race for any last-minute advice. Fitzgerald still remembers Gunn looking solemnly at him and saying: "You gotta dance with the one that brung you!"

Good advice from a good coach.

Truth Number 9: Tapering—reducing your training in order to be better rested for an upcoming big race—is both an art and a science.

Few coaches agree on how many days or weeks before a marathon runners should cut back on training and begin resting for a race. Depending on the individual, the prerace taper can vary from 3 days to 3 weeks. Al Dimicco, who since 1984 has directed a training clinic for the Vulcan Marathon in Birmingham, Alabama, finally settled on a 2-week taper for his charges. I recommend a 3-week taper, although when I was running my fastest times and running 100 miles a week, I tapered 10 days before the marathon, with the final 5 days featuring little or no running.

"Too many runners want to train right up to the marathon, but you need to let your body recover after all the hard training." Dimicco recommends a 50 percent cutback in mileage during the last 2 weeks, with very little running the final 2 or 3 days prior to the race. "Just enough to keep from going crazy," he says.

Tapering not only permits any damaged muscles to heal; it also promotes maximum glycogen (the fuel used by working muscles) storage within your leg muscles on race day. "You don't want to go into the race depleted of glycogen," warns Dimicco. He believes that it matters little whether you're an elite runner or a beginner; you still need a 2- or 3-week taper. Research by David L. Costill, PhD, of the human performance laboratory at Ball State University in Muncie, Indiana, actually pinpointed 6 weeks as best for tapering, although the study was done with high-intensity swimmers, not runners.

Although your mileage drops during the taper, the speed at which you run that mileage should not. The taper period is a good time to practice race pace, but at much shortened distances. One way to cut mileage is to convert "easy"-run days into days of complete rest. You may want to jog easily the day before the marathon just to reduce nervousness, but don't go too far. Arrive at the starting line rested and ready to go.

Truth Number 10: You'll go only as far as your motivation will carry you.

Bill Wenmark is among the most successful coaches when it comes to motivating runners. Bruce Brothers of the St. Paul, Minnesota, *Pioneer Press* once wrote of him, "Wenmark could motivate a penguin to fly."

But Wenmark claims he does not supply motivation. "The motivation has to come from within," he says. He feels that people sometimes underestimate the effort it requires to run 26 miles. He says that finishing a marathon requires courage, perseverance, and commitment: "If running marathons were easy, everybody would be doing it—but they're not. You've got to be committed to your training. If you're not focused on being a success,

IF YOU WANT TO SUCCEED IN THE MARATHON, YOU NEED TO BE READY TO PAY THE PRICE.

you won't be successful. You'll never succeed if you're not willing to prepare."

While Wenmark believes you can't teach commitment, he knows how to facilitate it by providing runners—beginners and experts—with a supportive environment. "People can enroll in a class," says Wenmark, "but unless they have that desire, there's nothing I can do for them. I can't run the marathon for them. I can't train for them. I can't stay out of the refrigerator for them. If you want to succeed in the marathon—or in any other activity in life—you need to be ready to pay the price."

Running 26 miles is one activity for which it's true that you get what you paid for. Runners willing to train properly, taking careful note of the 10 truths listed in this chapter, will find that the marathon can be an experience that provides much more joy than pain.

CHAPTER 8
STRIVING TO IMPROVE

BECOMING A BETTER RUNNER

How do you improve as a marathoner? How do you run faster? These are key questions for many runners. Getting to the finish line of your first marathon is just a matter of preparation—as we prove every year with the Chicago Marathon training class. Either through talent or with the help of a well-structured and progressive training program (or both), most people who set their minds on becoming marathoners succeed.

If they're hooked on the sport, their next goal is to get better. They seek to run their fastest marathon, whether it's their 3rd or their 33rd race. It's not that simple, but it's also not that difficult.

For the October 1991 issue of *Runner's World*, I wrote an article with Doug Kurtis, a 2:13 marathoner from Northville, Michigan, who, after he retired as a competitive runner, served for several years as director of the Detroit Marathon. The article was touted on the magazine's cover as "26.2 Proven Ways to Run a Better Marathon." Let me focus on four specific points that address the task faced by all of us as we seek to improve our performance. Here, in Kurtis's words, are these major points.

Consistency. The biggest key for Kurtis was his consistency. His mileage remained the same week after week: no downtime, no up time, no breaks. When you're consistent with your training week after week, there's much less chance of entering a race undertrained or overtrained—both reasons that runners get hurt or perform poorly. This is true for athletes in other sports as well.

Mileage. In his prime, Kurtis ran twice daily, averaging 105 miles a week: High mileage permitted him to run sub-2:20 marathons rather than run somewhat slower. Because of this, he won races and received invitations to travel all over the world with expenses paid, but Kurtis concedes that for someone trying to run 3:20 or 4:20, the incentive

> EVERYBODY HAS A MILEAGE LEVEL THAT'S BEST FOR THEM.

might not be quite so high. Each person has to determine what's important to him and use that as a guide to dictate training level. Everybody has a mileage level that's best for them.

Intensity. A lot of people believe they have to train hard all the time. Kurtis comments: "They feel they're not getting anything out of a workout unless they're running race pace." Yet Kurtis felt 7:00 pace was fast enough for him, though nearly 2 minutes slower than his race pace, and he often started a workout running an 8:00 or 9:00 pace. He ran at a relaxed pace to avoid burnout and injury. You can burn out if you run hard every day, or you can be injured. Message: You can achieve a lot with slow workouts.

Rest. Kurtis claims that he averaged 15 to 20 rest days a year. "I don't plan them in advance," he says, "but it's usually when something comes up: travel, or illness, or a family outing." He concedes that he probably should rest more often. One of the advantages of keeping your training consistent year-round is that when you do take a short rest, you lose very little of your training edge. Don't be afraid to take days off.

STAYING UNDERTRAINED

If you're a beginning runner who has just finished your first marathon, you'll continue to improve if you do nothing else but train consistently. Most established training programs for first-time marathoners last 3 months or more. Class leaders guide their students through a graduated schedule, the main feature being a long run that gets progressively longer (usually from 6 to 20 miles) as marathon day approaches. Students are usually sent to the starting line undertrained and well-rested because experience has shown that to be the best way to ensure that they finish.

Better to be safe than sorry. And who can argue with success? Thus, most well-coached first-time marathoners run their races without the training necessary to achieve peak performance and run comfortably slower than their talents might allow. They finish thinking they probably could have run somewhat faster if they had trained harder. They're right. They can. And so can you.

Even without adopting a refined training schedule, most marathoners can improve merely by continuing to train at or near the same level. After 3 months, you will have only begun to reap the benefits of that level of dedication. Your undertrained body will continue to improve, as long as you don't overtrain it. So keep running those long runs on the weekends, whether 20 miles or somewhat less.

Keep doing a sort of long run in the middle of the week. An hour is a good length for a midweek workout. Run somewhat longer on the weekends: 90 to 120 minutes, although no more than two or three times a month. Take those 1 or 2 rest days weekly as suggested in my Novice training schedule. Fill in the rest of the week with runs at various short distances and mix in some running at near your marathon pace. The accumulation of miles over a period of time will help you to improve. You will get better.

The important thing is to maintain your fitness at a steady level. Research by Edward F. Coyle, PhD, of the department of kinesiology at the University of Texas at Austin, suggests that runners begin to "detrain" (lose their fitness) after 48 to 76 hours and that it takes 2 days of retraining to regain the fitness lost for every single day of training that is skipped. That doesn't mean you should never rest, but if you take long periods off, it will take you longer to come back.

That is why consistency is so critical to marathon success. You don't need to maintain continuous peak condition, but settle on a consistent level of training that you know you can maintain for 12 months of the year. When it comes time to aim for a specific marathon, you can increase your level of training—slightly. The important goal is to maintain an effective endurance base.

The American College of Sports Medicine (ACSM) guidelines for fitness suggest 3 or 4 days of exercise a week, 20 to 60 minutes a day. That's the minimum fitness formula for maintaining good health, beyond which Kenneth H. Cooper, MD, president and founder of the Cooper Aerobics Center in Dallas, suggests you're exercising for other reasons. For the marathoner, that will be true: Your reason is to stay in shape to run marathons. You'll need to— and want to—run more than the time allotted in Dr. Cooper's formula. But the basic pattern offered in the ACSM guidelines still applies to marathoners.

For 4 years, I coached the boys' and girls' cross-country teams at Elston High School in Michigan City, and I also worked with the distance runners during the track season. Between seasons I encouraged my runners to keep diaries, and I tried to examine those diaries periodically to monitor the students' conditioning programs. I discovered that the less dedicated ones would train

THE STUDENTS WHO TRAINED CONSISTENTLY IMPROVED; THE OTHERS DID NOT.

hard for 3 or 4 days, but then they would miss 3 or 4 days of running. They thought they were staying in shape, but they were actually sliding backward—as they proved when they appeared for practice the first day of the season. The student who trained consistently improved; the others did not.

As a result, I told them: Never go 2 days without running. One day of missed training was no problem. That qualified as rest. But 2 or 3 lost days in a row (taking into account Dr. Coyle's research) equaled lost conditioning—and inevitably meant poorer performances once the season began.

FINDING YOUR MILEAGE LEVEL

At peak training, most top runners average 100 miles or more a week. You can't compete successfully as an elite runner in the marathon, or even as a near-elite, unless you run a lot of miles. Most runners would crash if they attempted to run 100 miles weekly, even half that many miles. Determining the level that is best for you is tricky and may take several years of experimentation, but once you have reached a comfortable level, you can reap the benefits of success.

Norm Green, a Baptist minister from Wayne, Pennsylvania, who ran his first marathon at age 49 (eventually achieving a PR of 2:25:51 at age 52) succeeded on 55 miles a week. During my years of peak performance, I found that I competed well in marathons on a weekly training level around 75 miles. On those one or two occasions when I could edge my training mileage above 100 and hold it there for several months, I achieved peak performances. But I risked injury by doing so. And also I risked boredom because I found the twice-daily workouts necessary to achieve that mileage robbed running of much of its joy. It also robbed me of time away from running, since fatigue forced me to sleep more.

Today I find 15 to 25 miles weekly a more acceptable training level when I'm running 5-K races or simply maintaining fitness. When I'm aiming for a marathon, I try to push that level to 40 miles, with most of the extra mileage gained by adding one progressively longer run once a week. Think about it: All you need to do to increase your weekly mileage from 20 to 40 is add a single workout of 20 miles.

The best way to determine your optimal mileage level is to keep a training diary, as I advised the Elston runners. You can find various diaries at bookstores for recording your training, or record daily workout records in your computer. An online training log is one of the features of my Inter*Active* Training Guide. It allows you to record everything from your heart rate to a map of the course you ran. Or you can simply mark mileage on a wall calendar.

The advantage of even a simple diary is that when things go wrong—or right—you can analyze your training and determine the reasons. My training diaries, which fill a shelf of a bookcase in my office, prove very valuable when I am writing articles for *Runner's World* and books such as this.

During special periods of time—such as when I'm preparing for a marathon or peaking for maximum performance at the World Masters Championships—I take poster board and a black marker and make my own diary calendars showing 3, 6, or 9 months, whatever the training for that particular race requires. I tack the poster-size calendar to a cork wall in my basement that I pass each day before and after running. It serves as both a visual record of what I have done and a reminder of what I have to do. In addition to what I write in my diary, I mark weekly mileage totals and sometimes specific key workouts, such as the distance of my long run.

I use my record-keeping system as motivation, but also as a safety net. If I notice that I have run 4 consecutive weeks at the 40-mile-plus level (which is high for me now), I may think, "Hmmm. Maybe I should back off my training for a week to avoid getting injured."

Finding the appropriate training level is not easy—particularly because that level may change as you get stronger or get older—but it is essential if you want to improve as a marathoner.

SLOWING IT DOWN

If there's one difference between fast runners and those who finish back in the pack, it's that the fast runners seem to have no qualms about running slowly. They're not embarrassed about it. One year at the Boston Marathon when I was in town appearing at the expo, not running the race, I went out the day before the race for an easy jog of a few miles along the Charles River. Returning, I arrived at a pedestrian bridge across Storrow Drive at the precise moment as did two Kenyan runners.

I had seen them at a press conference the day before, so I smiled and nodded, and they smiled back. After we crossed the bridge and continued to jog up a side street toward our hotels, I realized I was jogging faster than

I WAS JOGGING FASTER THAN THE KENYAN RUNNERS.

they were. In fact, I had to slow my pace to avoid embarrassing myself by passing them. The following day I saw them on TV at the front of the lead pack. If runners capable of sub-2:10 marathons are not embarrassed to jog very slowly, you should not be, either.

As an aging marathoner, I now do many of my workouts at a pace slower than 12:00 per mile—often much slower. If you station yourself near my house with a spyglass, you may even catch me cruising in at the end of a long run at 15:00 a mile. On a recent visit to Chicago, I stayed overnight at the Hilton Towers and went out for an early-morning run to the Adler Planetarium and back. It's about a 3-mile run, and if you time it right returning, you can catch the rising sun lighting the Chicago skyline. Returning from that run, I hit a path beside Michigan Avenue at the same time as a woman walking to work, carrying a briefcase. I was amused to see we were moving at almost the same pace. She would have been able to maintain pace with those Kenyan runners, too. That pace is quite different from the pace I or they might run in a 5-K or 10-K, or even a marathon, but the goal is to perform well in important races, not in every daily workout.

The important message is not that fast runners often run slowly but that they train differently each day. If I had to cite one mistake made by inexperienced marathoners when they seek to improve their performance, it is that they run too many of their miles at the same pace and over the same distance. There's little variety, and that limits their improvement.

If I'm running slowly on one day, it's probably because I ran hard the day before—or want to run hard the next day. To improve, you need to add intensity to your program. You may not necessarily need to run sprints on the track, but you need to at least run as fast as race pace. Very

> **VERY FEW RUNNERS CAN RUN RACE PACE DAY AFTER DAY.**

few runners can run race pace day after day. Green was one of those rare runners: At his peak, he averaged faster than 6:00 miles in training. I did too, in my peak years. Most runners, however, would break if they attempted to duplicate that feat—which Norm is the first to admit. (The last time I saw Norm, at a masters track meet in Barbados, he conceded that he had abandoned his practice of running every workout hard.) In order to train at a high level of intensity on certain days, most of us need to train at a low level of intensity on other days. That's where slow running comes in.

SCIENTIFICALLY SPEAKING

From a scientific standpoint, slow running is important for several reasons.

Caloric burn. This varies from runner to runner and depends on size and metabolism, but most of us burn 100 calories for every mile we run. Burn 3,600 calories by running 36 miles, and you lose 1 pound. But it doesn't matter how fast you run those miles. You can even walk and burn nearly the same number of calories per mile. Scientists quibble over the precise numbers, but calorie loss is related to foot-pounds: the amount of effort (that is, energy) it takes to push a body of a specific weight forward. You can run a 5:00 mile or a 10:00 mile, and you'll still burn approximately 100 calories for covering the identical distance.

One means of attaining maximum performance is to achieve optimal body weight and an optimal percentage of body fat. You can do that just as easily with long, steady distance: It will take you somewhat longer than if you ran those miles fast, but you'll be less likely to become injured.

Sparing glycogen. Exercise physiologists also say that when you run slowly, your body has time to metabolize fat as a source of energy. When you run fast, your body burns glycogen, a derivative of carbohydrate, as its preferred energy source. Glycogen is stored in the muscles and is a more efficient fuel, in the sense that the body can metabolize it more rapidly than fat. But by training slowly, you apparently teach your muscles to become more efficient at also metabolizing fat, thus sparing glycogen stores for those last few miles in the marathon.

REST IS BEST

With that idea in mind, realize that *not* running is as important a part of the marathoner's training guide as resting. That may sound somewhat confusing at first, but running a short distance at a slow period would qualify as "rest." A day when you cross-trained by swimming or cycling also might qualify as rest. But sometimes active rest is not enough; you need to take a day off when you do not run, or do much of anything. Although I promote consistency as critical to success, there are times when you simply have to kick back and do nothing. And I mean nothing! Take a week off. Take a couple of weeks off. Yes, you will lose some fitness, but you will more than make up for it if you return to training refreshed and ready to run hard again.

In *Lore of Running*, Timothy Noakes, MD, analyzed the training patterns of several dozen expert runners. He looked at reasons they'd failed and reasons they'd succeeded. For those who'd failed, often the reason was that they'd trained too hard and been too unwilling to take days off.

A prime example is Ron Hill, a British marathoner with a 2:09:28 best, who Dr. Noakes suspected was as much interested in keeping his streak of double workouts unbroken as he was in winning the 1972 Olympic marathon. An earlier British runner, Jim Peters, trained relentlessly, day after day, almost without pause, once running half a dozen miles at a 5:00 pace the day before setting one of his world records. Yet in two of his most important races (the 1952 Olympics and the 1954 Commonwealth Games), Peters failed to finish. In the 1954 race, on a hot day in British Columbia, he collapsed while leading by several miles, even though he was in sight of the finish line. He retired after that race, out of fear that his intense will might cause him to seriously hurt himself. Dr. Noakes suggests that had Peters alternated hard and easy training days, and tapered for his races—common practices among marathoners today—he might have achieved even greater success.

Knowing when to back off and take a complete day off—or even more—is one of the secrets of marathon success. It is not easy, since the traditional work ethic that has proved successful for many people suggests that more is better. That training calendar on my basement wall would be more of a hindrance than a help if it pushed me to run extra miles just to achieve mileage levels I might have planned months ago—without considering whether I have a cold, failed to get enough sleep the night before, or am overly fatigued because of having spent most of the previous day on an airplane.

Rest is essential to success. In our Chicago class, we program 2 days of rest into each week for first-time marathoners. Most experienced runners understand that tapering before a marathon—cutting training mileage the last week or two before the race—is important to ensuring success. Less recognized is the necessity for rest and mini-tapers all through the marathon training program. Take a day off; it won't hurt.

Does this message contradict the earlier one related to consistency, the importance of maintaining a steady schedule? Not at all, because who can better afford to take days off than someone who trains consistently?

If you hope to get better as a marathon runner, you need to pay attention to the basic elements—consistency, mileage, intensity, and rest—but those are only four of the routes available to you. Let's consider next the benefits and challenges of building up mileage.

CHAPTER 9

BUILDING UP MILEAGE

BALANCING TOO FEW AND TOO MANY MILES IS NOT EASY

Most marathon coaches agree that building up your weekly mileage is essential for achieving success in any long-distance event. "You need time on your legs," says Susan Kinsey, a coach from La Mesa, California.

But how much time? Atlanta's Jeff Galloway, a former high-mileage Olympian, has made a very successful career of teaching runners to finish their first marathons on the least mileage possible. Three or 4 days a week of training, coupled with some long runs, are all you need, according to Galloway. And it works. More than 98 percent of the people in Galloway's marathon program finish their first marathons, some on as little as 20 to 30 miles a week. (In recent years, many first-time marathoners in the Galloway program have used a run/walk method to complete the marathon. They use once-per-mile walk breaks, each lasting several minutes, to refresh their legs before they resume running again.)

Coaches surveyed for this book agreed that a high of about 35 miles a week was adequate to finish a marathon, 55 miles to finish well. Most elite runners believe 100-plus-mile weeks are necessary to excel, but some research suggests anything more than 75 miles a week may be a waste.

A survey of runners who used my online bulletin boards showed that 52.6 percent thought they had run too few miles before their

THE RIGHT NUMBER

In a survey of runners participating in my online bulletin board, I asked whether or not they were satisfied with the amount of training they had done before their last marathon. "Did you reach the starting line undertrained or overtrained?" I asked. "Too few miles, too many miles, or just right?"

More than half (52.6 percent) felt they had run too few miles, but almost as many (42.1 percent) believed they had gotten it just right. Only 5.3 percent felt they had run too many miles.

"Life just kept intervening during my last training cycle," sighed Mark Felipe of Arlington, Virginia. "All went well up until my 18-miler; then I had to improvise, adapt, and overcome. Then, after my 20-miler, I decided it was just as important to be well rested as it was to be well trained."

But Brent Sinclair of Grayslake, Illinois, said: "I think I hit the mileage right because my legs couldn't take it anymore."

Ironically, both runners had the same time goal of 4:30, although Sinclair said he would be happy with anything under 5 hours. He finished Chicago in 4:40 with a smile on his face. Felipe, too, was pleased to finish the Marine Corps Marathon in 4:47 on a very hot day.

last marathons, and 42.1 percent thought they'd hit it right. Only 5.3 percent felt they'd run too much.

How many miles do you need to run each week? It depends on your goals, your abilities, and your schedule—and in some cases, whom you listen to.

WHAT 100-MILERS SAY

Before the 1980 U.S. Olympic marathon trials, a survey of the American contenders showed that nearly all of them trained more than 100 miles a week—somewhat disheartening for the aspiring marathoner now doing 30 miles a week and hoping to work up to 50 or 60.

Bill Rodgers and Frank Shorter, 1976 Olympians and two of the most successful and consistent American road racers at that time, trained 140 miles a week. "I always felt best when doing high mileage," says Rodgers. Alberto Salazar ran 130 miles a week before the 1984 marathon trials. Portugal's Carlos Lopes, the 1984 Olympic champion, ran 140 on average. Joan Benoit Samuelson, the women's gold medalist in the 1984 Games, also ran more than 100. Norway's Ingrid Kristiansen ran as much as 125 miles weekly prior to breaking Samuelson's world record in the 1985 London Marathon. Uta Pippig, winner of the 100th Boston Marathon and a German Olympian, was a high-mileage trainer. A survey of the current crop of elite marathoners probably would reveal similar mileage totals.

Tom Fleming, a 2:12:05 marathoner with several second-place finishes at Boston, claims that such high mileage is necessary for achieving excellence. "You have to do 140 miles a week to get into the 2:12 bracket," he says. "And you have to main-

ANYONE CAN RUN 140 FOR 3 OR 4 WEEKS, BUT THAT'S NOT ENOUGH.

tain that mileage. Most people can't do it. Anyone can run 140 for 3 or 4 weeks, but that's not enough. I'd love to be able to have 10 months of 140-mile weeks." Fleming points out that Bill Rodgers ran at that level during his best 3 years: "His body held up under the stress of the hard training, and the result was that he was the best marathoner in the world."

But not every elite distance runner thinks you need to run so many miles. Don Kardong of Spokane, Washington, finished fourth in the 1976 Olympic marathon (2:11:16) with less mileage than most top marathoners, averaging 80 to 90 miles most weeks. "My feeling is that people pick 100 because it's a nice, round number," he says. "But 88 is an even rounder number."

Consider Benji Durden, a top runner from Boulder, Colorado, and a coach of elite and midpack runners. When he ran 110 miles a week at an average pace of 6:30 per mile, Durden had PRs of 29:21 for the 10-K and 2:10:41 for the marathon, and he made the 1980 U.S. Olympic marathon team.

But Durden found the stress of that much training too intense. In 1983 he cut his mileage to a still-demanding 85 to 95 miles a week—and set new PRs. He improved to 28:37 for the 10-K and 2:09:58 for the marathon, finishing third at Boston. "I believe you can be a successful performer on low mileage, as little as 70 to 80 miles a week," Durden now says. Granted, most of us wouldn't consider 70 to 80 miles a week low mileage, but it is for an elite runner.

Craig Virgin, a three-time Olympian and two-time world cross-country champion, was another relatively low mileage runner. While setting PRs of 27:29.2 for 10,000 meters and 2:10:26 for the marathon (in a second-place finish at Boston in 1981), Virgin averaged 90 to 95 miles a week. He didn't run his first 100-mile week until his junior year in college and, except when training for his infrequent marathons, rarely strung 100-mile weeks together.

"I don't think they give any awards for workouts," says Virgin. "To the best of my knowledge, there are no gold medals for 'most mileage.' If it was the end of the week and I had 98 miles in, I didn't go for a third workout that day to get 100. That won't make the difference between winning and losing. It's what you do with that 100 miles a week, and I think people forget about that."

Yet by the end of the millennium, American distance runners—once dominant on the world scene in the era of Shorter, Rodgers, Salazar, and Samuelson—had become second-rate performers. Kenyans, who sometimes run three workouts a day, fill the front ranks of most major marathons. In 1997 and again in 1998, the New Balance shoe company put $1 million on the line for any American man or woman who could break the national record. While the U.S. women's record of 2:21:21 set by Samuelson was very close to the world record, the men's mark of 2:08:47, set by Bob Kempainen, was "soft," nearly 2 minutes off the world record. Nobody collected the prize. The closest anybody came was Jerry Lawson, a high-mileage runner, who ran 2:09:17 at Chicago in 1997. Then Lawson failed to complete three out of his next four marathons.

Meb Keflizighi and Deena Drossin Kastor—the two American runners who won silver and bronze medals in the marathon at the 2004 Olympic Games in Athens—proved that it is less how many miles you run than what you do with those miles. In the 9-month buildup to the Olympics, Keflizighi and Kastor averaged 120–140 miles a week, high by any standard, but Kastor emphasized it was less the quantity of miles, but the quality that resulted in their strong Olympic showings by her and Keflizighi. "Over a period of years, I had matured as a runner," Kastor says. "This permitted me to increase the intensity of my training. That's what took me to the next level."

While most recreational runners cannot even comprehend the talent and training required to reach mileage levels of 120 to 140, similar improvements can be made if they can solidify their base at 20 to 40 miles a week. Train comfortably at that level over a period of time, solidify your ability to do long runs between 10 and 20 miles, and then you can concentrate on intensity to improve. Interesting about Kastor's training is that during the winter, she ran many of those miles on snowshoes. Both Kastor and Keflizighi do much of their training at Mammoth Lakes, California, where the altitude of 8,000 feet makes running fast difficult. Kastor often would drive down the mountain in the morning for workouts several thousand feet lower below the snow line. Afternoons, she often would don snowshoes and go to 9,000 feet for runs through the woods, "If you live in a ski area, you need to learn to embrace winter," she says. "The mechanics of running on snowshoes are slightly different, but there's less impact, plus stopping in a snowy meadow beneath a fir tree and taking in the mountain scenery is a great way to relax the mind and avoid the tedium of all that high-mileage training."

WHAT HIGH MILES ACCOMPLISH

The late physiologist Al Claremont, PhD, an exercise scientist from the University of Wisconsin, claimed that high mileage helps you better utilize glycogen, the starchlike substance stored in the liver and muscles that changes into a simple sugar as the body needs it. Carbohydrates in the diet are our main source of glycogen—one reason spaghetti is such a popular prerace meal for marathoners. Glycogen is the preferred fuel for running, but your levels can become depleted within 60 to 90 minutes. Thereafter, your source of fuel is fat, which is metabolized less efficiently.

Claremont believed high-mileage running in essence teaches your body to burn more fat along with the glycogen, stretching your reserves from 60 to 90 minutes to 2 hours or more. He explained: "Top marathoners are probably so efficient in metabolizing both fats and glycogen throughout the length of their races (because of the vast volume of their training) that they probably rarely deplete their stores. As a result, they don't hit the wall."

William J. Fink, a researcher at Ball State University's human performance laboratory in Muncie, Indiana, suggests that volume training may result in a more efficient use of your muscle fibers. "When a runner doubles his training mileage, we often see no change in his maximum oxygen uptake, the ability to deliver oxygen to the muscles," explains Fink. This, he says, indicates that something else—perhaps improved muscle fibers—causes the better performances.

Jack H. Wilmore, PhD, an exercise physiologist and professor emeritus in the department of kinesiology and health education at the University of Texas at Austin, suggests there is a psychological effect to high mileage as well. "When you do 100 miles a week, your legs are chronically fatigued," he comments. "Then, when you finally do taper before an important race, it makes you feel all the stronger. The same would hold true for a 30-mile-a-week runner who, through a gradual buildup, achieved an ability to train comfortably at 60."

Finally, Dr. Wilmore says, mileage helps your body adapt to the punishment that occurs during marathons—in ways that scientists can't yet explain. "When I'm out of shape and I race at long distances, everything

WHEN I'M READY FOR A MARATHON AND HAVE PUT IN THE MILES, EVERYTHING MOVES SMOOTHLY.

hurts," he says. "It feels like my connective tissues are coming apart. But when I'm ready for a marathon and have put in the miles, everything moves smoothly."

Research from exercise laboratories suggests that many of the long miles done by runners in the past may have been wasted—and, in fact, running too many miles may have contributed to chronic overtraining, which resulted in poorer, rather than better, performances. "You may run far," says David Martin, PhD, a U.S. Olympic Team consultant from Atlanta, "but you don't run far long."

David L. Costill, PhD, founder of the human performance laboratory at Ball State University in Muncie, Indiana, has measured beginning, average, and elite runners, as well as athletes in other sports. He believes that there exists a finite limit beyond which athletes cease to improve. For runners, he suspects the limit is 50 to 75 miles per week. "The amount of physiological improvement beyond that is almost insignificant," says Dr. Costill.

In one case documented in Dr. Costill's book *Inside Running*, his lab studied two marathoners who resumed training after 6-month layoffs due to injuries. Dr. Costill supervised muscle biopsies and treadmill tests for max VO_2 (the ability of the body to utilize oxygen during exercise) as the pair gradually increased their weekly mileages.

Dr. Costill wrote: "As one might have predicted, the muscles showed dramatic improvements in aerobic capacity with as little as 25 miles of running per week. [Their] max values increased when they increased their weekly mileages to 50 and then 75 miles per week. Beyond that level of training, however, our laboratory tests found no additional gains in endurance. During a 1-month period they even trained at 225 miles per week, with no improvement in endurance."

In tests of other athletes, Dr. Costill was unable to detect any differences in oxygen uptake scores between runners who ran 60 miles weekly and those doing twice that mileage. "There may be some psychological reasons for running high mileage," he concedes, "but we haven't been able to measure it."

When working with swimmers, Dr. Costill found that they improved when their mileage was cut. When Ball State University swimmers cut their daily mileage from 10,000 yards to 5,000 yards, everyone on the squad set new PRs—some by significant margins.

FITTING THE MILES IN

So what does all this mean to those of us who dream only of qualifying for Boston or setting a new PR? "There's no mystery about how you improve your endurance," says Lee Fidler, a running coach from Stone Mountain, Georgia, with a marathon PR of 2:15:03. "You just increase volume. I ran 110 miles a week 10 years in a row, but not everybody can do that. For most people, 60 is plenty."

But for someone running his or her first marathon whose weekly mileage may have been expressed in single digits before sending in their entry blank, the thought of running 60 miles in a single week may seem frightening, while 110 weekly miles ranks as beyond comprehension. The average reader of *Runner's World*, according to

TRAINING MILES

How many miles do you run a week? If you're like most viewers of the *Runner's World* Web site, you probably run about 25 miles weekly. The magazine asked that question of its readers and learned that most ran at least 15 miles a week, with a large number (36.9 percent) running between 20 and 30 weekly miles. After that point, numbers began to decline somewhat to where only a few runners (13.3 percent) averaged more than 40 miles weekly. The survey included runners who competed at all distances or ran no races at all. A later survey suggested that marathoners ran much more.

Miles per week	Percentage
1–9	3.99%
10–14	11.78%
15–19	16.37%
20–24	18.46%
25–29	18.46%
30–39	17.56%
40+	13.37%

surveys by that magazine, runs 20–25 miles week. When preparing for a marathon, that same individual bumps that mileage by another 10 weekly miles. My novice training program peaks at 40 miles in the 15th week, but runners reach that lofty goal in only that 1 week. In the half dozen weeks before the peak, the weekly mileage is in the thirties.

Although you can finish a marathon on only 30 miles a week, in order to finish well, you may need to push your mileage up to near the 60 miles that Fidler suggests. Brian Piper, founder of the Chicago Marathon training class, was running 70 miles a week when he broke 3 hours and qualified for Boston. To get anywhere near that

level of mileage, you should make a gradual progression in increments of 10 percent a week, says Fidler. Every 3rd or 4th week, drop
back close to the starting point to recover. Fidler says: "If you build
constantly week after week, you get stronger, but you also find
your break point. It's best to approach your break point without
reaching it. You advance in steps. Go up two or three steps, drop
back one or two steps, then hop back to where you were and start
stepping again."

Joe Catalano of East Walpole, Massachusetts, has coached
everyone from beginning jog-
gers to his former wife, Patti
Lyons Catalano, who had a
marathon best of 2:27:51. He believes people vary in their ability to
increase mileage. Joe recommends a gradual climb, adding 5 extra
miles a week for a top runner but fewer for others. "The endurance
base is the single most important factor in getting fit," he advises.
"People worry about speed, but if you concentrate first on mileage
and improving your strength, you can move to the speed phase later."

> **PEOPLE VARY IN THEIR ABILITY TO INCREASE MILEAGE.**

Thom Hunt, a coach from San Diego whose best marathon time
was 2:12:14, often varied his mileage from week to week and from
season to season. He usually ran between 85 and 105 miles a week,
slightly more when training for marathons. Hunt's secret was variation. "I might run 105 one week, 115 the week after that, then go
down and run a 90," says Hunt. "Rest is an important part of a
training program. There are times of the year when you just go to
the beach."

THE PERILS OF THE NUMBERS GAME

What you need to beware of is concentrating on how many miles
you're running to the exclusion of everything else. Some runners become fixated on high mileage, feeling that if they fail to reach their
weekly mileage goals, they remain unfulfilled. They begin worrying

by Wednesday or Thursday: "Am I going to make it this week?" At this point, they're running more for their training diaries than for themselves. They're also spending a lot of time running "junk miles"—miles that have no effect on fitness or performance.

Although high mileage may help produce better times, simply adding mileage may not guarantee success either for the world-class athlete or for the dedicated fitness runner who dreams of one day running the Boston Marathon. Quality must be mixed with quantity to produce maximum results. Don Kardong says: "People are too conscious of high mileage and not conscious enough about quality. It's a natural outcome of keeping a running diary. You become very concerned with how many miles you ran this week, but not with how fast you ran them."

Dr. Martin believes that much of the so-called rehabilitative running that elite runners do between hard runs may simply deaden their legs. "One of the secrets to remaining fresh," he says, "is to limit impact time, the number of times your feet strike the pavement."

Some runners jump from 50 to 75 miles to the "magic" 100 by simply adding a second workout to their day. Dr. Martin has his doubts about the gains from multiple workouts. "Run 5 miles each morning, and multiply that by 7, and you get 35 miles," he says. "If you add that to 65 miles of hard training in the afternoon, you can write 100 in your training diary. But does that make you a better runner?"

Dr. Martin continues: "It is not how much training you do as much as it is how well you recover from it. Because if you do not recover adequately, you'll either become injured, or sick, or chronically fatigued with resulting poor performance. Thus, while everyone has a different number of miles per week that they can tolerate (due to weather, terrain, biomechanics, lifestyles) without breakdown, the secret to success is not to exceed that threshold."

Invariably, people who achieve the highest level of success for their ability—regardless of whether they are winning marathons or merely running in the middle of the pack—are those who minimize the destructive effects of high mileage and maximize the efficiency of the miles they run.

FINDING THE MILEAGE
THAT WORKS FOR YOU

Top marathoners talk about redlining, a term borrowed from auto racers. The redline is the mark on the tachometer that delineates the safety zone from the danger zone. If you consistently rev your engine higher, it disintegrates.

In running, redlining means pushing your training to achieve maximum efficiency and your best performances. But if you push past your redline regularly, you risk injury or breakdown.

A beginning runner might redline after a gradual buildup at 30 miles. Or 45. Or 60. There are physiological limits: Running too many miles too soon results in injuries, such as strained tendons and ligaments, stress fractures, chronically tired legs, and a persistent feeling of fatigue.

There are also psychological limits. Some runners can't cope with dressing, running, and showering all the time—as well as the need for extra rest. Not only does 100 miles weekly require 10 or more hours of actual running time; it also requires a lot of recuperative time. One of the coaches in our survey suggested that elite runners need 3 to 4 hours of rest daily on top of 7 to 8 hours of sleep each night.

Scientists haven't been able to define the precise point—between undertraining and overtraining—where optimal benefits occur. And this point certainly differs for different athletes. While one runner might thrive on 30 miles a week, another might need 60, and a third might need 120 to excel. It's also possible that the optimal mileage level may change at different points in a runner's career. I consider this especially to be true when it comes to masters runners. Pass age 40—and particularly age 60—and you simply can't train as hard or as much as you could as a youngster.

In general, runners who can increase training mileage should expect to improve as long as they don't sacrifice quality for quantity. The key is to increase mileage gradually and to pay careful attention—very careful attention—to how your body reacts.

CHAPTER 10

RUNNING LONG

ENDURANCE IS ESSENTIAL FOR SUCCESS AS A MARATHONER

It is the staple of every distance runner's diet: the long run. If you're a seasoned marathoner, workouts up to 20 miles are de rigueur. If you call the homes of most distance runners on a Saturday or Sunday at 7:00 a.m., you'll find they're either already out running or just about to head out the door. Running long will get you ready to perform. In my programs, first-time marathoners use a single 20-miler as a confidence builder before tackling the full 26 miles 385 yards. Advanced runners do multiple long runs as one means of improving their PRs. Even 5-K runners find that running long regularly helps them run faster. And even if you're interested only in fitness, a longer-than-usual training run with friends on the weekend can be fun.

But what is the purpose, in both physical and psychological terms, of the long run? What function does it serve in getting you ready for a marathon? What is the perfect distance for running long, how often should you do it, and at what pace?

Most coaches agree that running long is not only enjoyable but also essential to achieving success in distances from 5-K to the marathon. "The single long run is as important as high mileage in a marathoner's training program," says Alfred F. Morris, PhD, a health and fitness manager for the Department of Justice in Washington, D.C. Tom Grogon, a coach from Cincinnati, ranks it second only to "raw talent."

Robert Wallace, a 2:13 marathoner who placed ninth at Boston in 1982 and is a part-

> RUNNING LONG IS NOT ONLY ENJOYABLE, BUT ALSO ESSENTIAL TO ACHIEVING SUCCESS.

time coach in Dallas, says, "I still love those long, easy runs on Sunday. They're the mainstay of any training program. You don't get results immediately. It's like saving pennies: Put them in a jar, and over a year, you accumulate $50 to $60."

Wallace favors slow workouts rather than fast ones for the long runs. "High-quality (fast) runs are too hard on a weekly basis," he says. "Run low-quality, and you can get out every weekend. I like to see 10-K runners go 14 to 16 miles; marathoners go 20 to 22 miles, several minutes slower than race pace."

Joe Friel of Scottsdale, Arizona, who coaches runners in person and online, considers the long run essential for building an endurance base. He has his runners do at least one long run every week, or every other week. "Every 10 days would be perfect," says Friel, "but that's tough to fit into a work schedule."

David Cowein, an ultramarathoner from Morrilton, Arkansas, runs long once a month for 2 to 6 hours. "I'll usually run trails," he says. "If I did a run that long on roads, I'd be sore the next day, but trails are easier on my body. I'll run far, but I'll also run slowly, walking up hills if necessary."

Runners often do their long runs in groups. "It's great to run with a group because it can be lonely out there," says Wallace. "Even when I ran fast times, I always trained with slower runners," he says. "I just wanted to run long and didn't care at what pace."

While working on an article that appeared in the August 1998 issue of *Runner's World*, I posed some questions on long runs to a number of top coaches. Each coach agreed that the long run was the key to marathon success. "Shun long runs in training and you'll pay the price for your neglect," warned Al Lawrence of Houston, a former world-class runner from Australia. But not all coaches surveyed agreed on every detail of marathon preparation. Here is what the top coaches had to say about running long.

1. What is the main purpose for the long run?

Running long offers a dress rehearsal for the race. "It's a test," says John Graham, who coaches runners on the Internet.

Atlanta-based coach Roy Benson agrees: "Running long gets you used to the stress of lifting your feet up and down nearly 5,000 times per hour." It allows you to practice skills you will need in the race, such as taking fluids. Long runs build confidence in your ability to succeed, and, maybe equally important, you learn patience.

"Many runners push too hard on daily runs," says Bob Glover, coach for the New York Road Runners Club. "The long run forces them to slow down and pace themselves wisely—just as they must do in the marathon."

But apart from practical and psychological considerations, there are strong physiological reasons to run long. Robert H. Vaughan, PhD, is an exercise physiologist who trains both elite athletes and first timers for the Dallas White Rock Marathon. Vaughan offers the scientific reason:

> The long run serves to increase the number of mitochondria, as well as capillaries in the active muscles, thereby improving those muscles' ability to remove and utilize available oxygen. In addition, the long run recruits muscle fibers that would otherwise go unused. This recruitment insures a greater pool of conditioned fibers that may be called upon during the later stages of the race. There are certain psychological barriers and adjustments to central nervous system fatigue that also are affected by the long run.

That's deep, and difficult for a layman to understand—but it's also the single most important reason you should run long.

2. What is the best long-run training distance for marathoners?

There is no "perfect" distance. Twenty miles is the peak distance used in most training programs, if only because 20 is a round number. That's the peak distance we use with our training class in Chicago—even for advanced runners. But in countries outside the United States, 30 kilometers (18.6 miles) is equally round and as frequently used. Most coaches feel that once you reach 16 miles, you're in long-run territory. That's the point where the psychological and physiological changes Dr. Vaughan mentioned kick in. But a few coaches prefer prescribing "time" rather than distance: hours rather than miles. Benji Durden of Boulder, Colorado, points to 3 hours as the equivalent to running 20 miles.

That was probably true in the 1980s and into the 1990s, when the median time for most marathoners was closer to 4 hours than it is now. Given the greater number of "slower" runners completing marathons, the median time now seems to be marching backward, aimed at 5 hours, with increasing numbers of marathoners taking that long or longer to finish. For a first timer hoping to finish in 6 hours, a 3-hour workout would result in only about 13 miles of running, hardly enough to condition that person for the full distance. Common sense must dictate whether you choose time or distance to measure your long runs.

Running much farther than 20 miles increases the risk of injury, particularly for first timers. For experienced runners, the suggested top number is about 23 miles, said the coaches. Bob

RUNNING MUCH FARTHER THAN 20 MILES INCREASES THE RISK OF INJURY.

Glover, who trains runners for the New York City Marathon, peaks first timers at 20 miles, experienced runners at 23 miles—but also puts a cap at 4 hours of running, regardless of how many miles you've covered. "The goal," says Glover, "is at least three long runs of 18 to 20 miles for novices and five or six runs of 20 to 23 miles for experienced runners."

Jeff Galloway, coach in Atlanta and a columnist for *Runner's World*, peaks participants in his nationwide training programs at 26 miles—but they do a lot of walking to get that far. At the furthest end of the spectrum, elite Japanese runners do 5-hour runs, which probably take them past 30 miles. Former world record holder Rob DeCastello and training partner Steve Monighetti, Australians, used to peak with a 30-miler 5 weeks before the marathon, but that's after a steady diet of 23-milers nearly every weekend. Most runners would self-destruct on that much mileage. At one point in my career as an elite athlete, I pushed the distance of my longest runs up past 30 miles, seeking increased endurance, but I failed to reap any benefits. Runs that long simply took too much time and increased my fatigue level.

The greatest danger, however, is that doing long runs much longer than 20 miles increases the risk of injury. I am haunted by the memory of a party I attended one year before the Chicago Marathon. One woman hoping to run Chicago as her first marathon had followed a program, designed by another coach, that peaked at 26 miles. In her last long run a month before the race, she pulled a muscle at 24 miles and had to stop. "What a shame," I thought. If the same had happened in the actual marathon (which the injury forced her to miss), the woman surely would have been motivated enough to walk or limp the final 2 miles and earn her finishing medal.

Nevertheless, I don't disagree with Coach Bill Wenmark of the Twin Cities, who encourages his most experienced runners to push past marathon distance for their longest runs. Wenmark defines "ex-

COACHES' CONSENSUS

Runners differ in their backgrounds and their abilities. There is no single workout, or training program, that works best for everyone—and this certainly remains true when it comes to doing long runs. Yet in surveying coaches, I did find a consensus about how far and how often you should run long, specifically during the marathon buildup. The answers and numbers differ according to whether you are a first-time marathoner or an experienced runner hoping to better your time at that distance. Here is what the coaches advise.

Category	First timers	Experienced
Longest run	20 miles	23 miles
Frequency	1 time	3–6 times
Pace (per mile)	Race pace	30–90 seconds slower than race pace
Weekly mileage	40 miles	55–60 miles
Walking breaks	Yes	No
Speedwork	No	Yes

To summarize the feeling of the coaches on two important issues: Walking breaks are okay in a marathon if your main interest is in finishing and you don't care about time. Experienced runners seeking to run fast, however, may want to skip the walk breaks (except through aid stations to assure proper fluid intake). Speedwork (training faster than race pace) is considered too risky for first timers. Experienced runners, who do their long runs slower than race pace, are likely to benefit from midweek speed sessions, including long repeats at race pace.

perienced" as having previously run 10 or more marathons, someone who probably regularly runs 50 to 60 miles a week. If such a marathon vet suffers an injury and loses training time—or maybe even misses the race—it is not as shattering an experience as it would be for people doing their first marathons.

3. How many long runs at, or near, peak distance should distance runners do?

If you're a novice following my program, you run only one long run at peak distance: the traditional 20-miler mentioned previously. Nearly every training program gradually builds runners up to near that distance, rests them 2 to 4 weeks, then sends them off to the starting line with a pat on the fanny. And it works! Most runners who follow the marathon training schedules on my Web site jump fairly easily from 20 miles in practice to 26 in the race. The excitement of the event coupled with several weeks' rest during the taper period helps them bridge the gap. First timers often surprise themselves when they discover that running the marathon can be easier than training for it. (That's assuming you train for it correctly.)

But finishing that first marathon and racing subsequent marathons are two different beasts. To improve, you probably need more long runs, not merely longer runs. Experienced runners don't need to emulate the Aussies mentioned earlier and run 23-milers every weekend, but in the closing stages of their preparation, they probably need to run between three and six workouts that are between 18 and 22 miles, according to the marathon coaches I consulted.

As with novice marathoners, the reason is psychological as much as physical. "The more peak-distance runs runners achieve in their marathon preparation, the more confidence they radiate," states Bob Williams, who prepares runners for the Portland Marathon.

Run long too often, however, and you raise your risk of not only injury but also staleness. Only experienced runners should venture often into that 18- to 22-mile window, and even they risk making mistakes.

4. Should you incorporate walking into your long runs, whether you plan to walk in the race or not?

Here's where I encountered some disagreement. Not all the responding coaches bought the idea as expressed in an April 1998 *Runner's World* article by executive editor Amby Burfoot titled "The Run/Walk Plan." Burfoot recommended that taking regular walking breaks is helpful both in workouts and in races.

"No!" thundered one coach.

"I thought the name of the magazine was *Runner's World*," grumbled another.

Al Lawrence of Houston was the most diplomatic dissident, when he said, "Runners seem to feel better about themselves when they say 'I've run a marathon,' rather than 'I've done a marathon.'"

That was the reaction in 1998, but as we moved into the new millennium, most coaches began to concede that walking was not that bad a strategy, particularly if your goals were less than Olympian. When you're running 10:00 miles or slower, the difference between that pace and a brisk walking pace may not be that much.

And just because you break to walk in a marathon, that does not mean you're a slow runner. A brief walking break (notice that I said "brief") may actually allow you to gather yourself and continue at a faster pace. On a warm day, I ran a 2:29:27 and won an M45 title at the World Masters Championships, walking through each aid station. My son Kevin used the same strategy to run 2:18:50 and qualify for the 1984 Olympic Trials. Bill Rodgers walked several times and even stopped to retie a shoe while winning the 1975 Boston Marathon in 2:09:55. So no apologies needed, you walking runners.

If you do plan to walk during long runs or in the marathon, here is how and when to do it.

• It's a good idea to walk through aid stations. You can grab more fluids and drink more easily while walking.

• Walk if you can't run any further, although it's best to walk before you're forced to.

• Do some walking in training, if only to learn how to start running again after being brought to a halt.

• Take walking breaks in training and races if the coach of your program tells you to do so.

The last piece of advice is a nod and salute to Jeff Galloway, the Atlanta coach who pioneered regular walking breaks for people he trained, sometimes referred to as "Gallowalkers."

5. How much recovery do you need after long runs?

Dr. Vaughan summarizes the consensus of the coaches when he says, "An experienced marathoner with years of training may recover in 48 to 72 hours, while a novice may require 2 weeks." Most runners in training will benefit from a day's rest after doing their weekend long runs, and

> MOST RUNNERS IN TRAINING WILL BENEFIT FROM A DAY'S REST AFTER DOING THEIR WEEKEND LONG RUNS.

probably an easy day after that, before taking another hard workout at a shorter distance. Thus, we arrive at the following pattern.

Sunday: Long run
Monday: Rest or easy run
Tuesday: Easy run
Wednesday: Hard run

That doesn't mean that the "hard" run on Wednesday should be another 20-miler. Most first timers should probably choose a medium-length run of between 5 and 10 miles for their midweek (hard) workout. In coaching marathoners, I describe this as the "sorta-long run." Experienced runners might be more likely to do their next fast workouts on either Tuesday or Wednesday.

Most marathon training programs, including ours in Chicago, allow 2 weeks between long runs near peak distance. The programs schedule medium-long runs (10 to 14 miles) on the weekends between.

Rest before the long run is as important as rest after. If you program a day or two of easy running and/or rest before your long runs so that you are not overly fatigued prior to the long runs, recovery afterward will be easier. This is particularly true for first timers.

6. Are there any tricks to recovery?

No tricks, just sound training and nutritional practices. The three best strategies cited by our coaches were gels, energy bars, and massage. Use the first two during the long runs, the last after. "Taking gels and bars during the long runs speeds recovery," says running guru Joe Henderson, author of two dozen books, including *Marathon Training*. "You need to keep your glycogen stores continuously high if you want to maintain training effectiveness."

Bob Williams considers dehydration to be one of the major sources of muscle soreness and also a source of muscle cramps during long run. "Drinking during workouts is as important as drinking during races," he says.

Massages can be expensive, but when you decide to train for a marathon, you make a major time commitment and also a financial commitment, considering the cost of entry fees, not to mention the cost of travel if you pick a marathon not in your hometown. Given that commitment, you might as well do right by everything connected with the marathon. Schedule a massage for 48 hours after your long run, since that's often the peak point of muscle soreness.

The massage will help you ease your way back into your regular routine. More frequent massages during the final 6 weeks leading up to your peak long run may help reduce the risk of injury by keeping you loose and relaxed. For that reason, massages also work well as preventative therapy 24 hours before a hard workout or long run.

7. How fast should you run during long runs?

Speed is of limited importance during long runs, according to the coaches I contacted. More important is time spent on your feet. One long-run strategy for runners following time-based programs is to set as their goal for the longest run approximately the length of time they plan to run in the marathon itself, not worrying about the distance or the speed at which they cover the distance. That's handy if you plan to run on unmeasured courses, particularly ones that would take you off roads and into the woods. "Sub-2:10 marathoners (who race faster than 5:00 pace) have been known to run their long runs at over 7:00 per mile," says Vaughan.

Novices in most training programs connected with major marathons run the same pace in their long runs as they will run in the race. "That's because we encourage first timers to select a conservative time goal to guarantee their finish," says Bill Fitzgerald, one of the leaders of the CARA Marathon Training Class in Chicago. Fitzgerald adds, "If you can't hold a conversation during the closing miles of your long run, the pace probably was too fast." Glover says: "If you can chatter, the pace doesn't matter."

Experienced marathoners who continually run long at race pace can get into trouble unless they slow down. They risk both injuries and overtraining. While the law of specificity suggests that you need to do some running at race pace to condition your muscles to the specific pace you will attempt to hold in the marathon, this is best accomplished during midweek workouts at shorter distances. "It's better to err on the slow side," says Lawrence.

On several occasions, I've experimented by doing long runs at race pace or faster, wondering whether it might make me stronger. I found that I could maintain this level of effort until the long runs got up to about 12 or 13 miles. After that, I began to encounter problems, the most serious being an inability to maintain the quality of my workouts during the rest of the week. It became an example of robbing Peter to pay Paul.

Not every long run needs to be done at the same pace, nor does the pace within each run need to be the same. Denis Calabrese, director of USA FIT, who trains marathoners in many cities, believes runners should do the second half of their runs faster than the first half both in practice and in the actual marathon. "The discipline of going out slow rather than allowing the excitement of the marathon to burn you up is very valuable," says Calabrese.

> **NOT EVERY LONG RUN NEEDS TO BE DONE AT THE SAME PACE.**

For experienced marathoners, I often recommend the 3/1 approach taught to me by New Zealand's John Davies, bronze medalist in the 1500 meters at the 1964 Olympics and a respected disciple of Coach Arthur Lydiard from that country. Davies advised doing the first three-quarters of a long run at a slow pace, then picking up that pace in the last quarter of the distance—although not quite to marathon pace. In a 20-mile run, this would mean slow for the first 15 miles and faster for the final 5 miles. Davies didn't recommend converting every long run into a 3/1 effort. He felt once every 2nd or 3rd week was sufficient.

How slow is slow, and how fast is fast? If you're looking for numbers, do your long runs 30 to 90 seconds per mile (or more) slower than the pace per mile you expect to run in the marathon. Notice that I qualified the time prescription with "or more," meaning I really don't care how slow you run as long as you cover the distance. Always be aware that inclement weather can render irrelevant any plans to train at a specific pace. Fatigue from activities related to your life away from running also can be a factor.

In a 3/1 workout, you might run the first three-quarters at a pace 90 seconds or more slower than marathon pace, then pick up to 30 seconds slower. But that's getting almost too precise for comfort. The most important point is to run slow enough at the beginning of a long run so that you can run somewhat faster at the end. This strategy works well in the actual marathon, too.

8. Is there any advantage for nonmarathoners doing long runs?

All the coaches we surveyed believe there is. "Endurance is a factor at all racing distances," says Henderson. "Even 5-K and 10-K runners can benefit from 1- to 2-hour runs, but anything much longer might drain energy away from their more specific work."

Running long regularly also is an effective way to both lose a few pounds and maintain weight. Don't overlook the psychological value of a regular, weekly long run, particularly if it gives you an opportunity to run in the company of friends whom you might not get a chance to see during the week. One reason that many runners continue to run marathons is that preparing for that long distance provides both focus and structure to their training. It gives them an excuse to do long runs, which is something that they want to do anyway.

Whatever the reason, the long run is here to stay as a regular part of our training diets.

CHAPTER 11
SPEEDWORK FOR DISTANCE RUNNERS

IF YOU WANT TO RUN FAST,
YOU HAVE TO RUN FAST

Dark clouds hovered on the horizon late on a spring afternoon as I drove eastward, toward Eagle Lake in Michigan. The temperature was in the sixties but was dropping. Thunderstorms had rattled through the area sporadically during the past few hours. Only a few drops of rain had hit my windshield, but I found out later that others in the class had driven through downpours.

It was a Thursday in mid-April, and I was running with Ron Gunn's Marathon 101 class. Gunn is the dean of sports at Southwestern Michigan College in Dowagiac, and he regularly conducts training classes for beginning and experienced runners. That spring's version of Marathon 101 was designed to prepare people for a June marathon in South Bend, Indiana. Class members were scheduled to run 16 miles that day in their progression to a maximum long run of 20 miles before tapering to marathon day. But I didn't want to run that far, or that hard. I had already done my long run earlier in the week, so I decided to cut that night's distance to 11 and do some speedwork.

We were to run a prepared course circling Eagle Lake, along which Gunn had chalked mile marks, an advantage to me in doing my speed session in that it provided set distances for creative workouts featuring repeat miles. While driving toward the lake, I decided to slice 5 miles from the planned workout and start at the 11-to-go mark. (Gunn drives class members to different starting points, depending on how far they want to run.)

I started slowly, as part of a planned warmup. I ran the first 2 miles at an 8:30 pace, allowing several class members to move out ahead of me. I weighed how I felt: decent, but fatigued and a bit stiff from my long run earlier in the week. I also planned to run a 15-K race in Kalamazoo, Michigan, on Saturday. It made sense to cruise comfortably and save energy for that race, the last formal test of my conditioning before the marathon. But at the 9-to-go mark, I started to push hard. I shifted gear into what Jack Daniels, PhD, exercise physiologist and coach at the State University of New York at Cortland, once called "cruise control." This is fast (but controlled) running, a phrase familiar to most serious runners.

I swept past several class members and continued at that pace until I crossed the 8-mile mark on the road. I punched my watch: 6:09 for the mile. I floated through the next mile, taking nearly 10 minutes, and then spurted again. Twice more I did the same at a nearly equal pace. Finally, I finished with 2 slow miles, coming in with a pair of runners I had caught who had started at a different point along the course.

Later, I recorded that workout in my diary as: 4 × 1 mile (1-mile jog between each fast mile) with a 2-mile warmup and a 2-mile cooldown, a classic speed workout featuring repeats.

WHO NEEDS SPEEDWORK?

Speedwork! That's a scary word, a frightening concept to a lot of marathoners, who reason that there's nothing speedy about the pace at which they run 26-mile races. If that is so, why *do* speedwork, with its ultimate threat of injury? Most marathoners want to run far, not run fast. One runner who picked up a copy of my book with that title (*Run Fast*) at a race expo where I was selling copies grunted, "I don't want to run fast."

Fair enough. If you're a marathoner, you probably need to do speedwork only if you want to improve your performances.

Did that get your attention? If so, let's discuss some of the ways marathoners can benefit by doing speedwork.

First, speedwork is an effective means for improvement, even though by running fast at Eagle Lake, I ruined my race in Kalamazoo that weekend. With sore muscles, I failed to run any 1 mile as fast as I had that Thursday in practice. Bad judgment on my part? Perhaps, but I rationalized that my goals were long-range: the marathon later that spring, and still other races beyond. But in all honesty, I had operated on instinct when I'd chosen to run fast because it was a good night for running.

That's not a bad reason, but the more pressing reason to include speedwork in your training program—even for marathons—is to improve performance. "Speedwork coupled with overdistance can bring a runner to any goal," says Paul Goss, a coach and duathlete from Foster City, California. Duathletes typically compete in races that include both running and cycling; triathletes add a swimming leg.

IF YOU'RE A MARATHONER, YOU PROBABLY NEED TO DO SPEEDWORK ONLY IF YOU WANT TO IMPROVE YOUR PERFORMANCES.

According to Alfred F. Morris, PhD, a health and fitness manager for the Department of Justice in Washington, D.C., "It is important for runners to learn to run fast, so that the marathon pace feels comfortable." Adds Frank X. Mari, a coach from Toms River, New Jersey: "You will never see full potential as a marathon runner until you develop your full potential as a sprinter." Coach Keith Woodard of Portland, Oregon, adds: "You have to be able to run fast at short distances before you can run fast at long distances."

As mentioned in earlier chapters, first-time marathoners need give little attention to speedwork. Their main goal is to gradually (but gently) increase their mileage so that they can finish a 26-mile race. Improving marathoners probably should also focus their attention on determining what level of high-mileage training works best for them. But after you've been running for several years and you begin to shave seconds instead of minutes off your PRs, or if you start to slip backward, it's time to turn to speedwork.

Most experienced marathoners know the value of speedwork, whether or not they practice it regularly. "Speed was my weakness, and I always felt I needed to concentrate on it even more than distance," says Julie Isphording, a 1984 Olympic marathoner. One time when I was visiting Cincinnati on business, I met her and a friend at 5:30 a.m. downtown near my hotel, and we ran across the Ohio River into Covington, Kentucky, to a high school track. The three of us had to climb a fence to get in, and it was still dark, but Isphording ran 8 × 800 meters, jogging 400 between. Soon after, she won the Los Angeles Marathon. (Another favorite workout of hers is 5 × 1600 meters, also jogging 400 between.)

BENEFITING FROM SPEEDWORK

Although long-distance runners concede that speedwork forms an integral part of any well-designed training regimen, not all marathoners use it as part of their training. One reason is unfamiliarity. Many of today's adult runners didn't compete in track or on cross-country teams in high school or college, so speedwork and running tracks feel foreign to them.

There is also an element of fear, both of the unknown and of injury—with good reason, since by training at a high intensity, you can hurt yourself. Speedwork also can hurt, and the burning sensation you get in your lungs, and the ache in your legs, may seem more threatening than the less piercing fatigue you encounter on the roads. Usually after a hard workout on the track, particularly early in the season, my legs are sore for several days.

Also, you can't carry on a decent conversation while zipping

SPEED FREAKS

Should marathoners do speedwork? The answer is similar to what you might hear if you asked at a boat show, "How much is that yacht?" If you have to ask, you can't afford one.

When first-time marathoners ask if they should do speedwork, because someone told them it can improve their speed, I answer no. If you haven't done fast running before embarking on your marathon quest, it's no time to start. And unless you are following one of my Advanced programs, which offer 1 or 2 days a week of speedwork, you're better off reserving speedwork for what might be called the off-season.

Nevertheless, even though so-called experts warn that speedwork can increase your risk of injury (not always true if you do it right), most runners seeking improved performance do head to the track now and then. While researching the book *Masters Running*, I surveyed more than 500 older runners and, to my surprise, discovered that 71 percent included at least some speedwork in their training. And in a later survey on my online Inter*Active* bulletin boards, I discovered that an even higher percentage (87.5) confessed to being speed freaks. I don't vouch for the methodology of the latter survey because most of the respondents were familiar with my views on speedwork for marathoners, as stated in this chapter.

Nevertheless, some comments by responders are worth sharing.

Nicole Henry, McHenry, Illinois: "I've never done speedwork

through a speed session. When I did those early-morning interval halves at the Covington track with Isphording and her friend, I was hanging on for dear life. Only later, jogging back across the river into downtown Cincinnati, could we resume our conversation.

Nevertheless, there are 10 good reasons every long-distance runner should do speedwork on a track.

before. I've mainly been concerned with covering the distance and staying injury-free. But I plan to incorporate speedwork into training for my next marathon, the Flying Pig. I'll dedicate one day a week to it."

Michele Keane, Westlake, Ohio: "I've done speedwork for years, partly because I'm a former track runner and like the feeling of running fast. I've always benefited from the short stuff (200s, 400s), but lately I've done longer repeats (1000s, 2000s, 3000s) to build my endurance, and it has helped. I also make a point of finding hills and running them. I try to get adequate rest the day after speed sessions. That has helped prevent injuries."

Geoff Wilson, Long Grove, Illinois: "I have done speedwork for 4 years, the last 2 in organized groups at a track with a coach. I've begun to see results. The group causes me to push myself harder than I would have done running alone."

Amanda Musacchio, Villa Park, Illinois: "I suspect almost everyone who qualifies for Boston does some sort of speedwork, whether they admit it or not. If every one of your workouts has a purpose—as they should—then you probably should select 1 or 2 days a week to run faster than normal. I did completely unfocused speedwork this summer and wound up with a nice 5-K PR."

Lori Hauswirth, Merrill, Wisconsin: "I've never done speedwork on a track, but occasionally on short training runs, I add some interval training: fast running between telephone poles. I feel it helps."

1. Performance. This is the most valid reason. With speedwork, you will run faster. That's guaranteed. Numerous laboratory studies have proven that adding speed training to an endurance base can take seconds off 5-K times and minutes off marathon bests. And runner after runner will testify to the value of including regular speed sessions in their long-distance programs. Melvin H. Williams,

PhD, a professor of exercise science at the human performance laboratory at Old Dominion University in Norfolk, Virginia, only began training seriously in his midthirties. After half a dozen years of mainly long-distance training, his performance times

> **BY TRAINING FASTER, YOU IMPROVE SPECIFIC MUSCLES USED AT HIGHER SPEEDS.**

stalled in the 2:50s for the marathon. After Dr. Williams cut mileage and added speedwork, he dropped his PR to 2:33:30 at age 44. "By training faster," says Dr. Williams, "you improve specific muscles used at higher speeds. You also improve your anaerobic threshold, which allows you to run a faster pace and remain aerobic. If you can run faster at short distances, you can increase your absolute ability at longer distances, too."

2. Form. One of the best ways I know—in fact, the only good way—to improve form is by running fast in practice. If you can learn to run more efficiently (exercise physiologists prefer the term "economically"), you will perform better at all distances and levels. I'm not sure why speed training improves your running form. Maybe you recruit different muscles. Maybe you force yourself to move more smoothly. Maybe by learning how to run at speeds faster than race pace, you're more relaxed when you do run that pace in a marathon. Maybe it's all of these reasons. Whatever the reason, running fast works.

3. Variety. Running the same course and the same distance at the same pace day after day can become tedious. To keep running exciting, you need variety. "Keeping workouts varied is one way to ensure success," says coach Joe Catalano from East Walpole, Massachusetts. Catalano has his runners do speedwork on the roads, on trails, and on the track. Many road-running clubs organize weekly speed sessions as a benefit to their members. When my wife and I stay at our Florida condo during the winter, I often train with the group that meets Wednesday evenings at the Bolles High School

Track in Jacksonville under the direction of coach Bob Carr. I go there as much for social reasons as to improve my speed, but I notice that many of my training companions take their Wednesday-night track workouts very seriously.

4. Excitement. Running alone through scenic trails provides its own pleasure, but tracks can have a level of activity that can stimulate you during your workouts. "Usually I preferred to do my fast running at a track where something is going on, even if it's only soccer practice and nobody's watching me," says Doug Kurtis of Northville, Michigan. "It's often hard to run when nobody's around."

During my early career, I trained frequently at Stagg Field on the campus of the University of Chicago. There always seemed to be half a dozen activities going on simultaneously: rugby in the infield, tennis behind the stands, several softball games on an adjoining field, kids playing in the sand of the long-jump pit, people doing yoga, and track athletes practicing multiple events. There was an electricity about being in the middle of this whirlwind of athletic activity that I found enormously appealing.

5. Convenience. "There are tracks in every city and town," says Catalano, "so it's very convenient to find one to do your workouts." Another important point: You can obtain maximum benefit in minimum time by doing speedwork.

> YOU CAN OBTAIN MAXIMUM BENEFIT IN MINIMUM TIME BY DOING SPEEDWORK.

"My clients don't have much time," notes Robert Eslick, a coach of adult runners from Nashville, "so short workouts appeal to them."

Here's a workout Fred Wilt, one of my former coaches, taught me. Head to the track and run eight laps, which is 2 miles (3,200 meters). Run the first four laps (1,600 meters) at a comfortable warmup pace. Then, without stopping, run the next 200 meters hard and the following 200 easy, and repeat this pattern for a total of three more laps (eight laps total for the workout). You're done, and your workout will have taken only about 20 minutes. That interval workout would be expressed as 4 × 200 (200 jog). The final 200 jog serves as your cooldown, and then you're in the car, heading home for dinner. (The same workout—once you learn the pattern—can be done on the road or on trails as well as on a track.)

6. Concentration. One of the skills that separate the good runners from the almost-good runners is an ability to focus their attention for the entire period of the race, whether it's a mile or a marathon. Dissociating is a good strategy for beginning marathoners, but not for people who want to run fast. When your mind wanders during a marathon, inevitably you slow down. If you stay focused, you learn how to concentrate all body systems to sustain a steady pace, conserve your energy, and maintain your running form. Eslick suggests that repeats between ¾ mile and 1½ miles simulate the concentration and pacing feel needed in a marathon. It takes total concentration to run fast on a track; once you master this skill, you can transfer it to your road runs.

7. Safety. You can't get hit by a car while running on a track, and you probably won't be chased by a dog, either. If you're in the company of others, the danger of being mugged is reduced. On a hot or cold day, if you become overheated or chilled or fatigued, you can just walk off the track and head for your car or the locker room; you don't have to worry about being caught 3 miles from home and trudging those final miles at a diminishing pace. Also, there are usually drinking fountains at running tracks, and toilets nearby.

8. Companionship. Willie Sutton was once asked why he robbed banks, and his response was "Because that's where the money is." Well, tracks are where the runners are. On a track you can seek company and training partners, and partners are important if you want to run fast. It sometimes becomes difficult to motivate yourself to train hard when you're alone. With someone running those interval quarters with you, you may get a better workout and improve. But beware: A companion danger is that you may train too hard, resulting in staleness (aka "burnout") or injury. On balance, however, your running will improve if you find running partners with whom you enjoy training.

9. Motivation. Your running also will improve if you can find a coach to guide you in your training. A second variation of the Willie Sutton rule is that you find coaches at tracks. Because it's difficult to watch runners and monitor their strengths and weaknesses when they are scattered all over a road, most coaches prefer to gather people in groups for speedwork sessions. Probably the single most important asset a coach can offer any runner is motivation. Any runner can select one of the many training programs offered in this book or on the Internet, but a skilled coach can motivate you and guide you to follow that program properly.

10. Pleasure. Just as it feels good for a tennis player to hit the ball perfectly over the net or for a golfer to loft a well-aimed chip shot to the green, it also feels good to run fast. There's a certain tactile pleasure in doing any activity well, an experience that in running I call "feeling the wind in your hair." One way to achieve the pleasure of fast running is to run short distances interspersed with adequate periods of rest. In other words, speedwork. And because speedwork inevitably will help you to improve your performance on race day, that boost will add to your pleasure, too.

SPEED VARIETIES

I defined speedwork in *Run Fast* as "any training done at race pace or faster." In that book I was offering advice for runners seeking to improve their 5-K and 10-K times, so I related race pace to how fast they ran those distances. If you run the marathon in 4:30, you run at a pace of 10:18 per mile, but to go out and run half a dozen miles at your marathon pace—which most experienced runners could achieve easily—would not necessarily constitute speedwork. Speed-

LONG REPEATS

Most marathon coaches believe runners should do their long runs slower than race pace. To do otherwise is to risk injury. Yet they agree on the need to do *some* running at the pace you plan to run your marathon so you can familiarize both your mind and your muscles with that pace. So when and how do you run race pace?

The answer is long repeats.

Just as milers go to the track and do interval workouts of 10 × 400 or 15 × 200 at fast pace, jogging or walking in between each rep for recovery, experienced marathoners can do long repeats as a form of speed training. Runners training for 5-K and 10-K races can also benefit from long repeats, although this workout is not advised for first-time marathoners.

Long repeats are best done on the roads on a course featuring mile markers. If there is no such course nearby, you can always use your car to make measurements, even though they won't be precise. Good distances for long repeat workouts are the half-mile, mile, 1.5-mile and 2-mile. Run one of those distances at race pace once, rest for 2 to 3 minutes by walking and/or jogging slowly, and then repeat. Over a

work for marathoners is training done at a pace significantly faster than they would run in a marathon. Your 10-K pace still remains an excellent benchmark.

To further define speedwork, I probably should add that it usually involves bursts of fast running (at race pace) followed by periods of slower running, or rest. That's essential because most runners probably can achieve race pace for long distances only when motivated and well rested—in other words, during the race itself. To achieve race pace in practice, they need to cut their race distance into segments and rest between those segments. If you were a com-

period of weeks and months, you can gradually increase the number of repeats, but you should always run race pace because familiarization is one of the most important reasons for this workout.

Here are several patterns for runners training for different race distances. Over a period of weeks and months, begin at the lower numbers and increase to the higher numbers.

Goal race	Starting workout	Goal workout
5-K	3 × half-mile	6 × half-mile
10-K	3 × mile	6 × mile
Half marathon	2 × 1.5-mile	5 × 1.5-mile
Marathon	2 × 2-mile	5 × 2-mile

Taper the workout 2 to 3 weeks before your important race. If your goal is not a specific race, you can vary your training by alternating between different repeat distances week to week. Or if your goal is a fast marathon, begin with the 5-K repeat distances and gradually progress to those for the marathon.

petitor at 5000 meters, you could run 12 × 400 meters in a workout, resting short periods after each 400, and simulate some of the stress of your race as well as practicing race pace. A marathon runner probably wouldn't do 26 × mile in a single workout, but the principle is the same.

There are different ways to do speedwork. Some ways work better for marathoners than for runners competing at shorter distances. You can run repeats, intervals, sprints, strides, surges, fartlek, or do tempo runs (terms I am about to define). You can run these workouts on the track, down the road, or on a path in the woods.

You don't even need a measured distance and a stopwatch; you can measure intensity by using a pulse monitor or even by perceived exertion. And now we have global positioning system (GPS) watches that track the length of your fast burst with reasonable precision. In *Run Fast*, I devoted a chapter to each of the speedwork variations, describing them in detail. In summary, here are the various types of speedwork and their applicability to marathon training.

Repeats. In a repeat workout, you run very fast, usually over a very short distance, and take a relatively long period of time to recover before repeating that distance. The fast (or hard) run in repeats is referred to as a repetition, or a rep. The runner recovers almost fully between repetitions, either jogging or completely resting. When I coached high school distance runners, I often had them walk a timed 5 minutes between reps. That allowed them to recover sufficiently so they could run each repetition at near maximum speed. There's nothing magic about 5 minutes, but resting for that precise amount of time at each workout offered them a familiar benchmark.

Interval training. In interval training, you carefully control the period of rest time, or interval, between the fast repetitions. Usually there are more reps than in repeat workouts, and the distance (or time) of the interval is shorter. Key to this kind of workout is that your heart rate not be allowed to drop too low before you surge into action again. Please note that the "interval" is the period between reps, not the repetition itself. Interval training is a more stressful form of training

INTERVAL TRAINING IS PROBABLY THE MOST EFFICIENT WORKOUT FOR DEVELOPING SPEED.

than most other forms of speedwork because you are never quite allowed to relax, so the result is a steady buildup of fatigue. For this reason, many veteran long-distance runners shy away from this type of speedwork. On the other hand, interval training is probably the most efficient workout for developing speed. I titled my chapter on interval training in *Run Fast* "The Magic Workout," quite accurately so, I might say.

Sprints. A sprint is just that: an all-out run for a short distance. The maximum distance a runner can run at full speed is probably around 300 meters, and that only if the runner is extremely well trained. Most sprints run by distance runners in practice are probably shorter than that:

> THE OBJECT OF RUNNING SPRINTS IN TRAINING IS TO DEVELOP STYLE AS WELL AS SPEED.

50 to 100 meters, a straightaway on a running track or a fairway on a golf course. The object of running sprints in training is to develop style as well as speed, economy more than endurance. It's also a good way to stretch muscles and learn to lengthen your stride.

Why should marathon runners run sprints, when at no time during the race will they run anywhere near that speed? The reason is that sprints develop speed. And speed is basic to success in running, regardless of the distance. If you can develop your base speed at distances of 100 meters to a mile, inevitably you will become a faster marathon runner.

Strides. Strides are simply slow sprints. I frequently use strides as part of my warmup to get ready for a faster workout, or before a race. Typically, I might jog a mile or two, stretch, then do 4 × 100 meters near race pace. Or I'll sometimes do strides at the end of a workout. Or, on a "rest" day, I'll do an easy workout that consists mainly of stretching and a few strides. Particularly during summer months, I like to do these stride workouts barefoot on the fairway of a golf course in the early morning before the golfers appear.

I like to do strides at race pace, regardless of the race distance from 800 meters to the marathon. Doing so reminds me of how fast I plan to race. The day before a marathon, I usually will jog a mile or so for a warmup, pick a grassy place where I can run three or four easy strides at marathon pace, then jog a mile or so for a cooldown. It relaxes me for the race the next day. And on race day, I may do a couple of warmup strides, although as marathon fields grow in size to near 40,000, it's often hard to warm up because of the crush of numbers.

Surges. Surges are fast sprints thrown into the middle of a long run or a long race. Well, not too long a race. You probably don't surge too frequently in a marathon, or you'll surge yourself into the pickup bus for runners who can't finish. Although surging at the right time might win you an Olympic gold medal (as Joan Benoit proved in 1984), it's probably not a good race strategy for midpack runners, whose goal is to spread their energy evenly throughout the race to maximize their performance. Nevertheless, surging is an effective and enjoyable training strategy.

Surging is also one way to get yourself out of those "bad patches" that develop in the middle of even the best-trained runner's marathon. Sometimes a surge to a slightly faster pace allows you to recover as much as if you jogged along slowly. You may surge for any distance. Tim Nicholls, a coach from Pembroke Pines, Florida, recommends 1-mile surges in training, as well as 2-mile repeats, but a surge can be as short as 100 meters.

Fartlek. Fartlek is all of the above thrown into a single workout, usually done away from the track, preferably in the woods. It's a Swedish word that roughly translates to "speed play." Fartlek includes fast and slow running—maybe even walking. Basically, you jog or sprint or stride as the mood strikes you, generally alternating fast and slow running. One of my favorite T-shirts was one I saw worn by a woman in a race. On the front of the shirt it said "fartlek." On the back of the shirt it said, "It's a runner's thing."

Although fartlek is best practiced on wooded trails, marathoners can adapt this type of workout to their own needs on the roads. This is an unstructured form of speed training that appeals particularly to experienced runners who have become very adept at reading their bodies' signals and thus don't need the discipline of a stopwatch and a measured distance.

Tempo runs. Exercise scientists now tell us that doing tempo runs is the most efficient way to raise your lactate threshold—that is, your ability to run at a fast pace without accumulating lactic acid in the bloodstream, which eventually will bring you to a halt. You train at the theoretical point between aerobic and anaerobic running.

A tempo run is one in which you begin at an easy jogging pace, gradually accelerate to near your 10-K race pace, hold that pace for a period of time, then gradually decelerate to your earlier jogging pace. A 40-minute tempo run might follow a pattern like this: Jog for 10 minutes, accelerate for 10 minutes, hold near 10-K pace for 10 minutes, decelerate for 10 minutes. There's nothing magic in the pattern of 10 + 10 + 10 + 10 = 40. A tempo run can follow any pattern as long as you take yourself up to near the edge of your lactate threshold.

I find tempo runs to be not only the most effective form of speedwork but also the most enjoyable. I love to do tempo runs on the trails of Indiana Dunes State Park near Chesterton, Indiana, about a 20-minute drive from my home. The surface of Trail Two circling the marsh near Wilson Shelter is smooth, flat, and conducive to very fast running. Maybe it's partly the scenery (often I spot deer in the woods), but I usually finish my tempo runs invigorated and ready to beat the world.

All forms of speedwork can make you a better runner, and a better marathoner. If you want to improve at any level of running, you have to learn to run fast.

CHAPTER 12
DEFENSIVE RUNNING STRATEGIES

YOU CAN'T SET PRS IF YOU'RE INJURED

When it comes to automobile accidents, one of the most dangerous strips of pavement in the world is Chicago's Dan Ryan Expressway. Whoever designed this expressway, with its intersecting lanes, failed to consider the mindset of Chicago area drivers. They speed, they weave, and they cut each other off, in their desperate attempts to get where they're going 30 seconds faster than the other guy. Maybe if these motor maniacs ran a couple of miles before jumping into their cars, they'd be less likely to inflict damage on each other.

One evening while heading home after a marathon training class, I was driving in a middle lane on a four-lane stretch of the Dan Ryan when I noticed in my rearview mirror that two cars were approaching rapidly. Either the drivers were racing each other or they were simply clueless. One passed on my left; the other passed on my right. Then each decided he wanted to occupy the same middle lane. I can still see the moment in instant replay. Their sides touched. Locked together, the cars began spinning in front of me.

I reached deep into my bag of defensive driving techniques. I stayed in my lane. I hit the brakes, but gently. I was as worried that I would be hit from the rear as that I would hit the two spinning cars. I watched as they skidded off to my left, crashing into the guardrail.

I believe in defensive driving, which is why I stay especially alert when driving the Dan Ryan, an expressway I can't easily avoid when heading home to Indiana.

As a runner, I also know what I need to do to avoid injury—not necessarily encounters with automobiles, but injuries that may be caused by overuse, training errors, and so forth. You can call these defensive running techniques. If you want to have a long running career, determine what activities most often cause you to become injured; then avoid them—just as I try to avoid high-risk highways.

FASTEN YOUR SEAT BELTS

Some physicians order injured runners to give up running. Several doctors offered me that advice earlier in my career, until I stopped going to doctors who weren't runners themselves. For most of us, stopping running permanently is not an option. We want to learn to run injury-free.

We also want to run long distances. And to run marathons is to court injury—if not from the race itself, then from the high mileage that's necessary for training. Jack H. Scaff Jr., MD, founder of the Honolulu Marathon, director of the highly successful Honolulu Marathon Clinic, and author of *My First Marathon*, says marathon running by definition is an injury. Dr. Scaff isn't

MOST RUNNING INJURIES ARE THE RESULT OF TRAINING ERRORS.

advising people not to run marathons; he's just stating what he considers to be a fact.

The late Michael L. Pollock, PhD, who directed the University of Florida Center for Exercise Science in Gainesville, identified intensity as the most common cause of running injuries. "People who only walk or jog short distances at slow paces don't become injured," said Dr. Pollock.

Stan James, MD, the orthopedist from Eugene, Oregon, who performed arthroscopic surgery on Joan Benoit months before her

Olympic Marathon victory, claims that most running injuries are the result of training errors. Avoid those errors, suggests Dr. James, and you can run injury-free. Lyle J. Micheli, MD, founder of the Sports Medicine Division at Boston's Children's Hospital and author of *The Healthy Runner's Handbook*, agrees: "Many of the injuries we see could have been prevented. There is usually some type of training error."

Nevertheless, most successful training programs—including the ones presented in this book—are based on variations of the progressive overload theory. You gradually overload the system with more mileage or the same mileage at faster paces. To achieve peak performance, you train to just under the point that your body would break down if you went further.

For most elite runners, their breaking point is somewhere beyond 100 miles per week, but not everyone is blessed with superior athletic ability. Podiatrists tell us their waiting rooms are filled with average runners who run 30 miles or more a week. Above that magic 30 miles seems to be where chondromalacia, plantar fasciitis, Achilles tendinitis, and other major injuries occur.

Logically, you just wouldn't run beyond that 30 miles a week, but that won't suffice for marathoners. Surveys by *Runner's World* have suggested that when runners commit to running a marathon, they increase their weekly mileage over a period of time by 10 to 15 miles—from somewhere around 20 miles to between 30 and 40 miles a week. If podiatrists are correct, that's when many of those runners call for appointments.

If you're a runner seeking peak performance, whether in the marathon or in some other event, the ideal is to determine—within 1/10 mile, if possible—the weekly mileage at which your body self-destructs. Then you can train to the edge of disaster, occasionally pushing slightly (and I emphasize the word *slightly*) over that edge to determine whether months and years of steady training (or a new

MILES RUN BY MARATHONERS

When preparing to run a marathon, most runners logically increase their weekly mileage. According to an online survey by *Runner's World*, 4 out of 10 responders ran between 30 and 39 weekly miles in the last 8 weeks of their marathon training. Compare this with the survey of all runners by that magazine that suggested weekly mileage in the 20-to-29 range, 10 or more miles less.

Interestingly, a survey I took of visitors to my Inter*Active* bulletin boards, a group I call my "V-Team," showed slightly higher numbers. (This survey was done simultaneously and in cooperation with the *Runner's World* survey.) Fewer than 10 percent of those runners I surveyed trained less than 30 miles weekly, compared with 25 percent for *Runner's World*. I also had more runners in the 40-to-49 mileage bracket. Possibly this was because those responding to my survey were following a specific online marathon training program of mine that dictated that mileage. This may have been less true among *Runner's World* responders.

Neither survey addressed the question of whether or not increased mileage resulted in increased injuries.

Miles per week	*Runner's World* survey	V-Team survey
10–19 mi	2.25%	1.89%
20–29 mi	23.87%	7.55%
30–39 mi	39.41%	43.40%
40–49 mi	21.06%	33.96%
50–59 mi	8.33%	9.43%
60–69 mi	3.83%	3.77%
70+ mi	1.24%	0

pair of shoes) have allowed you to nudge your breaking point to a new level and to permit you to run a marathon, or run that marathon faster.

Pushing to that edge has to be done over a period of time. Elite runners spend many years gradually adapting their bodies to accept the stress of 100-mile weeks. They don't increase from 50 miles a week one month to 100 the next without getting hurt. First-time marathoners

FIRST-TIME MARATHONERS WHO TRY TO INCREASE THEIR WEEKLY MILEAGE TOO RAPIDLY ARE LIKELY TO GET INTO TROUBLE. THEY WILL DEVELOP INJURIES.

who try to increase their weekly mileage too rapidly, from fewer than 20 to more than 30, also are likely to get into trouble. They will develop injuries.

When I began coaching track at the local high school in Michigan City, Indiana, a student named Tony Morales rejoined the team midway through his junior year. He had run well as a freshman under a previous coach but had suffered a series of discouraging injuries and had missed most of his sophomore year.

The previous coach told me, "Tony has a lot of talent, but whenever I got his weekly mileage up over 35, he'd get injured."

"Then I'll train him at 34 miles a week," I said.

That statement didn't endear me to the previous coach, but that's what I did, and Tony was able to run pain free. By gently pushing his limit over a period of nearly a year, Tony eventually nudged his training mileage to nearly 55 a week. As a senior, he made the All-Conference team in cross-country.

But midway through the season, Tony developed mild tendinitis in his upper thigh that limited his performance over a period of several weeks. Maybe if we had stopped at 54 miles a week, this injury would not have occurred. Or maybe not. That's the secret to injury prevention: to straddle the line between undertraining and overtraining.

ARE YOU OVERTRAINED?

Overtraining isn't an injury per se. You're not hurt. Nothing is swollen; nothing is broken. You don't limp. It's just that when you run, your legs feel dead most of the time, both your workout and your race times start to deteriorate, and you enjoy running less and less. By overdoing it, you may be predisposing yourself to injury. If you overtrain, something bad will happen; not can happen—*will* happen.

Marathon runners probably are more prone to overtraining than other runners simply because of the volume of training required. It stands to reason that if you train more, you increase your chances of becoming overtrained.

Probably the key cause of the symptoms of overtraining is the loss of glycogen, the sugarlike substance that fuels your muscles and provides the readily available energy that permits them to contract efficiently. Glycogen debt can occur if you're not eating enough carbohydrates to match the amount of calories burned—or if you're not synthesizing enough glycogen. Excessive training appears to inhibit the body's conversion of fuel into energy, although why this occurs is not fully understood. This condition might be compared to having fouled spark plugs in your automobile. The engine still runs, but not as well as it would if you bought new plugs.

MARATHON RUNNERS PROBABLY ARE MORE PRONE TO OVER-TRAINING THAN OTHER RUN-NERS SIMPLY BECAUSE OF THE VOLUME OF TRAINING REQUIRED.

Some runners increase their training levels to reduce weight. They sometimes train for marathons to provide the incentive to slim down. But one common mistake is to combine an increase in mileage with a decrease in calorie consumption. Frequently, I get questions on the Internet from runners training for marathons who complain of energy loss. Inevitably, when I inquire, I discover that they were either dieting or following a low-carbohydrate regimen, which provides insufficient carbohydrates for high-mileage training. (For more information, see Chapter 16, The Distance Runner's Diet.) They became overtrained as much from their eating habits as from their training habits.

The overtrained runner may maintain speed, but with poorer form and with greater expenditure of energy. David Costill, PhD, of the human performance laboratory at Ball State University in Muncie, Indiana, cited one runner who, early in his training, could run a 6:00 mile pace at only 60 percent of his aerobic capacity. Later, when he became overtrained, the same runner had to use 80 percent of his capacity to maintain that pace.

As athletes enlist all available muscle fibers in an attempt to maintain their training pace, they invariably exhaust their fast-twitch muscles faster than their slow-twitch muscles. This is one reason runners lose speed: Their fast-twitch muscles have become exhausted through intensive training.

But glycogen depletion is not the only problem. Another is microscopic damage to the muscle fibers, which tear, fray, and lose their resilience, like a rubber band that has been snapped too often. Despite analysis of blood and urine samples, researchers find it difficult to identify how, or why, chronically overtrained muscles lose their ability to contract. Harm Kuipers, MD, PhD, of the University of Limburg in the Netherlands, researched the effect of overtraining for nearly a year by training racehorses on a treadmill, alternating hard days of interval sprints with easy days. Horse trainers warned that the animals would become overtrained, but this failed to happen. Finally, with time running out, Dr. Kuipers began training the horses hard on their easy days. "Almost immediately," he said, "the horses began to exhibit symptoms of being overtrained." The message to runners is, if you want to avoid overtraining, don't eliminate easy days.

RECOGNIZING THE SIGNS

The simplest defensive running strategy you can use is keeping a training diary. Determining where you made a mistake—that "training error" described by Dr. James—is the main reason for keeping a training diary, or a log if you record workouts on a computer. Learn the cause

THE SIMPLEST DEFENSIVE RUNNING STRATEGY YOU CAN USE IS KEEPING A TRAINING DIARY.

of that mistake and you are less likely to repeat it.

Your training diary can also provide clues that you're overtraining. For example, if you've noted that you feel tired all the time, you may be training too hard. "Perceived exertion may give us our most important clues," suggests William P. Morgan, EdD, a sports psychologist at the University of Wisconsin at Madison. Here are some other symptoms to watch for.

Heavy legs. Your legs lose their snap—and speed. A run at an 8:00 pace feels like a 7:00 pace. Depleted muscle glycogen may be the cause. "You feel like you're running with glue on your shoes," says Dr. Costill.

Increased pulse rate. This is easily measured: Record your pulse each morning before you get out of bed and cut back your training on days when it's higher than usual. After doing a research project for Athletics West, Jack Daniels, PhD, exercise physiologist and coach at the State University of New York at Cortland, and psychologist S. Scott Pengelli, PhD, advised that club's athletes to cut training on days when their pulse rates were high.

Sleep problems. You have trouble getting to sleep and may wake several times during the night. Then you have to drag yourself out of bed in the morning. On rising, you find your pulse is also elevated, as above. "Sleep dysfunctions often are a sign of overstress," says Dr. Costill.

Diminished sex drive. The romance has gone out of your life. Somehow you seem to have lost interest in sex. You're too tired to tango. Whether this is related to lowered testosterone levels caused by training or just to plain exhaustion, no one knows for sure. But overtrained runners of both sexes look and feel like zombies, according to Dr. Costill.

Fear of training. You have trouble pushing yourself out the door to run each morning. So you sit and stretch longer. Your body is telling you to back off. "This is part of the psychological effect of overtraining," says Dr. Costill.

Sore muscles. Your muscles, particularly your legs, seem sore and stiff. "They may even be sore to the touch," says Dr. Costill. The reason is muscle damage, caused by too much pounding on the roads. Some muscle soreness is natural after hard training sessions, but if it persists, you're working too hard.

I like to believe that individuals who use my online training programs, as well as those who sign up for the marathon training class in Chicago, have a relatively low rate of injury. Class founders Brian Piper and Bill Fitzgerald used to agonize over every single individual lost to injury, but I'm certain that local marathoners who don't join the class get hurt more frequently than those who do. When a class member does get hurt, it's often for one of three reasons.

1. They started the program with insufficient base mileage.

2. If first-time marathoners, they followed the Intermediate program, rather than the novice program, because they had been running for several years and didn't want to consider themselves "novices" or "joggers."

3. They ran their long runs at race pace or faster, believing it would get them in better shape to set a PR.

BEWARE THE COMMON COLD

Another early warning sign of overtraining is the common cold, particularly right before an important race.

Upper-respiratory problems, from colds to the flu, are common among overtrained runners, claims Gregory W. Heath, DHSc, an exercise physiologist and epidemiologist at the Centers for Disease Control and Prevention in Atlanta. He notes that runners normally experience only half as many upper-respiratory infections as the general population. We're a healthy lot because of our lifestyles. Up to a certain point, exercise does boost immunity. But you lose this protection, claims Dr. Heath, if you race, and particularly if you race in marathons.

David C. Nieman, DrPH, director of the human performance laboratory at Appalachian State University in Boone, North Carolina, surveyed participants in the Los Angeles Marathon and found that 40 percent had caught a cold during the 2 months before the race. By doing high-mileage training, runners lowered their resistance and became more susceptible to whatever cold bugs were floating around, even in the warm climate of Los Angeles.

Dr. Nieman discovered that if runners trained more than 60 miles a week, they doubled their risk of infection. He also found that in the week after the race, 13 percent of marathon finishers had caught colds, compared with 2 percent of runners who hadn't raced. Although Dr. Nieman's research failed to indicate this, I suspect that most of those 60-mile runners who became victims of cold bugs were individuals who normally trained much less but had cranked their mileage way up for the marathon.

I believe in undertraining runners, rather than overtraining them. The upper limit for my advanced marathon training programs falls somewhat below 60 weekly miles. I don't tell runners not to run more miles weekly; I simply believe they'd better know what they're doing be-

THERE'S A FINE LINE BETWEEN BEING UNDERTRAINED AND OVERTRAINED; FINDING THAT LINE IS NOT EASY.

fore they pursue a more aggressive program. Those who regularly run 60 miles a week, and whose systems have adapted to that high load, may not be at increased risk. Instead of being overtrained, they may be well trained. There's a fine line between being undertrained and overtrained; finding that line is not easy.

It makes sense, nevertheless, to save your high-mileage training for months when the risk of infection is lower (spring through fall). Obtaining a flu shot at least once a year, usually in the fall, is important. You may not be able to avoid the flu entirely, but the shot will help ward off its worst symptoms, says Dr. Nieman.

Also, build a strong training base so that a week lost to a cold or flu won't be a serious setback. You should start your taper early enough to prevent last-week problems. Finally, you need to be particularly wary following the race. "Spread of many viruses is hand to hand rather than airborne," says Dr. Heath, who recommends avoiding people with colds, washing your hands after contact, and, particularly, isolating yourself as much as possible before and after competition (avoiding crowded movie theaters, for example).

I caught a bad cold the week before the 1998 Chicago Marathon. It was less a result of the stress of training and more from the stress of a busy life. My wife and I had spent the weekend before visiting our daughter Laura. She and her husband, Pete, have two children. Kids are notorious for bringing germs home from school.

After I got back to Chicago, I had the mother of all colds, and I had to give final lectures to my marathon training class in four locations on the next 4 nights. I arrived at our biggest clinic, on the near North Side, with my nose running so much I could barely carry enough tissues in my pocket to contain the flow. Several hundred runners attended the last lecture, and I worried that each one of them would catch my cold and compromise their marathon. Afterward, class members approached me to thank me for helping them with their training. I tried to avoid shaking any hands, but didn't entirely succeed. My cold was gone by race day, but I hope I didn't infect too many others. Perhaps by confessing this indiscretion, I can

MOST COMMON RUNNING INJURIES

What are the most common running injuries? While writing *Masters Running*, I surveyed more than 500 athletes over the age of 40 to find out which injuries plagued them the most. Here are the results of that survey. In the survey, respondents were allowed to check more than one injury, which explains why the frequency numbers add up to more than 100 percent.

Injury	Frequency
Muscle pull	32%
Knee injury	30%
Plantar fasciitis	26%
Nonrunning injury	22%
Iliotibial band injury	20%
Achilles tendinitis	17%
Shin splints	16%
Stress fracture	9%
Health-related problems	8%
No injuries	10%

If you can determine which injury plagues you the most, you can figure out the best defensive strategies to avoid it. A running diary is often the best ally in figuring out what went on.

be absolved of my sin. Since we carefully taper class members the last 3 weeks before the marathon, it's likely that the runners' immune systems had rebounded from the hard training enough to avoid my germs.

It's important to cut your training during a cold and cease it entirely if you have the flu (with elevated temperature) because you may increase your chance of an injury while in a weakened condition. You can run a marathon with a cold without its greatly affecting performance (dehydration may be your worst problem), but running a marathon with the flu is definitely unwise. You may finish, but you can significantly compromise your immune system and incur health problems that can extend not merely weeks but months and even years, according to Dr. Nieman.

EASE INTO THE SEASON

One of the first lines of defense against injury is to quash your instinct to start training at full steam. Coaches have noted that many athletic injuries occur in the spring. "Usually I find that after a very sedentary winter, runners want to get out and start training at the same mileage level as in the fall," says one coach of adult runners. "As a result, they get hurt."

In my work for *Runner's World*, I discovered that high school runners, particularly, were susceptible to injuries in both the spring and fall a few weeks after track or cross-country season had begun. This was because they failed to train properly between seasons, and then they were forced to do too much too soon. The most common injury: shin splints. "It's like an epidemic at the start of each season," says Debbie Fray, an assistant coach at Valparaiso High School, who frequently trained with our club at Indiana Dunes State Park. Running through the park one Sunday, she told me, "Kids go from zero miles to high miles, and they get injured."

It happens to adult runners, too, particularly those who have never run before but suddenly get inspired to run a marathon. If inspiration comes a year before your marathon date, you probably have time to ease into a gentle training program that will take you from zero to 26 miles. If much less than that, you might want to pick as interim goal a 5-K, 10-K, or half marathon race and save for later your first marathon.

Cross-training can lull even experienced runners into a false sense of security. Don't overvalue off-season training that doesn't involve running. During the period of my life when I remained in the Midwest all winter, I cross-country skied, and it got me into fabulous cardiovascular shape. But when the snow melted, I had to be cautious about bringing the same intensity to the running trails as I did to the ski trails. The one or two times I pushed right into running, I suffered injuries. In 1984, I entered several cross-country ski races in Norway, then headed south to Italy, where I ran surprisingly well in the famed Cinque Mulini race north of Milan. "Wow," I thought, "I'm in great shape." But 2 weeks later, I was limping.

My cardiovascular system had been in better shape than my running muscles. It was like putting a Porsche engine into a Volkswagen chassis: The chassis couldn't handle the power.

Since then, I've used two strategies to help prevent this problem. First, instead of shifting completely from running to skiing as soon as snow covers the ground, I maintain a maintenance level of running, at least every other day. And once the snow melts, I cut the intensity of my training during that transition period between winter and spring.

ADD SOME VARIETY

Cross-training can be an important means of preventing injury—if used wisely. Hector Leyba of Raton, New Mexico, a track coach and a sub-3:00 marathoner, skis winters and bicycles summers. "Cross-training helps my endurance," he says. "After many years pounding the streets, I feel I need variety."

One of the main causes of running injuries is the stress caused by the literally thousands of times your feet hit the ground when you run. If you've ever seen any slow-motion photography of what happens to the leg muscles during a single running stride, you'd wonder how we survive even a single lap on a track, much less a marathon. Swimming, skiing, cycling, and walking don't generate this ground impact.

It follows that if you want to maintain a high level of intensity in your training, you can shift to swimming, skiing, cycling, walking, or other activities on your off days. Or select nonimpact exercises that mimic running movements. Melvin H. Williams, PhD, a professor of exercise science at the human performance laboratory at Old Dominion University in Norfolk, Virginia, and a top-ranked 50-plus runner, spends one day a week cross-training and does supplemental training on his off days. His 1-hour off-day routine includes running in deep water, wearing a flotation belt, and riding standard and recumbent exercise bicycles. On the standard bike, he likes to stand up on the pedals frequently, figuring that this more closely exercises the muscles used in running, but without the impact. His recumbent workout exercises the quadriceps, which are sometimes overlooked in running. Again, he uses an interval approach: hard and easy. When Dr. Williams runs less than his usual 1 hour, he uses cross-training to fill out the exercise period to a full 60 to 70 minutes.

> IF YOU WANT TO MAINTAIN INTENSITY IN YOUR TRAINING, SHIFT TO SWIMMING, SKIING, CYCLING, WALKING, OR OTHER ACTIVITIES ON YOUR OFF DAYS.

When my wife, Rose, and I acquired a condo in Ponte Vedra Beach, Florida, so we could escape winter's worst winds, we picked a location only a few minutes' walk from an ocean beach that provided a perfect running surface, flat and firm but also springy enough to minimize impact. Fortuitously, between condo and beach, there was a fitness center with both weight room and swimming pool. After running (or biking) on the beach, I could pump iron, then use the pool to both swim and run laps. Afterward, I could soak in the whirlpool and stretch to relieve sore muscles.

I tried to select exercises that simulate running as much as possible, but most cross-training fails to exercise the muscles specific to running. In order to succeed as a runner, you need to train as a runner.

There is also the danger that you can cross-train yourself into an injury if you do so excessively. Coach Roy Benson of Atlanta warns that runners who cross-train on days between hard running bouts may do too much because they're using different (read "unfatigued") muscle groups. "If you're not careful," says Benson, "you can convert an 'easy' day into a 'hard' day, and it will eventually catch up with you. It's a myth to believe that you can't get hurt cross-training."

One woman training for the marathon posted a message to my online bulletin boards, worried that she would lose fitness during the 3-week taper. She wondered if she could cross-train to compensate for the lost miles while tapering.

My response was that if she was used to cross-training, she could continue with her alternate activities, but it was unwise to suddenly add new cross-training activities during the premarathon taper. The whole purpose of the taper is to rest your muscles—*all* your muscles—by exercising significantly less. Cross-training the week after the marathon because you're too sore to run is also a very bad idea. I created an online postmarathon program primarily to discourage runners from returning to hard training too soon after their marathon efforts. The first 3 days after the marathon feature no running, and no cross-training either. Nothing! Nada! Zilch!

Nevertheless, if you're prone to overuse injuries, substituting less stressful cross-training for some of your running may decrease your injuries and therefore your downtime. And if you can avoid gaps in your training caused by injuries, inevitably you'll perform better as a runner.

USING SPEEDWORK CAUTIOUSLY

Every running expert I know recommends speed training as the most effective means for improvement. But this can be dangerous advice if applied too zealously, particularly in training for a marathon. "Don't read what an elite athlete does in terms of mileage and attempt to do the same," advises John E. Tolbert, a coach from New Haven, Connecticut. "Get advice and train at your own level."

A frequently asked question to my online bulletin boards comes from runners who have heard that speedwork can help them improve their marathon times. Should they start doing some fast running at the track? No, I respond, if they have never been to the track before starting to train for a marathon. Definitely no, if the person asking the question is training for a first marathon. Even if that person has done speedwork in the past—such as someone with a track or high school background—I say no. Only my advanced programs include speedwork, but these programs are for experienced runners used to that type of training.

It isn't the speedwork itself that causes marathon runners to injure themselves in training, but speedwork coupled with the progressively longer distances run during the marathon buildup. Early in my career, I learned that I could improve by increasing either the intensity of my workouts or the distance, but I couldn't do both at the same time without risking injury. Marathoners should include speedwork in their training programs only after an initial buildup to high mileage and a subsequent cutback.

In *Your First Marathon*, Dr. Scaff advises that racing or speedwork make up no more than 10 percent of your mileage. "After you've run a marathon," he warns, "you need 260 miles of training before you enter your next event, or start doing speedwork."

Although I dislike formulas and don't want to suggest 10 percent as the absolute limit to speedwork—particularly because when you cut mileage to train for short-distance races, speedwork could become a predominant part of your training—Dr. Scaff's basic advice is sound.

CHOOSE RUNNING SURFACES CAREFULLY

I'm a believer in trail running, partly because I love to run in the woods but also because there's less chance of getting injured on soft surfaces. Yet I've noticed that runners who are not used to varying trail surfaces are prone to injury when they take to the woods. This was borne out by my cross-country team at the beginning of the fall season, and the track team when it trained on trails after the long winter hiatus. The less dedicated runners, who had failed to work out during the off-season, tripped over roots or twisted ankles while stepping in holes, but this never seems to happen to those runners who train on trails year-round.

In addition to running trails, I like to train on the smooth fairways of golf courses. To avoid interfering with golfers, I rise very early in the morning during the summer—a marvelous time to train if you can motivate yourself to get out of bed. Living as I do near Lake Michigan, I also find that the beach (particularly the day after high waves have flattened it) provides an ideal training surface.

In training top Dallas runners, including five-time Olympian Francie Larrieu Smith, coach Robert Vaughan avoids interval running on a track. "We do all our interval work on grass," he says. "We do repeats on the track, anything less than six reps. Anything more, we run on grass." Since switching to grass, Vaughan has virtually eliminated the problem of stress fractures, even though his runners do two speed workouts a week.

Asphalt may be slightly less unyielding than concrete, but let's face it; neither surface is soft. Nevertheless, if you're going to race on roads, you need to train on the roads to accustom your muscles to the impact. When preparing for a marathon, I usually do a much higher percentage of my running on the roads than when I'm training for shorter events, such as track and cross-country races.

With the increase in the number of fitness centers, and in the number of treadmills at those centers, many runners have begun to train indoors on such devices, particularly when winter winds blow. Or in the summer, as an air-conditioned option, when it gets too hot. Christine Clark of Alaska won the 2000 Olympic Marathon Trials despite having done most of her training on a treadmill. But not *all* of her training.

Making the switch from treadmill to pavement in spring sometimes can be tricky. There's a subtle but important difference between running on a moving belt, which can carry you along, and running on pavement, where all of the propulsion is yours. Runners who trust the numbers related to pace on their treadmills are sometimes surprised to find that they have to work harder to maintain that pace outdoors. Nevertheless, treadmills generally provide a more cushioned running surface than the roads around the fitness center. Treadmill running can help prevent impact injuries, but if you set the treadmill angle too high, so that you are running more on your toes, you can develop other injuries, particularly plantar fasciitis and Achilles tendinitis.

FOOTWEAR TO REDUCE SHOCK

One way to diminish road shock is to wear properly cushioned shoes. Running shoe companies spend millions of dollars on research and technology to design shoes that help prevent injuries. Various energy-absorbing materials, and air built into or pumped into your shoes, can decrease the impact of running on either asphalt or concrete.

One possible reason that men's marathon times have improved by nearly 20 minutes in the last half century may be better footwear and, as a result, fewer training injuries. A word of caution, however: Shoes that are too spongy (so soft that they offer little support) may destabilize the foot and contribute to injury. One shoe company some years ago came out with a marvelously comfortable shoe that was half the weight of other shoes. But the shoe was so spongy, I suspected it could contribute to injuries.

Spending more money does not guarantee you will obtain the shoe most likely to help you prevent injury. When I used to visit the office of a cardiologist in Elkhart, Indiana, who ran for relaxation, I found that he spent as much time pumping me for running advice as I did pumping him for medical advice. During one visit, he asked me what shoes I would recommend. I learned that he owned a very expensive model. Physicians earn good money, and the cardiologist had not skimped when selecting a running shoe. But the expensive shoes he'd purchased were designed with extra features to protect much heavier runners. That's why they cost more. By paying too much for a pair of shoes that were stiffer than he needed, he had actually increased his risk of injury.

It is of paramount importance to choose your footwear very carefully. Among other considerations, heavier runners certainly do need shoes that offer more support than those designed for lighter runners. You may also need more than one type of shoe. I have a built-in rack on one basement wall where I stack my various athletic shoes, each pair for a specific purpose.

I wear heavy, protective shoes on those easy days when I run slow. When I run fast, I prefer a light shoe, and I often wear racing flats for my speed workouts, and a semilight pair for long runs. When I run smooth trails, I wear a flexible, light shoe; uneven trails may require shoes with studs on the bottom. At the track, I may don spikes for repeats. I also have cycling shoes and ski boots and Aquasocks for the beach.

Every shoe has its own place in a runner's shoe inventory, and certain shoes that work well in one setting may not perform well in another. Runners who wear inflexible road shoes in the woods may increase their chance of injury on the uneven ground. Cross-training shoes may be suitable for weekend warriors, who exercise infre-

MAKING THE MOST OF YOUR MILES

Sometimes even a conservative runner who tries to ease gradually into a routine of high mileage just can't do so without injury. This is where the unfairness doctrine enters in.

The unfairness doctrine says that just when you increase quantity to the point where you feel you really are getting in shape, something happens. You catch a cold. You twist an ankle. Your knee starts aching. You suffer a stress fracture.

You may be one of those runners who just can't handle high mileage. If so, there are still ways to improve.

Mixing miles. In the marathoning world, this means running different distances on different days. A runner who can't safely do more than 35 weekly miles need not run 5 miles every day 7 days a week. That runner may be able to train more efficiently by running more than 5 miles on some days and less than 5 miles on others, or even taking days off.

By altering your daily running schedule, you can increase the intensity and duration of certain workouts without necessarily increasing your weekly time commitment. (In fact, you might save time.)

Here is a week's training schedule that involves mixing miles.

Sunday—15 miles
Monday—1 mile

quently, but I'm not convinced they belong in the inventory of any serious endurance athlete.

Listing makes and models of running shoes makes little sense in a book such as this. Even shoe surveys by *Runner's World* frequently lose relevance as shoe companies continue to change and update their models (not always improving them). The best source of in-

Tuesday—10 miles
Wednesday—3 miles
Thursday—read a spy novel
Friday—6 miles
Saturday—rent a movie

Mixing in miles is simple. But there are other ways to prevent injury and still excel in your marathon goals.

Speeding is another variation that can help runners improve. When you're unable to push past a certain mileage because of lack of talent, time, or determination, simply run those miles faster. A runner limited to 35 weekly miles might have a training program like this.

Sunday—15 miles steady pace
Monday—2 miles recuperative jogging
Tuesday—fartlek in woods: 6 miles total
Wednesday—2 miles easy jogging
Thursday—100-yard sprints on golf course
Friday—rent a movie: *Chariots of Fire*
Saturday—6 miles hard, or race

For real improvement, combine the principles of mixing miles and speeding while also running farther.

formation on running shoes is—surprise, surprise—running shoe stores. This was not always true in the 1980s and into the 1990s, when runners were forced to patronize chain sports stores in the mall, whose clerks often were high school football or baseball players and had little understanding of runners and their footwear needs. But as we nudged into the new millennium and as running continued to increase in popularity, more and more runner-owned specialty stores materialized to serve our needs. These stores often employ clerks who are runners, like us. Some stores use treadmills so the clerk can observe the runner running in the shoes before sealing the sale. Or they'll watch you run on the sidewalk out front—as long as you don't run too far!

Since many of the runners using my training programs live in Chicago, I frequently recommend that they go to the Fleet Feet store on North Avenue, run by David and Lisa Zimmer, because I know they'll be well served. But specialty running stores have begun to appear elsewhere in the city and in the suburbs, providing competition for David and Lisa and service for us all. I notice this trend as I travel from city to city. Finding a good running store is akin to finding a good running doctor. Ask other runners for their recommendations; then arrive at the store prepared to ask knowledgeable questions.

Although I have been sponsored at various points in my career by different shoe companies, I sometimes run shoeless, at least during warm weather. When I run on grass or sand, or sometimes in deep water, I'll go barefoot because I believe that it stretches and strengthens the muscles in my feet. At least a few innovative coaches prescribe a certain amount of barefoot running for their athletes, specifically at Stanford University, whose cross-country teams achieved success recently at the NCAA championships. I've even raced without shoes, running 5000 meters barefoot on London's Crystal Palace track in 1972 in 14:59.6, a masters record that lasted a quarter century. Telling you that I run barefoot won't endear me to the shoe companies, but it's all part of my defensive running approach.

KEEP MUSCLES LOOSE AND STRONG

Stretching and strengthening is another way to minimize injury. The best time to stretch a muscle is after it's warmed up. Track runners typically jog a mile or two, then stretch or do calisthenic exercises before beginning the intense part of their workout.

Long-distance runners are less likely to pause in the middle of a long run to stretch, although this practice is becoming more common. I'll stretch before long runs and in the middle of

STRETCHING AND STRENGTHENING IS ANOTHER WAY TO MINIMIZE INJURY.

intense workouts, but my preferred time to stretch is after the workout, usually while relaxing in a whirlpool, even though some experts advise against this approach, saying it's too easy to over-stretch when the hot water dims your senses. Every runner should adopt a stretching regimen that is convenient and comfortable.

Strength training is important for both conditioning and injury prevention. I lift weights and/or use exercise machines regularly in the off-season when I'm not racing regularly, but I limit strength training during the competitive season. It is wise to cut back on your strength training during the marathon mileage buildup as miles increase. Light weights and high repetitions seem to work best for marathoners. Do not—repeat, do not—overdo strength training if you want success as a marathoner. I recommend no lifting the last 3 to 6 weeks before the race at the time when you are peaking near 20 miles. You may be able to continue lifting safely, but why take a chance? If a specific injury threatens, I'm quick to seek advice from a trainer or physical therapist about which strength training exercise will help.

Part of my long-term success as a runner has come from avoiding those injuries that require extensive rehabilitation. During a half century of running, I've had very little downtime. A sore Achilles tendon now and then, a strained knee once, plantar fasciitis on another occasion. Nothing much. No surgery. Either I'm smart or lucky, or I have what Dr. Costill describes as a "bulletproof body," one that is biomechanically sound. (Or maybe it's a combination of all three.) Although two of these factors are out of your control, you can be smart about your training by including stretching and strengthening as part of your routine.

PREVENT REINJURY

After suffering an injury serious enough that standard remedies such as ice, anti-inflammatories and rest fail to provide relief, a runner needs not only to seek medical advice but also to consult his training diary to identify the training patterns that contributed to the injury. Coming off an injury or a period of reduced training mileage, runners often reinjure themselves, says Russell H. Pate, PhD, chairman of the department of exercise science at the University of South Carolina in Columbia. "Runners think, 'I can do 40 miles a week again,' but their bodies aren't ready," he says.

After following the daily training of 600 runners for a year, Dr. Pate identified two major predictors for injuries: a previous injury and heavy training. "If you got injured once and don't modify your training, you probably will get injured again.

For runners doing heavy training, three factors determined whether they would be reinjured: frequency, mileage, and whether or not they ran marathons. A critical problem was the runners' approach to training. "Too rapid a buildup is a critical factor in injuries," says Dr. Pate. "You need to know your limitations." Once you determine that, you can modify your training to prevent future injuries.

One additional strategy I use in preventing injury is to obtain therapeutic massages. I am a frequent client of the Harbor Country Day Spa in New Buffalo, Michigan, founded by Patty Longnecker Van Hyfte. I've been a client of Patty's for several decades, beginning when she used to travel by car to her clients, carrying a massage table in her trunk. The table could be pretty cold after being pulled out of the trunk in winter, so I didn't complain when she opened her spa, which meant that I now had to travel to her.

Typically, I schedule a massage once every 2 weeks, more frequently if I am training hard for a specific race. And I'll often schedule a massage for a day or two before or after the race, particularly if it's a marathon. I've also found that a massage is the perfect anecdote to jet lag, although it sometimes requires skill to locate a massage therapist in a different city or country. Before arriving in Australia for the 2001 World Masters Championships, I scheduled a massage with a therapist in Sydney the day after I arrived. Although free (or low-cost) postrace massages available at marathons feel good, it's better to obtain a massage 24 to 48 hours after the race, while your muscles are recovering.

Professional athletes often get more frequent massages. Tennis player Pete Sampras had daily massages from a personal trainer. In the 1980s, Nike sponsored a club called Athletics West for several dozen athletes who trained in Eugene, Oregon. Team members, including Alberto Salazar and Mary Slaney, were able to benefit from massages three times a week. If I were a professional athlete whose income depended on my performance, I would get massages more frequently than I do now. Therapists sometimes suggest that massage can soothe and heal fatigued muscles, but research on the subject is scanty. I'm convinced that the most important benefit from massage is the relaxation effect. A relaxed muscle is less likely to get injured.

ADJUST YOUR PROGRAM TO YOUR AGE

Basic training principles apply to all runners, but the specifics may vary greatly. Although running offers a marvelous means of diminishing the effects of aging, as I point out in my book *Masters Running*, the body eventually begins to slow, and as you get older, certain cautions are in order.

Instead of 1 day's rest after a hard speed session or a long run, you may need 2 days, or more. And standard training programs may not work for you if they predispose you to injury. Tom Cross, a coach from Tulsa, Oklahoma, describes a discussion he had about training with three other runners, all over 60, who had just finished an 8-K race with times faster than 35:00.

"We decided that we should just keep a steady pace and forget about the frills," says Cross. "At our age, the consensus was: Don't run intervals, don't try hills, just be consistent. Run the same every day, although the pace might vary depending on the distance. This is what older runners learn because the secret of endurance is to stay uninjured. All you need to do is run steadily every day, and whether or not you improve, you'll at least maintain your ability as well as you can."

REST—IT'S GOOD FOR YOU

"Dynamic repair" is a fancy title for rest coined by Bob Glover, a supervisor of coaches for the New York Road Runners Club. Glover considers rest to be a commonly overlooked component of any successful training program, and he believes that less training is sometimes best. "When in doubt, the coach should suggest less, and I've gotten softer and softer every year," he says. "By minimizing injury and getting a person to improve gradually, instead of rapidly, you'll have the most success. The old coach's mentality was to get out there and crack the whip: survival of the fittest. But how many people ended up on the junk heap along the way?"

Inevitably, if you can avoid injury, you can run long distances for the longest time. Defensive running may be the best training strategy.

CHAPTER 13

AUGUST INJURIES

AS MILES GO UP, SO DO INJURIES

Many of the runners who utilize the bulletin board I manage online under the identity Inter*Active* Training have as their goal the Chicago Marathon, a race held the second week in October. This is because the Chicago Marathon sponsors the board as a service to entrants in its race, even though runners training for other marathons and shorter races also use it.

It is in August (8 to 10 weeks before Chicago) when a significant number of runners begin to suffer injuries, minor and major. August, not too coincidentally, is also when runners using my Novice program increase their long run to 15 miles, their weekly mileage to 30. By the end of the month, they will be running 18 and 36 respectively. This elevated mileage causes a certain number get hurt, not too surprisingly, since surveys suggest that when you push your training mileage beyond 30 miles weekly, you do increase your risk of injury.

My bulletin board has half a dozen different forums so that questions can be separated by subject. One of the forums, Body Shop, is dedicated to questions about health and nutrition, but also about injuries. Traffic remains relatively light to Body Shop for much of the year, but August brings with it an explosion of calls for help.

AUGUST BRINGS WITH IT AN EXPLOSION OF CALLS FOR HELP.

I sometimes refer to the injuries runners suffer 2 months out from the marathon as "August Injuries."

Here is a compilation of August Injuries, questions asked by runners about their ailments during that dangerous month of the year. I include the date the question was asked plus responses by me and other knowledgeable forum viewers, many of whom suffered the same injuries, thus learned from the experience.

SORE QUADS

The Problem: (August 1) A runner identifying himself only by the initials K.F. described feeling stiff and sore after starting his longer runs. "Short runs bother my quads even more," he said, "maybe because of the faster pace." The runner stretched before and after workouts, but did no strength training. "Is there anything else I should do?" he wondered.

The Response: Jon Dikinis of Park Ridge, Illinois, responded: "Those long runs stress the body. It takes a while to recover. A massage might help." Dennis Ryan of Boston suggested an ice bath. I recommended two quadriceps stretching exercises, both shown on my Web site, www.halhigdon.com. The most common one is to stand on one leg, grasp the other leg by the ankle, and pull your heel up toward your butt. But I cautioned against stretching too aggressively and recommended waiting until after the marathon to start strength training. "Running hilly courses can challenge the quads," I said, "but eventually, that same sort of training will strengthen them."

STRAINED HAMSTRING

The Problem: (August 6) Steve Blaine of Elmhurst, Illinois, strained his left hamstring but took immediate action to heal the injury: "I iced it, got a massage, took a couple of days off, then tested it with a short run and discovered I needed more rest. Tomorrow will be 10 days since the injury." Blaine wondered what to do next. "Should I go back to running? Is it too soon?"

The Response: Hamstring injuries vary in severity, so even a skilled physical therapist might not be able to answer that last question. Amanda Musacchio of Villa Park, Illinois, described having a severe hamstring injury, almost a tear, several years before. She recommended: "Lots of ice. Lots of ibuprofen. No fast speedwork." She found that it hurt most the first 20 minutes of a run, then

> **CONTINUED REST, IBUPROFEN, AND ICE SHOULD HEAL THINGS NICELY.**

gradually felt better. She could handle long runs, although at a slow pace. Musacchio recovered in time to PR with a 3:46 in Chicago, although 5 minutes slower than her Boston Qualifying goal. Nevertheless, the injury took 6 months to completely heal. I recommended that Blaine see a physical therapist, adding: "Yes, I know it costs money, but a good therapist who knows where to press and has access to ultrasound equipment that can cut your recovery time significantly." Coincidentally, my son Kevin suffered a hamstring pull about the same time. His therapist recommended cross-training: cycling, swimming, running in the pool, plus leg curls to cure a muscle imbalance Kevin had between quads and hamstring.

KNEE PAIN

The Problem: (August 8) "I suppose I've learned a valuable lesson," sighed Anissa Neely of Goldthwaite, Texas. "Don't do a 15-miler, then ride in a car for 7 hours. Not rocket science, I know, but I never would have imagined this would cause such ill effects. It has been almost a week since that workout, and I haven't been able to run since." Before posting her message, however, Neely already had visited a physical therapist, who diagnosed an inflammation between kneecap and joint. Neely added: "Continued rest, ibuprofen, and ice should heal things nicely, he said. But when and how do I pick up my training?"

The Response: Bob Winter of New Lenox, Illinois, noted that since the injury had come during a step-back week (when Neely

BROKEN FIELD RUNNING

The 100th running of the Boston Marathon in 1996 was a special event for many runners, but particularly so for Bob Sarocka of Lombard, Illinois, who completed the race despite his having twisted his left ankle after stepping in a pothole at mile 3. He was running with a friend, Tony McElligot. "I wanted to drop out, but Tony talked me out of it."

Sarocka discovered that if he ran on the right side of the road, the camber made the pain manageable: "I just focused on one mile marker at a time." He finished in 3:18, compared with his PR of 2:55.

Once Sarocka removed his shoe, the ankle began to swell. With the aid of his wife, Lori, he limped to the medical tent for treatment, including ice and a compression bandage. Sarocka purchased crutches at a local drugstore and after returning home checked into the emergency room at Loyola University Medical Center. X-rays revealed he had run the last 23 miles on a broken ankle.

But the story doesn't end there. Sarocka continues: "A few months later, after bottoming out on potassium following the Ice Age 100, Tony went to the same emergency room and got the same doctor. She started telling him about some idiot runner she had treated who had run a marathon on a broken ankle. Tony had to admit that he was the one who told me to keep running."

would have done only an 11-mile long run), she hadn't missed that much. "Rest was best," said Winter. He felt that once the knee healed, she could jump right back into the program, whether to run 17 or 18 miles on the weekend: "But go slow, slow, slow!" I suggested that since Neely was following my Intermediate-I program, she could compensate for lost miles by shifting down one level to the Novice program, with its slightly fewer miles. She didn't quite do that, but did cut back on her pace runs. In the Chicago Marathon, rather than push for a fast time, she decided to run with a friend and finished happily in 5:25.

SORE HIPS

The Problem: (August 13) "This is my first marathon," wrote Sarah Westbrook of Charlotte, North Carolina, "and I'm going further than ever before. Running is cool, but by about 14 miles, my hips and knees begin killing me." Westbrook, who was training for the Marine Corps Marathon, wanted advice for reducing the pain.

The Response: Most of us suspected Westbrook had a classic iliotibial band injury, ITB being the tendon that connects the outside of the hip with the inside of the knee. Cindy Southgate of Kanata, Ontario, recommended checking some yoga Web sites for stretching exercises. "I'm usually a bit achy after a long run, too," commented Southgate. "Unless you experience severe pain, it's probably just normal wear and tear." Icing and anti-inflammatories can reduce pain. Liz Reichman of Columbus, Ohio, added: "Strength training seems to help my hips. When I lift (especially squats), that helps limit the pain." Proper shoes may help, since the pain may be caused by foot imbalances. So might orthotics. If the pain worsens, I said, a podiatrist might provide a more proper diagnosis and treatment, possibly orthotics.

BACK PAIN

The Problem: (August 13) Julie Cagwin from Marion, Iowa, noticed that whenever she got finished running, she would suffer lower-back pain. "Nothing serious," she reported. "Just a bit achy. It usually happens only after I go more than 8 or 9 miles."

The Response: That's a common problem, I responded, noting that I had been running behind a woman in a 10-K recently who spent most of the middle miles with her hands on her hips, as though her back hurt: "It's caused by weak abdominal muscles, the core of your body." I recommended crunches, situps where you don't sink all the way back to the floor. *Runner's World* frequently promotes cover stories offering exercises so runners can develop a "six-pack," or "killer abs," but you can't beat crunches for strengthening the core. Kathleen Wahlgren of Washington, D.C., seconded the motion: "Work on your abs, and you'll notice a great difference." Jim Fredericks of South Milwaukee recommended frequent massages. We all, however, warned about starting a radical strength training routine during the middle of her mileage buildup.

BACK PAIN

The Problem: (August 16) It started with a 5-K that Paul Jankowski of Valparaiso, Indiana, ran in April. "I started having sharp pain at the top of my right leg, both front and back," he wrote. Despite cross-training, the problem continued into the summer, but worsened after a 14-mile run. "That's it," said Jankowski. "I'm going to a doctor." The first doctor diagnosed the pain as an adductor and gluteus problem, said take 2 weeks off, ice, and take ibuprofen. That didn't work, so Jankowski visited a chiropractor, who offered electrical stimulation, ultrasound, massage, and stretching. With recovery imminent, Jankowski worried about loss of speed because of his enforced recovery.

The Response: I cited research that suggested it takes 2 days of retraining to regain fitness lost from 1 day of missed training. "Of course you've lost your speed," I said somewhat unsympathetically. "You lost training time!" Fortunately, Don Pocock of Winston-Salem, North Carolina, had my back, offering more practical advice. Pocock experienced a hip flexor injury before the Marine Corps Marathon the previous year and spent 3 months resolving the problem. "What got me going," said Pocock, "was some weight training. My injury stemmed from muscle weakness and was prolonged by scar tissue that built up in the muscle. After a few light workouts, I was able to break up the scar tissue and begin running normally again." Jankowski recovered enough to run Chicago, albeit in 4:19, compared with the 3:32 he'd run the previous year. He attributed the slower time to lack of fitness because of the injury.

OVERTRAINING

The Problem: (August 18) "I overtrained," confessed Jean Domel of Batavia, Illinois. "With a trainer, no less." Domel began getting bizarre pains in her body. "Now the pains are gone, but I just don't feel like working hard again." Domel reduced her mileage and cut back on speed workouts but still found herself without focus. "Even though I just ran a 5-K personal best, it just didn't thrill me." She wanted advice to help herself get back on track.

The Response: Alan Ford of Loganville, Georgia, got right to the point: "Stop running! A day, a week, a couple of weeks, whatever it takes. Find new routes. Make each new run an exploration. Have fun. Even if your body feels better, you still have the mental aspects of overtraining to deal with." I agreed with Ford, suggesting that overtraining was as much psychological as physical, although physical problems can

> **MAKE EACH NEW RUN AN EXPLORATION. HAVE FUN.**

create psychological problems. Melissa Vetricek of Tampa commiserated with Domel. "I've been in the same boat for months. I'm even entered in a marathon, but have no burning desire to tear up the course." Vetricek felt Domel—and she herself—just needed to take time to relax, not always easy for well-motivated runners. Personal trainers, I said, should know better than to push their clients too hard; otherwise, those clients soon become ex-clients, as was true in this case.

PLANTAR FASCIITIS

The Problem: (August 23) After a few weeks of pain in his right arch, Russ Bartlett of Salt Lake City began to suspect that he had plantar fasciitis. An article in *Runner's World* recommended stretching, icing, and anti-inflammatories, but Bartlett wondered: "Can I 'run through it,' or do I need to take a break from my training?"

The Response: Plantar fasciitis is a very common injury among runners who do speedwork, run very hilly (uphill) courses, or even run on a tilted treadmill. Getting up on their toes stretches the tendon that connects the ball of the foot and the heel. In fact, piercing heel pain is the most common symptom, particularly at the start of a run. What worked for Mark Felipe of Arlington, Virginia, was to never go barefoot. "The moment you get out of bed," he advised, "put your shoes on. The minute you get home from work, shift from dress shoes to running shoes." Paula McKinney of Between, Georgia, recommended inserts and training on soft surfaces. "I cut back on distance," said McKinney, "but never stopped." She also found that rolling a tennis or golf ball under her foot felt good. Plantar fasciitis usually proves most painful at the beginning of a workout. Once you get warmed up, the pain begins to diminish. If you can stand the early pain, keep running; if not, see a podiatrist.

SHIN SPLINTS

The Problem: (August 25) "I've been suffering from shin splints for the last few weeks," revealed Gordon Booth of Bloomfield Hills, Michigan. "Standard treatment has allowed me to keep running with minor pain at the start, shifting to dull pain, then fading away as the run gets over 5 miles." Discomfort when not running, however, forced Booth to skip the (step-back) week after his 18-mile run. He wondered whether to cut back on his training or run the next 20-miler as planned. "I hate not running for a week," he added.

The Response: We felt Booth's pain. Shin splints quite frequently are a beginner's injury, although he was following one of my Intermediate schedules. Paula McKinney commented: "Shin splints are nothing to sneeze at. They are a sign that the muscle is weakening and placing stress on the bone. Ignoring them can lead to fractures." McKinney told Booth to relax, to take time off—and not to panic! She recommended cycling or swimming during the off time. I agreed and suggested reducing mileage. Booth responded that he would follow our advice, adding that he felt better already. "I sold my bike a few years ago," he said, "but I think it's time to get a new one."

STRESS FRACTURE

The Problem: (August 29) A new runner (whose name I will omit) pleaded for help because of what she identified as "a strain, or sprain, or something." She wrote: "Toward the end of my 11-mile run, I felt a small pain above my ankle. Within a few days, the pain became intense." During a midweek 5-mile run, the leg hurt so much, she cried. Ice and stretching failed to help, forcing her to skip 15- and 16-mile runs the next two weekends. "What should I do?" she asked. "Financially, I am not able to see a doctor."

The Response: Several of us considered that unfortunate because her injury sounded more like a stress fracture than a strain or sprain. Kousik Krishnan, MD, of Glenview, Illinois, works as a cardiologist. He advised rest from running for a long time. "If you still have pain," said Dr. Krishnan, "you will need to see a professional or stop training and let whatever injury you have heal, which would likely put you out of this year's marathon." I also recommended not starting, saying: "The right sports medicine professional might be able to help, or might not." After the Chicago Marathon, we heard again from the injured runner, who trained in a pool and using an elliptical trainer for 8 weeks without running. Indeed, she had suffered a stress fracture, although she said it was healed by the time of the race. Unfortunately, by the 9-mile mark, she had pulled a quadriceps muscle and finished in pain. Her time was 6:25:22.

Some August Injuries respond to treatment—the most popular

being ice, anti-inflammatories, and rest—and runners resume their training in September, leading to that October marathon. But other injuries do not, causing runners to make the unfortunate decision to postpone their dreams of marathon glory for another time and place. Dropping out is never fun, before or during the race. But while mileage in excess of 30 miles weekly has been identified as one cause of running injuries, more of a problem is jumping into that high level of training with an inadequate base. If you train properly, and increase mileage gradually, your Augusts should be filled with sunshine and success.

CHAPTER 14
PLANNING FOR PEAK PERFORMANCE

SUCCESS REQUIRES BEING TOTALLY FOCUSED ON ONE GOAL

Aiming at key races is the best way to achieve peak performance in long-distance events, says Russell H. Pate, PhD, chairman of the department of exercise science at the University of South Carolina in Columbia.

Yet Dr. Pate (a man with several top-20 Boston Marathon finishes to his credit when he raced in the mid-1970s) concedes that the buildup to a goal carries with it a degree of risk, which escalates as the race gets closer and the workouts more intense. "Experience indicates that high-intensity workouts are more demanding and stressful," he says. "Training hard for prolonged periods is risky in terms of overtraining and even riskier in terms of injury."

This is where progressive training aimed at a certain event comes in: You start from a low point of conditioning and build to a high point. You compete in a race or a series of races. You then relax your training and begin to contemplate your next goal. And maybe in between, you do some speedwork aimed at improving your basic speed before going back to an endurance-based program.

This is what coaches call "periodization." At different periods of the year, you use different training approaches, sometimes setting interim goals while still focused on your ultimate goal. For most of the readers of this book, given its title, that ultimate goal would be either finishing or running a fast time in the marathon.

More than any other event, the marathon lends itself to this approach. Although some runners run a dozen or more marathons a year, most distance runners are content to run one or two during any given 12-month period. Many runners will run a single marathon in a lifetime. Usually, these races are selected well in advance, allowing ample time for a buildup to peak performance.

How do you plan for peak performance? How do you adjust your training schedule in anticipation of a specific race? How do you guarantee that you can follow that planned schedule and maximize your chances for success—and enjoyment?

PERIODIZATION

"Periodization" is a name used by coaches to describe a system of training—actually, the planning of that training—that extends over a period of weeks, months, and even years. Although New Zealand coach Arthur Lydiard didn't invent the term, he certainly pioneered the division of a runner's training into different periods of time leading to a specific goal, which for some of his athletes (Murray Halberg, Peter Snell) was winning an Olympic gold medal.

"If you want to improve your performances, you can't train the same way all the time," writes Owen Anderson, PhD, editor of *Running Research News* (www.rrnews.com). Dr. Anderson suggests that runners who resist change stagnate and fail to improve.

Here is how periodization might work for runners coming off one marathon who want to prepare for another. Some periods may blend with others.

Rest: After a marathon, you need an extended period of active rest for 3 to 6 weeks before beginning to train hard again.

Endurance-I: Miles, and lots of them, is the key to success in long-distance running. Lydiard even had half-milers like Snell running

"There is no magic formula," warns Keith Woodard, a coach from Portland, Oregon. "There is no magic mileage, no magic mold to put runners into. Runners are too individual for that." Nevertheless, there are certain guidelines all runners can follow to help achieve peak performance.

TIMING IS EVERYTHING

If you're planning to run a marathon in the next month or so, skip ahead to the chapters on nutrition and tapering, which will do you more immediate good. You don't have time to execute the advice in

23-milers for their base training. Most endurance-trained marathoners may be able to skip this period—or postpone it to later.

Strength: To run fast, you need strong muscles. Lydiard's athletes ran hills. Interval training on the track also can improve strength and speed. To run fast, however, you need to cut back on mileage during this period.

Speed: Marathoners can improve their speed by racing at shorter distances, specifically 5-K and 10-K. The best time to do this is during a period of time when you are not increasing mileage. The speed period and strength period may overlap.

Endurance-II: This is the final mileage buildup leading to the marathon itself. My 18-week training program allows novice runners to increase their longest run from 6 to 20 miles.

Taper: Don't overlook this important period. You can't achieve peak performance unless you are well rested.

The marathon: Run your fastest; then periodize your training again for your next major effort.

this chapter. Instead, place a bookmark here so you'll remember to return. After you've finished that race and have begun to plan your next major running campaign, then come back and read this chapter.

If you expect to peak for a specific race—whether a mile or a marathon—you need time. You need time to plan, time to establish a base, time to progress, and time to taper properly.

How much time? For a short-distance event on the track or an important 5-K or 10-K on the roads, you probably need at least 2 to 3 months of preparation. If you're talking marathon, 4 to 5 months is probably enough time for most first timers. (My marathon training programs last 18 weeks but assume you arrive at the starting point with some level of fitness.) For experienced runners seeking improvement, 6 months is probably minimum, and 12 would be better. Former world-class marathoner Benji Durden of Boulder, Colorado, designed an 84-week schedule for me to use in my book *How to Train*. It involved a preliminary buildup to one test marathon, then a peak buildup to a second PR effort. Those with Olympic aspirations must think 4 years ahead. I planned 18 months for one of my best races, a sub-2:30 marathon I ran to win a gold medal at the 1981 World Masters Championships in New Zealand.

Doug Renner, a coach from Westminster, Maryland, suggests you develop a 2- to 4-year game plan. "Goals must continually be refined," Renner says. "Runners need to know the big picture, rather than just haphazardly go from race to race."

You want enough time to execute a well-organized plan that will bring you to the starting line in the best shape of your life. If you don't do that, you're not peaking. And you haven't learned to apply the principles of periodization.

WHY YOU NEED A GOAL

Before you make a plan, you need a goal. "The ability to adhere to a specific well-thought-out and long-term training program is the

most necessary factor leading to success in the marathon," advises
Clark Campbell, a coach and professional triathlete from Lawrence, Kansas.

BEFORE YOU MAKE A PLAN, YOU NEED A GOAL.

In other words, when you have no destination, you can take any road. If you want to float along from week to week, training the way you feel, racing whenever you want to, that's fine. Running need not always be the relentless pursuit of one Big Event after another. We all need downtime to renew ourselves psychologically, to gather ourselves for the next push. Sometimes I'll take a year or more off from serious training and racing.

Bill Bowerman was the late—and great—track coach at the University of Oregon. I've written often about the Bowerman approach, which features hard days and easy days; I'll often plan hard years and easy years. Sometimes not having a goal might even be considered having a goal.

Usually I set goals at the beginning of each year, when I'm starting a new training diary. Sometimes my goals will be a set of times I want to better at various distances—or maybe there are a number of races I want to do well in. Most frequently, I attempt to peak for the World Masters Championship, which comes at 2-year intervals. Other times, I'll peak for a marathon.

Marathons lend themselves to goal setting because of the extra effort required both to train for them and to compete well in them—and simply because of the magic of the marathon itself. But setting a goal involves not merely selecting an

MARATHONS LEND THEMSELVES TO GOAL SETTING BECAUSE OF THE EXTRA EFFORT REQUIRED BOTH TO TRAIN FOR THEM AND TO COMPETE WELL IN THEM.

event or events but also deciding what you expect from your participation in that event. Is your goal just to finish? Is your goal a PR? Is your goal victory—or at least placing high in your age group?

Or maybe you're just out to have a good time. You need to determine your principal goal first, and only after that can you begin to make plans.

It is also possible to have subgoals, or a series of goals. You may want to run some preliminary races—and run them well—as interim contests before the main race that interests you most. First-time marathoners probably need a few races under their belts at distances from 5-K to the half marathon, if only so they can get some hint as to what their marathon finishing time might be. Sometimes I select a primary goal (such as running a fast marathon), expecting to use it as a stepping-stone to a greater goal (running a faster marathon). Michigan marathoner Doug Kurtis says, "Marathoners need short-term goals, other races leading up to the marathon. I'm amazed when I meet people and their first race is a marathon. It's hard to focus on a marathon 2 or 3 months away, so focusing 2 or 3 weeks ahead on a 5-K can help keep you motivated."

On the other hand, if your goals are too many or too diverse, you may have difficulty achieving your main goal.

DEVELOPING YOUR GAME PLAN

Once you set your goal, you can make a plan to achieve that goal. Here's where training diaries come in handy, particularly for those of us who have been running for more than a few years. Whether or not I actually pull individual diaries down from the shelf, I'll at least mentally review what has worked for me in the past and what hasn't. Even if I decide to take a totally different approach—say, low-mileage training instead of high-mileage—it will be pursued after considerable reflection.

I do a lot of my preliminary planning on airplanes as I return from major events. If, as so often happens, it's an overseas flight, I have plenty of time trapped in a tight seat with nothing better to do than think. Invariably the food is terrible, and I've already seen what is probably a bad movie, so what better time for considering future goals? Sometimes I'll pull out a notebook and jot down dates and times. Or I'll tap away at my laptop computer, which I sometimes take with me on trips.

Inevitably, however, I fine-tune my plan after returning home. On a large sheet of poster board, I draw a homemade calendar with large blocks for each date. I'll list major events in appropriate boxes, usually drawing a red border around the important box, the day on which I want to hit my peak. I may list certain workouts I want to run, or distances (daily or weekly) I want to achieve. Or I may use the calendar to record how my training is going. I'll record the distance of my long runs and my weekly miles, and I may plot key speed workouts in advance, or record them after they occur. I'll do the same with races and my times at those races. (This is in addition to my regular diary, where I record more specific details about individual workouts every day.)

The Internet has provided runners with many planning tools. For several years I would ask runners in my Chicago Marathon training clinics how many had Internet access. The first year I asked, it seemed half the people raised their hands; the following year it was more like 75 percent. Now I no longer ask because practically every runner has Internet access or knows a friend who can obtain training information for them off the World Wide Web. Many runners go to my Web site and print or download one of the training programs for Novice, Intermediate, or Advanced runners. Or they sign up for one of my InterActive programs, where I send them daily e-mail messages telling them what to run. Particularly on my Inter-Active programs, it's quite easy to modify the dates and numbers to fit your specific marathon training needs. In fact, I do this myself. To get ready for the 1999 Walt Disney World Marathon, where I was leading a pacing team for *Runner's World*, I grabbed one of my marathon training booklets and simply scribbled in changes. Now I simply choose one of my online programs for different race distances, from 5-K to the marathon. In planning for a marathon PR,

GOAL SETTING

Are runners good at setting goals? In an online survey of runners who had just finished a fall marathon, the answer apparently is yes. Several months before most people would make their New Year's resolution, 32 percent claimed they already had picked their spring marathons, and 21 percent had chosen both spring and fall marathons. "Why train if you don't have a goal?" asks Paula Sue Russell of Findlay, Ohio.

Brian Collins of Las Vegas planned to run the Sunburst Marathon in South Bend, Indiana, in June, more than 7 months away. "I've planned my training for the next 7 months," he says.

"My next year goals are already set in stone," said Michael Murphy of Ferndale, Michigan. "I'm already considering the year after that."

Nobody admitted to not having a goal, except one runner who said: "I alternate between periods of having goals and periods of not. If you don't have down periods, running becomes an endless treadmill of goal chasing."

Is there a disadvantage to goal setting? Possibly only when you achieve them because then you need to come up with another. Reinhold Messner, one of the great mountain climbers of all time, once said: "Each goal achieved is equally a dream destroyed." Runners need to keep resetting goals as well as reinventing themselves.

Goal	Percentage
Goals not yet set for next year	19.6%
Planned spring marathon	32.1%
Planned fall marathon	10.7%
Planned spring and fall	21.4%
Goals don't include marathon	13.6%
Goals extend beyond calendar year	12.5%
No goals planned for next year	0%

you're limited only by your imagination—although it helps to have the support of a good coach.

Planning is where time and goal come together. If you have a specific period of time in which to achieve a specific goal, you can plan accordingly—to a point, of course. You can't predict whether the wind will be in your face or the weather will be too warm. But you can plan almost every other aspect of your marathon training so you'll reach the starting line ready to perform to the best of your ability. If you can plan to achieve that goal, it won't matter how fast you run or whom you beat.

Goal setting is important if you want success as a runner. "To stay in shape, I need to have a goal," says Julie Koehler of Chicago. "I may enjoy several months of downtime, but before finishing one marathon, I've already planned the next. Without goals, my exercise routine lacks focus."

Smart runners look years down the road when setting goals. Toby LaFrance of Tigard, Oregon, hopes to nibble 5 or 10 minutes a year off his marathon time so that in 5 years, when he moves into another age group, he can get a Boston Qualifying time of 3:20.

For runners like LaFrance, Dr. Pate advises, "Figure out the key sessions you need for your program. Get them in there; then surround them with those kinds of recovery activities that allow you to continue over a period of time. Build your program on priorities. The highest priority is attached to the key, hard sessions.

"The secret to success in long-distance running is not what type of workouts you do, whether high or low intensity, but how those workouts are structured into a specific program and incorporated throughout a training year—and for the length of a career as well."

> **THE SECRET TO SUCCESS IS NOT WHAT TYPE OF WORKOUTS YOU DO BUT HOW THOSE WORKOUTS ARE STRUCTURED INTO A SPECIFIC PROGRAM.**

You might want to reread that paragraph. It may be the most important message you encounter in this book.

TAKING TIME OFF

How important is rest? It's more important than most of us realize, says Paul Goss, a top-ranked duathlete and coach from Foster City, California. Marathoner Benji Durden of Boulder, Colorado, makes rest an integral part of his training programs.

While you're choosing your goal and planning your attack, you may want to take time to relax: a planned vacation, not necessarily away from running, but away from training at maximum effort. "Rest" is a word you have encountered before in this book, and it is a word you will encounter again.

Rest isn't always entirely optional, of course. If you've completed a marathon, you may be forced into a period of recuperation that could last a week, a month, or more. This time is necessary not only to allow sore muscles to recover but also to permit rejuvenation of the spirit.

It may take more time for the spirit to recover than the muscles. Psychiatrists write about postmarathon depression. At a premarathon lecture in Chicago, Joan Benoit Samuelson referred to it as PMS. At first many of the women in the audience thought she was talking about premenstrual syndrome. When Joanie explained she meant postmarathon syndrome, women as well as men gave a nervous laugh.

At least in the aftermath of a marathon, there usually is a period of well-deserved euphoria after a peak performance, particularly one that involved much preparation. First-time marathoners are more susceptible than others because they have passed—for better or worse—through a unique experience. They wonder, "What do I do next?" and often there is no immediate answer.

One year, Ron Gunn of Southwestern Michigan College and I took a large number of runners from his beginning running class to the Honolulu Marathon. The morning after the race, we planned a short walk along the beach from our hotel to the Royal Hawaiian Hotel for brunch. Nearly everybody appeared wearing the "finisher" shirt they had won the previous day. Inevitably, of course, that revered shirt gets thrown into the dirty laundry.

Regardless of whether or not you immediately select your next goal, take ample time to rest before setting out to achieve it.

STABILIZING YOUR TRAINING

In many respects, the base period (when you run easy without worrying about pace or distance) is an extension of the rest period. Usually within a week after finishing a marathon, muscle soreness will have almost completely disappeared, and you can begin to run comfortably again. But you need time to stabilize your training. Don't rush immediately into all-out training for your next goal. If you do, you're liable to crash some weeks or months later.

Runners tend to have a comfortable base level of training, a weekly maintenance mileage that they can accomplish almost effortlessly. For me, this base level is about 15 or 20 miles. I don't have to aim at running that much; it just happens. I enjoy exercise. If I'm just going out the door 5 or 6 days a week without thinking about where I'm going or how far or how fast, I'll end the week with that many miles recorded in my training diary. That's my base maintenance level to which I return periodically: It's enough to maintain a reasonable percentage of my peak fitness level.

While exercising at this level, I often cross-train. If I've just finished a fall marathon, I'll swing eagerly into the cross-country ski season. Or at least that was true until we bought a winter home in Florida. This forced some shifts in my training. I spend more time now lifting weights or swimming, an excellent upper-body exercise. This is good, since I usually would eliminate strength training during the final countdown to a marathon.

I rarely peak for winter events, but after a spring marathon, I

50 MARATHONS, 50 STATES

After finishing their 10th marathon and having established a PR of 3:30, some runners might be tempted to call it a career. At that point, Mark Kramer of Lindenhurst, Illinois, had just gotten started. Kramer, who ran his first 10 marathons in five separate states, set as his goal running at least 46 more marathons, more specifically 50 marathons in 50 different states (plus the District of Columbia). "I like running different marathons," admits Kramer. "Big ones. Small ones." Kramer decided that by adding one to three states a year, it would force him to stay focused and continue to maintain a fitness program for several decades at least.

While Kramer was getting started on his quest, Bob Sarocka of Lombard, Illinois, was finishing his in Alaska, the Mayor's Midnight Sun in Anchorage. Sarocka says: "I wanted to save a prime destination for last. My wife ran her second there. My sister-in-law, her first."

Sarocka ran his first marathon in 1990 and spent 13 years chasing his 50th. He identifies Maui as his favorite marathon, with Napa Valley and Jackson Hole close. The most unforgettable moment came at Jackson Hole, when he had to stop for several minutes to let a herd of free-range cattle cross the road. "I was carrying a disposable

might do some cycling or swimming, compete in some triathlons, or run some summer 5-K races—which I like because hot weather offers you a built-in excuse for slow times. I'll sometimes run these races on impulse, deciding to enter on the race morning itself.

Quite often, my peak performances coincide with late-summer track meets. Once past the track season, I divert time and energy in the fall to road races such as the Scenic Ten (10 miles) in Park Forest, Illinois, or the Blueberry Stomp (15-K) in Plymouth, Indiana, or the National Heritage Corridor 25-K along a towpath beside the

camera," says Sarocka, "so I have the moment forever preserved."

Two separate organizations, the 50 States & D.C. Marathon Group and the 50 States Marathon Club, maintain Web sites and minister to those runners seeking to run in as many states. The former boasts 626 members, everyone from Bob Aby of Minnesota to Michael Zyniewicz of Georgia, each of whom has run more than 100 total marathons, including one in every state. You don't need to have run 50 states to join, but you need to have run marathons in at least 10 states, with the intent to someday run the remainder.

The 50 States Marathon Club has slightly more members. The Club's Steve Boone estimated that by the end of 2004, approximately 250 runners (both clubs plus nonjoiners) had run marathons in all 50 states. Only a fifth of them are women. "Ten times as many people have climbed Mount Everest as have run 50 marathons in 50 states," says Boone.

Another goal that inspires other runners is to run a marathon on all seven continents, including Antarctica. Thom Gilligan of Marathon Tours, who organizes trips every other year to that last continent, says that 95 men and 25 women have accomplished that end.

I & M Canal near Channahon, Illinois. Sometimes I've run a fall marathon with minimal preparation, with no goal other than having a good time or leading a pacing team.

Running many different races can take the edge off the period of base training, but it's important to slack off and give yourself some time when you're not too serious about anything connected with running—either racing or training. When it comes time to concentrate your training toward a peak goal, you move into a new phase.

MILO AND THE BULL

Practically every beginner's program depends on gradually increasing distance, usually weekly up to the day you do your longest run. Nobody has been able to come up with a better program, and I doubt anybody ever will. It's the old story of Milo (the ancient Greek wrestler) and the bull. You start lifting a calf when it is young, and by the time the calf grows into a heavy bull, you have the strength to throw people out of the ring in the Olympics.

The same is true with running: You take people running 15 to 25 miles a week, and by adding a few miles a week over a period of 18 weeks, you get them up near 40 to 50 miles weekly. You take people capable of running an hour (or half a dozen miles) continuously and help them to progress to where they can run for 3 to 4 hours (or about 20 miles).

If you're talking peak performance, however, you need to do more than spend 4 months adding a mile a week and increasing your final long workout to 20 miles. You need to take suffi-

> **IF YOU'RE TALKING PEAK PERFORMANCE, YOU NEED TO DO MORE.**

cient time (or have a sufficient base) to arrive at that level probably at least 2 months before the marathon—and hold at that level.

A single 20-miler isn't enough. For peak performance, you need to develop the ability to run 20-milers repeatedly (two or three times) without undue fatigue and without overtraining.

Some runners go beyond marathon distance in their training. At one point I progressed to 31-mile (50-K) workouts, but I eventually decided that it was counterproductive, at least for me. It took too much time, and I had to slow down too much to achieve that distance. During peak marathon training, however, I added a second, semilong run to my training week, usually about two-thirds of the distance of the longest run: 10 miles if my long run was 15; 13 to 15 miles if my long run was 20. Olympian Julie Isphording refers to these workouts as "sorta-long" runs. It's possible to increase your long and semilong runs simultaneously, but a more sensible approach is to stabilize your long run near 20 miles, then begin a progression featuring a second workout.

Don't forget that word I promised to use again in this chapter: rest. Every 3rd or 4th week, depending on how I felt, I would take an extra day or two of rest. I would back down from my weekly mileage and maybe skip my long run that week. That allowed me to gather strength so that I could progress to a still higher level.

NEXT, ADD INTENSITY

Another standard approach for elite runners is to increase the intensity of their training sessions. One way to increase overall intensity is to do your long runs faster. When I peak for spring marathons, this happens naturally. As the weather warms, I can run more fluidly in shorts and a T-shirt than I can in the multilayered outfit I wear in colder weather. Similarly, before fall marathons, I find I can run more comfortably (and faster) as the weather cools, at least to a point. Some natural speeding is acceptable as you increase distance and improve fitness, but to push too fast, too far, too soon raises the specter of overtraining and injury.

One training option for long runs that makes a lot of sense to me is the 3/1 pattern pioneered by the late John Davies of New Zealand, bronze medalist for 1500 meters in the 1964 Olympic Games. Davies suggested that runners do their long runs at a gentle pace for the first three-quarters of the distance (12 miles in a 16-mile run), then push the pace over the last quarter (the final 4 miles). This strategy pushes you to finish faster than you started, which is good both psychologically and physically. Davies didn't advise 3/1 long runs every weekend, only every other weekend: again, the hard/easy approach.

Another sensible approach is to run all your distance workouts at a steady pace and to increase intensity in separate speed sessions. In fact, most experienced runners decrease their mileage at least slightly when moving from the distance phases to the speed phases of their peak training plans. Various forms of speedwork, particularly interval training, lend themselves to progressive training of this sort.

A typical speed progression would be to start with running 10 × 400 in 90 seconds with a 400 jog between, then over 10 successive weeks lower the time 1 second a week until you are capable of running 10 × 400 in 80 seconds. Another approach would be to begin at 5 × 400 and add an extra repetition at the same pace each week until you achieve 10 × 400 or more.

But don't make the mistake I once made when I increased the speed and the number of reps simultaneously. While training in Germany in 1956, I began at 10 × 400 in 70 seconds and tried to add a 400 a week and drop a second a week. A few weeks before reaching my goal of 20 × 400 in 60 seconds, I suffered a sudden drop in performance. I had set the bar too high while planning my training. Sometimes you learn more from your failures than you do from your successes.

> SOMETIMES YOU LEARN MORE FROM YOUR FAILURES THAN YOU DO FROM YOUR SUCCESSES.

Don't let the numbers frighten you. Progressions such as those I've described work only if you begin conservatively and don't pick an end goal beyond your capabilities. Many runners (including me now) would find it difficult to run a single 400 in 90 seconds, much less use that as their starting point. No matter. We all play with the hands we are dealt and succeed or fail at various levels depending on our abilities.

HIT THE HILLS

Hill training is another means of increasing workout intensity. You can run sprints up hills as a form of speed training or shift to hilly courses for your long runs. Preparing for the Chicago Marathon,

HILL TRAINING

If you're planning to run a hilly marathon, you need to do at least some of your training on hilly courses. Even if you live in the flattest of flat-lands, hills can be found if you search hard enough and are willing to climb in a car. The city of Chicago is flat, but several suburbs offer rolling hills. Runners in Jacksonville, Florida, preparing for the Gate River Run, a 15-K, train over a 2-mile loop course that crosses two high bridges over the St. Johns River.

Increasing the angle of your treadmill to simulate uphill running is another option. Some high-tech treadmills can be adjusted to down-hill. Downhill training is de rigueur if you're preparing for a marathon such as St. George in Utah or Boston. The St. George Marathon drops 2,600 feet, promising a fast toboggan ride—but not if you haven't trained your quads to withstand the extra pounding they'll absorb. Boston is hilly overall, but with more down that up: going from 490 feet above sea level in Hopkinton to 10 feet near the finish.

As part of my strength training, I do hill repeats: starting with 3×400, adding one more repeat each week, climaxing with 8×400. (The hill that ends near my driveway is about that long.) I run hard up, jog back down easy, then repeat.

But preparing for the Boston Marathon, I also run downhill repeats, typically every second or third one. This is risky because the extra im-pact might cause an injury, but if you want to succeed at Boston, you need to prepare for the downhills as well as the uphills. Before the Boston Marathon one year, Olympic marathoner Rod DeHaven pre-pared by placing a 2×4 board under the rear of his treadmill. He ran 2:12:41 at Boston.

If you live in a hilly area and are training for a flat marathon, like Chicago, the problem is the same, but reverse. Find some flat areas for your training.

which has a relatively flat course, I would select flat courses for my long runs. When I prepared for a hillier marathon, such as Boston, I trained over hillier courses, at least during the closing stages of my training. I also included some downhill repeats, since Boston is a point-to-point course that drops in elevation. This can make for very fast times, but you need to be prepared for the pounding your legs (especially your quadriceps) get on the downhill portion of the race.

Since Joe Catalano coaches in New England, where the Boston Marathon is the annual focus of many runners, he has his runners do their long workouts on hilly courses because he feels that the combination of hills and distance increases endurance. "Many people shy away from hills," says Catalano, "especially when they go long. They make it easy on themselves, but that limits their improvement. It's a matter of strength: The more you repeat something, the stronger you get. We run long every week for best results. Wait more and you fail to improve. We start novice runners on courses as short as 3 to 6 miles. Very gradually we build: 8, 10, 12, 14, 16, then level off. We'll start on a series of small hills spaced apart. Then, as the runners get stronger, we seek steeper hills closer together." One advantage of the Boston area, he says, is that it's fairly hilly.

The advantage of training using an overload, or progressive, stage similar to that proposed by Catalano is that as you get tougher, you toughen the workout. This approach provides a strong psychological "carrot" for the runner trying to peak for a specific race. After the long runs to develop endurance, after the fast runs to develop strength, you use a shot of speed training to fine-tune your speed.

THE TROUBLE WITH NUMBERS

Blind application of any number-based training system can cause problems. One variable not mentioned in many coaching articles is weather. And "whether." Whether it's cold or hot, whether it's windy or rainy, can affect how fast or how far you run during any given workout. The number of miles you've run doesn't necessarily reflect the quality of your training.

The late Barry Brown, a top masters runner, was an invest-

BLIND APPLICATION OF ANY NUMBER-BASED TRAINING SYSTEM CAN CAUSE PROBLEMS.

ment consultant who commuted by air between offices in Bolton Landing, New York, and Gainesville, Florida. Brown trained with a heart monitor so he could measure the relative intensity of his workouts, regardless of other variables.

Brown once described to me an interval workout featuring mile repetitions, which he ran averaging 5:20 per mile in cool weather in New York, then averaged 5:40 in hot weather in Florida the following week. "The intensity measured by my pulse rate was exactly the same," he told me. "But if you just looked at the numbers in my diary, you would have thought I was taking it easy in the second workout."

Here's another example. A flight attendant with Delta Airlines lived in Boulder, Colorado, was based in Atlanta, and often flew to San Juan, Puerto Rico. She worried about managing and measuring the intensity of her training schedule, but sometimes you simply need to relax and not try to compare the numbers from one workout with those of the next, or one week with the next.

Fatigue, diet, and sleep can affect the intensity of your training. Monitoring intensity is probably the trickiest aspect of any training program, even for an experienced runner, and that is one reason a knowledgeable coach can help you shave minutes off your marathon time. Self-trained runners who are well-motivated can get themselves in trouble too easily. If they train in a group, where group dynamics sometimes take precedence over good sense, they can encounter similar problems.

For these reasons, I do not recommend doing interval training—or any form of speedwork—year-round. Nevertheless, it's a type of training that lends itself well to progressing toward a specific goal.

REVIEW WHAT YOU DO

At various points during the premarathon buildup, I like to review what I am doing. Am I on schedule? Am I training too hard and need to back off? What level of fitness have I achieved, and how will that affect my pace in the marathon?

In some respects, this review is ongoing because every day on my way out to train, I pass my training calendar on the wall, where I can see at a glance the number of weekly miles I've run and the distance of my long runs and whether I'm on schedule or not. My smaller diary provides me with the details of my training, and I sometimes thumb backward through it if I'm planning to progress in certain workouts (in either distance or intensity). I also look for key words and phrases, such as "tired," "dragging," or "legs dead," which, if they occur too often, are a clear signal to me that I need several easy days or a week of low mileage to avoid injury or overtraining.

One year at the Chicago Marathon, a runner approached the booth where I was selling books and said that he would log on to the marathon training program on my Web site to see what he was supposed to run that day. After the workout, he would log back on to make sure he had done the workout correctly. You're tempted to laugh, but what he achieved was positive reinforcement for his training. A lot of runners today who don't have easy access to good coaching in their area use the Internet as their coaches.

A LOT OF RUNNERS TODAY USE THE INTERNET AS THEIR COACHES.

During any review, I'll decide only to decrease the level of my training; I never decide to increase the level. If you think you're behind your premarathon schedule, you either need to lower your performance expectations or choose another race later in the year.

One way to determine your fitness level is to enter a race over a well-established distance. It's easy enough to find a 5-K or 10-K race to jump into, although I would prefer to test myself at either a 10-miler or a half marathon. A 25-K would be ideal, but there are only a few of those around. (One of the best in my area is the River Bank Run in Grand Rapids, Michigan, although its May date eliminates it as preparation for most spring marathons.)

I don't like to race too often during my peak buildup for any major event, but particularly not before a marathon. To race properly, I find I need to rest several days before the race, and it takes me several days after the race to recover. Before you know it, you've lost the equivalent of a week of productive training. For that reason, I try to limit any test races in the premarathon buildup to one a month. We used to list three to four test races for runners taking the CARA marathon training class, but then we decided against it, for fear that runners would feel obligated to run all of them.

Invariably someone in each early lecture would ask what Brian Piper, Bill Fitzgerald, and I used to refer to as "the triathlon question." There was a late-summer triathlon in Chicago, and some individuals would want to enter both that and the marathon. "You can do both," we would usually tell them, "but it's difficult to do both well. You need to establish which race is most important to you and concentrate your main energy on that event. This may mean cutting back on the biking and swimming you might normally do before a triathlon, and doing the triathlon as a hard workout rather than a race. Or do the marathon as an afterthought: 26 miles of low-pressure running without worrying about time."

Nevertheless, some racing is helpful. If you're a beginner, you'll learn where to pin your number (front rather than back) and what it feels like to go to a starting line. Your time in test races can help you predict your marathon time and guide you in selecting a pace. But in making comparisons, beware of overconfidence. You may also need to make adjustments depending on conditions, including weather and the difficulty of the course.

REACHING THE PEAK

Eventually, if you have planned well, you will reach a peak in your training. Running becomes easier and less of an effort. You are able to finish your weekly long runs at the same pace you started, and you don't feel as tired or worn-out the next day. If you are running speedwork on the track, your times are faster. You feel good. You look lean and mean. One of the best indicators of my fitness level was when my wife's mother would look at me and say, "You're too skinny!" It was then that I knew I was in shape.

All of these signals offer positive feedback and will provide a psychological boost when you run your big race. If you know you're in shape, you're more likely to feel confident that you can achieve a peak performance. To achieve peak performance, mental strength may be as important as physical strength, but you achieve mental confidence by training yourself physically.

Most first-time marathoners train to reach a quick peak—that final 20-miler before the race. But if they're well coached, they won't try to achieve a peak performance in their first marathons; they'll save that goal for future races.

Most experienced marathoners like to reach a peak, then hold that training level for 4 to 6 weeks. Once you get to the point at which you have the time and ability to run several 20-milers, you are more likely to achieve the peak performance you want. You will probably also chop minutes off the time you ran in your first marathon.

The final touch for any program designed to achieve peak performance is the taper, the gradual cutback of training immediately before the race. This is such an important subject that I've devoted an entire chapter to it.

The one factor critical to your taper is rest, something many dedicated runners have trouble doing. You need to arrive at the starting line Rested, Refreshed, and Ready to run, the three Rs of peak performance. More on this in the next chapter.

CHAPTER 15
THE MAGIC TAPER

THE FINAL WEEKS PROVIDE
YOUR KEYS TO SUCCESS

After months and months of training, after the steady buildup of weekly miles and a string of long runs on weekends, the big event is near. Many questions may spring to mind: What do you do the last few weeks before the marathon? How do you prepare yourself physically and mentally? How much should you rest? How do you cut back on training? How long should you taper?

In the critical, final weeks just prior to the race, many marathoners make a serious mistake. They fail to utilize one key ingredient in any training system that's mentioned many times in this book: rest.

David L. Costill, PhD, of the human performance laboratory at Ball State University in Muncie, Indiana, believes that runners often train too hard in the weeks immediately preceding a marathon. "They feel they need one last butt-busting workout and end up tearing themselves down," he says.

That probably was true at the start of the first running boom in the 1970s, leading into the 1980s. In decades past, runners rarely tapered, or cut back their training, for more than a week, even for a major marathon. But in the 1990s, leading into the new millennium, more and more marathons provided training classes for the convenience of their runners. Increasing numbers of coaches began to serve the large pool of new runners. And with the explosion of training advice on the Internet, especially for beginning runners, the word has gotten out: You need to cut back on your training for several weeks to obtain a peak performance. In fact, sometimes more than several weeks. In his research with swimmers, Dr. Costill noticed that they often set PRs when they'd tapered as much as 3 to 6 weeks before an event.

> **YOU NEED TO CUT BACK ON YOUR TRAINING FOR SEVERAL WEEKS TO OBTAIN A PEAK PERFORMANCE.**

He also found that swimmers performed better when undertrained. So when Dr. Costill worked with a group of runners, he

TAPER MADNESS

While 3 weeks of tapering can have a positive effect physically, it can have a negative effect psychologically. As runners run fewer and fewer miles during the final weeks before the marathon, they suddenly find themselves with too much time on their hands. Plus, they enjoy running and find that it relaxes them: either wakes them up in the morning or allows them to put the cares of their workdays behind them in the evening.

"During the taper, nervous energy takes the place of running," states Catherine Kedjidjian, a runner from Deerfield, Illinois. On the online Inter*Active* bulletin boards I manage, I notice a sudden increase in frivolous messages as people turn to their computers when not allowed to run.

We have a term for this: Taper Madness.

Three-fourths of the runners, when responding to an Internet poll asking if Taper Madness was real, answered yes. "I swear," says Jennifer Heemstra of Champaign, Illinois, "that the short runs during the

started their taper 3 weeks before a track race. During this period, they ran only 2 easy miles daily.

Two problems developed. Psychological tests showed that the runners, addicted to running and worried about losing conditioning, became anxious. It's what I call Taper Madness. In a preliminary 5000-meter trial, the runners—apparently so well-rested that they misjudged their abilities—started off too fast and faded at the end. But in a subsequent trial, the runners paced themselves better and ran their best times.

Dr. Costill eventually concluded that runners could best achieve success in long-distance running by preparing far in advance. "Base is important. Runners need to start their marathon training early

---

taper period felt tougher than the 20-miler, bringing on a panic attack that I would be unable to hold marathon pace for 26 miles."

"I become acutely aware of everything I have to do leading into race day," groans Mike Feliciani of Collegeville, Pennsylvania. "I question my preparation, my pace, my shoes, my socks, my health, my sanity, and everything else 3 weeks before my marathon."

There's no real cure. Cross-training is not the answer. Going on an eating binge as a mood reliever is a very bad idea. Using the extra time to reconnect with your spouse might be the best choice—unless your spouse is running the marathon, too. Yikes! In fact, twice yikes!

Nevertheless, David R. Fried of White Plains, New York, insists that the more often you are exposed to Taper Madness, the more you build up immunity: "It's a matter of confidence. Having completed a few marathons now, I'm less susceptible to going nuts."

Grit your teeth and get on with it, knowing that in 3 weeks the Big Day will come. Until then: Yikes!

enough so that they can afford to taper 2 or 3 weeks before the event. You need to realize that it is the training you do months before—rather than weeks before—that spells success."

That's a message we all should heed, but the drive that pushes us to success often pushes us to train too hard at the end. This is particularly true of seasoned marathoners. They become comfortable with their regular training routines—whether it's 40, 50, 60, or more weekly miles—and don't want to cut back.

You may not know what to do with the extra time. And you don't want to give up your long Sunday run with friends, even the last weekend before the marathon. Then there's the problem of diet. If you cut down on the number of miles you run, you'll also need to cut the number of calories you eat if you don't want to gain weight. And while many marathoners might believe that rest could benefit their performance in this marathon, they're afraid of the effect of 2 or 3 weeks rest on their overall conditioning.

CUTTING WAY BACK

Nevertheless, if you want to run well in the marathon, you will need to change your habits in five areas in the weeks leading up to the race.

Cut total mileage. Many of us are slaves to our training logs. We find security in the consistency with which we run week after week, month after month, recording a steady succession of miles in our diaries and on our calendars. That's fine, since steady and consistent training brings results, but for the last 2 to 3 weeks before the marathon, mileage doesn't count. In fact, high mileage may hinder your performance.

According to Owen Anderson, PhD, editor of the newsletter *Running Research News*, "Scientific evidence suggests that temporary training reductions bolster leg muscle power, reduce lactic acid production, and carve precious minutes off race times. In contrast, hard workouts just before a race can produce nagging injuries and deplete leg muscles of their key fuel for running—glycogen."

How much should you cut mileage? That's a tough question because all of us are different, and our goals differ. As a general rule, I'd say cut total mileage by at least 50 percent. Later in this chapter, I present specific programs for how to do this.

TEMPORARY TRAINING REDUCTIONS BOLSTER LEG MUSCLE POWER, REDUCE LACTIC ACID PRODUCTION, AND CARVE PRECIOUS MINUTES OFF RACE TIMES.

Cut frequency. The simplest way to cut total mileage is to reduce the number of times you train. When I was training at the elite level and running twice a day, I cut my mileage by eliminating one of those daily workouts for the last 10 days before a race.

You might not train twice daily, but if you follow a hard/easy pattern in your training, you have a similar option. Just eliminate the easy days. Instead of running an easy 3-miler on your in-between days, don't run at all. Take a day off. Your body will be able to recover more fully from the hard workouts, and you won't lose any conditioning.

Cut distance, not intensity. Research suggests that you need to continue to train at or near race pace on the hard days. At McMaster University in Hamilton, Ontario, a group led by Duncan MacDougall, PhD, compared different ways of tapering for well-trained runners who averaged 45 to 50 miles a week. For the taper week, some athletes didn't run, others ran 18 to 19 miles at an easy pace, and another group cut their mileage but continued running fast. The researchers decided that a taper including small amounts of fast running was superior to slow, easy miles.

Dr. MacDougall also worked with runners training for a 10-K race who started their tapers with 5×500 at race pace, then progressively eliminated one 500 for the next 5 days, ending with a 1-day rest. (In other words: 5 × 500, 4 × 500, 3 × 500, 2 × 500, 1 × 500, rest.)

Dr. MacDougall comments, "We still don't know what the optimal tapering plan actually is, but we do know that if you're going to be tapering for a week or so, it's important to keep the intensity of your workouts fairly high as you cut back drastically on your mileage."

Translated to the marathon, this would mean maintaining the pace of your runs but cutting their distance. A hard 8-mile run would become a 6-mile run at the beginning of the taper, then later get cut to 4 or 2. But you should keep the pace near the comfortable one you've used for most of your training. In speed workouts, cut the number of repetitions, similar to the McMaster's taper.

Cut the lifting. If you are a frequent visitor to the weight room and lift weights two or three times a week or more, that's good for your physical fitness and overall health, but you need to cut back on this discipline, too, as marathon day nears.

Certainly during the last 3 weeks before the marathon, you need to match what you do on the roads with what you do in the gym. No heavy lifting. Fewer repetitions. Grab your towel and head to the shower feeling exhilarated, not exhausted.

In fact, a 3-week taper for lifters might not be enough, particularly for those who didn't spend a lot of time in the gym before becoming runners. Start to taper your lifting 6 weeks out, at the time when you hit peak running mileage. That will decrease the chance of injury either running or lifting.

Cut back on calories. Finally, watch what you eat. If you're running less, you're also burning fewer calories. This could mean you gain a pound or so—no big deal, unless you also fill in your spare time by making extra trips to the fridge.

Robert Eslick, a coach from Nashville, says, "I tell my runners to watch their intake for the first 3 days of the marathon week to avoid weight gain and then to eat a little more than their normal intake, with the emphasis on carbohydrates the last 3 days." Sound advice.

To keep from piling on extra pounds, you could eliminate junk food from your regular diet during your taper week. Get rid of the soft drinks and sugar sweets that you may have used to boost your calorie intake during regular training. Rely on complex carbohydrates instead—potatoes, apples, pasta, bread, and so on.

PRECISION TAPERING

Knowing precisely how to modify your training during the last 2 to 3 weeks before a marathon takes experience. Even for seasoned marathoners, it may take a few bad starts before finding a specific routine that works. There are too many variables in the equation: how long you might have prepared for any one specific long race,

FINAL FOUR

The principles of tapering are the same whether you're a first-time marathoner or an experienced marathoner hoping to qualify for Boston. You run progressively fewer miles but maintain your usual pace and intensity. The last several days, you do next to nothing. Below is the final 4 weeks of my 18-week training schedule for Advanced-I runners, showing the peak week of training (week 15) followed by the 3 taper weeks (16, 17, 18). Novice and Intermediate runners taper similarly.

Week	Mon	Tue	Wed	Thu	Fri	Sat	Sun
15	5-mi run	10-mi run	5-mi run	8 × 800	Rest	12-mi pace	20 mi
16	5-mi run	8-mi run	5-mi run	6 × hill	Rest	4-mi pace	12 mi
17	4-mi run	6-mi run	4-mi run	30 tempo	Rest	4-mi run	8 mi
18	3-mi run	4-mi run	3-mi run	4 × 400	Rest	2-mi run	Race

how effective your training has been, whether you enter the closing stages undertrained or overtrained, and how confident you are.

A good coach who is familiar with your abilities and training patterns can tell you how to taper. A coach who has worked with you on a day-by-day basis could tell you precisely how to modify your training for the final countdown. Although I frequently get involved in writing training schedules on the Internet and for various books, one single program cannot be expected to fit all runners. Nevertheless, here's my spin on the last 3 weeks before the big race.

Three for the money. By 3 weeks (21 days) before the race, after your final 20-miler, you should have figured out what to do next. For all practical purposes, your marathon training is over. Avoid the trap of thinking that 1 additional week of training just might get you in really good shape. It's more likely to injure you or lower your resistance so you're at risk of catching a cold or the flu—a big liability when you have a race to run.

This is particularly important if illness or injury forced you to miss a week or two of training during your ramp-up to the marathon. You do not—repeat, not—want to make up that lost mileage now.

In Chicago, and for runners following my programs online, we do our final 20-miler on the Saturday or Sunday before the 3-week taper begins. On successive Sundays, we go from 20 to 12 to 8 miles with the 26-mile race falling on the 4th Sunday of our program. The more I work with both beginning and even experienced runners, the more comfortable I become with this pattern.

Most runners, even experienced ones, will benefit from a slight decrease in their mileage, to about 75 percent. The runner who ran 40 miles last week

MOST RUNNERS, EVEN EXPERIENCED ONES, WILL BENEFIT FROM A SLIGHT DECREASE IN THEIR MILEAGE.

should cut back to about 30 miles. An easy way to cut total mileage is to convert 1 or 2 of your easy days into rest days. Change 1 or 2 others into half workouts, decreasing your distance. But don't cut intensity or pace yet. You can cut the number of repeats during speed workouts, for example, but don't necessarily run them slower.

Two for the show. Two weeks (14 days) out. If you didn't cut mileage last week, cut it now. You need at least this much time to taper. In my peak years, I tapered exactly 10 days before marathons. Now that I am older and wiser, I take more time. If you feel you must run a final 20-miler 2 weeks before the race, it should be your final workout at this distance.

If you did cut your mileage to 75 percent the week before, now you should cut it to nearly 50 percent of your normal mileage. The marathoner who normally runs 40 miles a week should run maybe 20 miles this week.

But don't reduce your pace yet. You don't want to forget too soon what it feels like to train at near-marathon pace.

Remember that along with the decreased mileage, you'll be burning fewer calories, so if you're worried about gaining a pound or two, cut back on your intake of "empty" calories.

One to get ready. One week (7 days) before your big race. If you've resisted the idea of cutting your mileage before, you definitely need to cut it now. Even another-lap-around-the-park zealots will concede that maybe a little rest is helpful at this point. Okay, if you wouldn't taper

BEGIN CARBO-LOADING 7 DAYS IN ADVANCE.

for 3 weeks, how about 3 days? Did you really believe running 20 miles the final Sunday before your race was going to help you? I once did, but I've long since changed my mind.

Speaking of diet, begin carbo-loading 7 days in advance. Forget what you read years ago about depletion and 3 days of a low-carb diet before switching to a diet high in carbohydrates. Stick with a high-carbohydrate diet throughout the week. You don't need to eat spaghetti all 7 days: Focusing on fruits, vegetables, and grains will keep you near 60 percent carbs even if you have lean meat as a main course. If you haven't eliminated between-meal junk snacks, do it now.

This is also the week to eliminate hard training. There's no room in your training plan for hard, fast, or long runs. Forget them. If you run anything at or near race pace, don't run far.

Now is not the time to cross-train. According to Tom Grogon, a coach from Cincinnati, "One problem that often develops is that people in training sometimes use these easy/lower-mileage weeks to do something else equally stressful." Grogon recalls one tapering runner who rebuilt his barn and another who spent his "rest" time swimming and biking—and none of these activities exactly qualify as resting. Grogon recommends using the extra time to catch up on family and work responsibilities.

Time to go. Three days remain. For the final 3 days of the countdown, I shift to almost total rest. Notice I said "almost." During the final 3 days, I rest 2, run 1. This is my usual premarathon pattern:

Three days before is a day off.
Two days before is a day off.
One day before, I may do some light jogging and perhaps do a few strides, particularly if I've traveled a long distance to the race.

"Strides" are controlled sprints at race pace. I do a couple of miles of easy running to loosen up, particularly if I traveled to the race by car or plane. But by definition, strides are short: 150 meters at the most. Soft surfaces are best. Instead of jogging between strides, I'll walk. Before Boston, I'll head out to the Charles River and do my strides on the grass beside the bike path; in Chicago, there's plenty of grass in Grant Park near the start of the race. Most runners find prerace training areas without much prodding.

If possible, I prefer to travel at least 2 days before the race, not the day before. Travel fatigues me, and I prefer to get to the race city early. For international races requiring an overnight jet flight, I need to arrive much earlier. For a short overseas track race, I'll sometimes arrive a couple of days before I compete; for marathons, I need nearly a week to adjust. One rule of thumb is to arrive 1 day early for every time zone crossed—if the cost of hotel rooms isn't prohibitive. Ask yourself: How important is this race? Then plan accordingly.

THE LAST 24 HOURS

The important point to remember about the last 24 hours is that if you have prepared properly, nothing much you do on this day— except what you eat and drink—will have much effect on your race. Mental preparation is probably more important than physical preparation at this point.

One way to pass time the day before the race is to hang out at the exhibition of running equipment, which is as much a part of the marathon mystique as the pasta party. But don't spend all day on your feet, particularly given the hard concrete in most exhibition halls. If you want to chat with your friends, do it in your room, or sitting in soft chairs in the hotel lobby.

Another option is touring the course. Some runners feel it is important to see the course in advance so they know what to expect. But having been in the running business this long as both a participant and a reporter, I've either run over most of the courses I race or ridden them on press trucks. I don't need to see them one more time, particularly if it means committing myself to sitting for several hours on a bus. With several thousand people around you on race day, you're not going to get lost.

To me, the hills always seem steeper and the miles longer when you're riding over them rather than running them. If there are key points of a course I feel I need to see—such as a series of hills—I might make an effort to see them, but usually I'm content to wait until race day.

My all-time favorite running book title is *Spaghetti Every Friday*, written by Houston runner Bob Fletcher, who ran 50 marathons on 50 successive weekends. This title refers to the ritual spaghetti dinner the night before most major marathons. Often you can eat on the cheap at these affairs, but sometimes they're noisy and impersonal. My nominee for the best prerace pasta party is the Chicago Marathon, but I'm biased because I grew up in Chicago.

To avoid crowds, I'll sometimes sneak off to a local Italian restaurant—if I can find one without a 30-minute wait. Boston has some of the best Italian restaurants in the world in its North End. Or I may pick a Chinese restaurant, where I can eat a rice dish. Honolulu, as you might suspect, has excellent Asian restaurants.

Wherever or whatever you eat, your last meal needs to be high in carbohydrates. But don't overeat, thinking more is better. The night before a marathon in San Francisco, I sat next to a top runner who piled a world-record amount of pasta on her plate. Then she went back for seconds! She was only 5 feet 5 inches tall and weighed 109 pounds, so I don't know where she stored all that food. And I don't recall that she ran too well the next day.

Don't eat any more at the prerace pasta party than you're used to. Even though the second and third helpings are free, don't necessarily avail yourself of them. Eat a normal-size meal and drink what you usually drink. In the past, I noticed a lot of runners walking around expos with water bottles in their hands. I see that less often now, suspecting that the drink-until-you-drown approach to hydration is past its time. If you feel that's what you need to do to ensure that you go to the starting line well-hydrated, do it, but you may spend most of the last 24 hours before the race going to the bathroom. Most experts advise against beer because it's a diuretic, but if you're used to having an occasional beer with your meal and you think it will relax you, it probably will.

Research at Ball State University suggests that eating two small meals 4 hours apart the night before the race may be better than eating one larger meal. Logistically, that used to be difficult to do, but with so many energy drinks and bars on the market, carbo-loading has become easier. Dr. Costill sug-

EATING TWO SMALL MEALS 4 HOURS APART THE NIGHT BEFORE THE RACE MAY BE BETTER THAN EATING ONE LARGER MEAL.

gests that a high-carbohydrate snack just before going to bed may help assure a full supply of glycogen in your muscles. Avoid soft drinks with caffeine, which may keep you awake. My caffeine limit is normally one cup of coffee or one soft drink, but I won't have even that the night before a marathon.

With or without caffeine in my system, I may sleep fitfully or awaken in the middle of the night. This used to worry me; it no longer does. I thought I was losing energy by lying awake in bed, but as long as you're horizontal, you're still getting rest. More important than the night before the race is the night before the night before. For a Sunday race, make certain you sleep well on Friday, and don't worry about Saturday.

Another important and delicate question. Sex the night before: yes or no? It depends. It's your choice and your mate's choice. "Don't call me. I'll call you." Casey Stengel, the famous New York Yankee manager, used to claim that it wasn't sex before the game that caused declines in his baseball players' performance the next day; it was chasing all over town to find it.

One final item in my premarathon countdown: I know this sounds both silly and obsessive, but I always pin my number on my singlet before I go to bed. In deference to the sponsors, I no longer fold around the numeral to cut wind resistance (as elite runners used to do several decades ago), but I will fold the bar strip under. I usually bring extra safety pins in case there aren't enough in my race packet, as I don't want the number flapping in the wind.

With my singlet so pinned—and I'll try it on to make certain I haven't pinned the front to the back—I'll position it on a chair in my hotel room, along with my shorts, warmup clothes, and any other gear, with my shoes (socks inside) under the chair pointing in the right direction, as though I were seated in the chair. Sort of like a fireman having his boots ready before sliding down the pole. I once felt somewhat foolish doing this, but I've talked to enough runners to realize that I am not alone.

Be sure to check to make sure you have all of the necessary gear before you leave home. A friend of mine once confessed to putting on what he thought were his shoes the morning of the Boston Marathon and realizing that he had packed his wife's running shoes, which were the same model, instead of his own. Savvy marathoners also carry their shoes onto the plane just in case the airline loses their bags.

When it comes to the marathon, you don't want to leave anything to chance.

CHAPTER 16
THE DISTANCE RUNNER'S DIET

YOU NEED ENERGY TO RUN 26 MILES

It was difficult for those of us who ran long-distance in the 1960s. We were poorly served nutritionally because of our own lack of knowledge and because of an equal lack among event organizers. We didn't know what to drink—or whether to drink. Race officials rarely provided fluids on the course and frequently scheduled starting times so we ran during the hottest part of the day. Our motto could have been "Mad dogs and marathoners go out in the midday sun."

Somehow we survived, and the sport began to prosper, but only after major changes were made in the distance runner's diet.

A page from my 1963 training diary is particularly frightening. While being coached by Fred Wilt, I kept meticulous records of everything from temperature and humidity to what I ate. It was June 30, at the National Amateur Athletic Union (AAU) 25-Kilometer Championships in Detroit. The race started at 1:30 in the afternoon. It was 94°F; the humidity was high, and there wasn't a cloud in the sky. I recorded the weather as "hot!!" There was no drinking water on the course past 10 miles.

Most astounding was my prerace meal. For breakfast at 7:30 a.m., I had orange juice and cereal, which was a good start, but my choices for lunch several hours later seem strange today. I had more orange juice, bread, milk, and a 6-ounce steak! Little wonder I suffered problems that day. I kept pace for half the distance with the eventual winner, Peter McArdle, of the New York Athletic Club, then faded badly to barely salvage third.

Coach Wilt and I knew even then that good nutrition was essential for success in endurance events, but we hadn't yet fit together all the puzzle pieces. I usually had problems in the closing stages of marathons because I ran out of energy, so I experimented with several nutritional means of boosting energy stores. At various times, I taped dextrose tablets to the back of my shorts to take during the race, or drank a high-energy drink called Sustagen, a milkshake-like supplement often used for the elderly. It made me belch through the first half of the Boston Marathon one year and didn't help much during the second half.

I was on the right track, but my focus should have been less on nutrition during the marathon, and more on nutrition before.

BREAKFAST OF CHAMPIONS

Actually, where diet was concerned, some of the veteran runners from New England knew better. In the 1950s, New England was a hotbed of road-running activity. In fact, it was the only "bed." When I first arrived at Boston in 1959, I learned that the traditional breakfast for marathoners was "porridge," what I knew as oatmeal. I made fun of this strange New England meal in an article I wrote in 1963 for *Sports Illustrated* called "On the Run from Dogs and People" (later expanded into a book with the same title).

I should have kept my mouth shut. Or, rather, opened it and started to eat. Oatmeal is high in carbohydrates and, sweetened with honey and coupled with orange juice, was exactly the kind of pre-marathon meal I should have been eating. Porridge truly could have been my Breakfast of Champions.

By the end of the 1960s, we began to get an idea of what diets work best for distance runners. In 1966, David L. Costill, PhD, established the human performance laboratory at Ball State University in Muncie, Indiana, and I became one of his first guinea pigs. One of his early experiments involved fluid replacement. One summer, I ran 2 hours on a treadmill on 3 successive days in Dr. Costill's lab—the equivalent of three 20-milers—drinking either (1) nothing, (2) water, or (3) Gatorade.

When I was allowed to drink at the rate of 50 milliliters every 3 minutes, my core body temperature remained several degrees lower than when I ran without fluids. The replacement drink provided a glucose boost that theoretically would permit me to run cooler and faster.

Dr. Costill continued his research on race nutrition. Within a few years, in some of the earliest experiments on carbohydrate loading, his assistant Bill Fink was cooking large pots of spaghetti in the Ball State lab to feed to runners. The word soon leaked out to the sports world: Steaks were out; pasta was in. Several years later, I had an assignment to write an article for the *New York Times*

THE WORD SOON LEAKED OUT TO THE SPORTS WORLD: STEAKS WERE OUT; PASTA WAS IN.

Magazine on a quarterback for the Kansas City Chiefs. I noted with interest that Hank Stram, coach of the Chiefs, was already promoting spaghetti as a better pregame meal for his 280-pound linemen than the traditional lean beef. Today just about any runner knows that spaghetti is a better premarathon meal than, say, scrambled eggs or steak, but that knowledge was a result of the pain suffered by us guinea pigs.

We now realize that the preferred fuel for the endurance athlete is carbohydrates because they are easy to digest and easy to convert into energy. Carbohydrates convert quickly into glucose (a form of sugar that circulates in the blood) and glycogen (the form of glucose stored in muscle tissue and the liver). Proteins and fats also convert into glucose/glycogen, but at a greater energy cost. The body can normally store about 2,000 calories worth of glycogen in the muscle, enough for maybe 20 miles of running.

Can better nutrition create better athletes? Ann C. Grandjean, EdD, director of the International Center for Sports Nutrition in Omaha, Nebraska, frowns at the question and gives an indirect, one-word answer: "Genetics!" What she means is that great athletes are born with the ability to succeed, a gift of good genes that allows them—when properly trained and fed—to run and jump and throw faster and higher and farther than their less genetically gifted opponents. In suggesting better nutrition for long-distance runners, sports nutritionists can't promise you success—but at least you won't fail because of poor nutrition.

How important is good nutrition? Frederick C. Hagerman, PhD, of Ohio University in Athens, served as a nutritional consultant for the Cincinnati Reds baseball team. Dr. Hagerman led off a conference in Columbus, Ohio, on nutrition for the marathon and other endurance sports before the 1992 men's Olympic marathon trials by saying that the second-most-important question asked by athletes is "What should I eat to make me stronger, better, and faster for my sport?" (The most important question, he said, is "How do I train?") Dr. Hagerman claimed that too many athletes had no idea how to eat properly to maximize their performance.

There are three important areas of the distance runner's diet. One is overall nutrition, the ability to maintain high energy levels during training. The second is prerace nutrition, what you eat in the last few days before running to ensure a good performance. Third is what you consume (mostly liquids) during the race itself to make sure that you maximize performance—and get to the finish line on your own two feet. This chapter covers the first two, training nutrition and prerace nutrition. Your body's needs during the race are covered in Chapter 19, Drinking on the Run.

FINDING THE RIGHT FUEL

When you run long distances, your energy requirements increase. In an article on endurance exercise in the journal *The Physician and Sportsmedicine*, study authors Walter R. Frontera, MD, and Richard P. Adams, PhD, commented, "During sustained exercise such as marathon running, total body energy requirements increase 10 to 20 times above resting values." Runners need to eat more of the proper foods to fuel their muscles. They also need to drink more, particularly in warm weather.

At the sports nutrition seminar in Columbus, Linda Houtkooper, PhD, a registered dietitian at the University of Arizona in Tucson, made it clear that endurance athletes in particular should get most of their calories from carbohydrates.

No argument there. The only problem is that with 35,000 items in the supermarket, marathon runners sometimes need help determining which foods are highest in carbohydrates. Unless you plan to eat spaghetti three meals a day (and even pasta contains 13 percent protein and 4 percent fat), you may need to start reading labels.

Dr. Houtkooper explained that the body requires at least 40 nutrients that are classified into six nutritional components: proteins, carbohydrates, fats, vitamins, minerals, and water. "These nutrients cannot be made in the body, and so must be supplied from solid or liquid foods." She listed six categories that form the fundamentals of a nutritionally adequate food selection plan: fruits, vegetables, grains/legumes, lean meats, low-fat milk products, and fats/sweets (in descending order of importance).

The recommendations for a healthy diet suggest 15 percent protein, 30 percent fat, and 55 percent carbohydrates. But all carbohydrates aren't created alike. There are simple and complex carbohydrates. Simple carbohydrates include sugar,

THE RECOMMENDATIONS FOR A HEALTHY DIET SUGGEST 15 PERCENT PROTEIN, 30 PERCENT FAT, AND 55 PERCENT CARBOHYDRATES.

honey, jam, and any food, such as sweets and soft drinks, that gets most of its calories from sugar. Nutritionists recommend that these

CHANGING FOOD CHOICES

Has your diet changed since you became a runner? Four out of five people who responded to an Internet survey I initiated said yes. Deciding to become a runner, for many, signals a significant lifestyle change. Sometimes the motivation is to lose weight by exercising—and dieting. More often, it is simply a desire to run a marathon. Whatever the motivation, changing food choices becomes an important part of the package.

"Because of involvement in other activities, I had a good diet before starting to run," says Jennifer Heemstra of Champaign, Illinois. "But now I am able to eat more healthy foods, including my favorite high-carb ones, such as fruit, cereal, and granola bars."

A runner all his life, Kevin Robinson of Omaha, Nebraska, concedes that his diet sometimes swings from good to bad. Nevertheless, while training for his first marathon, Robinson pushed the pendulum back toward good. Robinson says: "I definitely made a point to resume good eating habits. With the marathon as motivator, I didn't find doing so that hard."

A friend approached Julie Koehler of Chicago, saying she wanted to start running, but planned to get her diet in order first. Koehler told

simple carbs make up only 10 percent of your diet. It's complex carbohydrates you should concentrate on—the starch in plant foods—which include fruits, vegetables, bread, pasta, and legumes.

Endurance athletes in particular benefit from fuel-efficient complex carbohydrates because of the extra calories they burn each day. You need to aim for even more total carbohydrates than people who fail to exercise. You can eat (in fact, may need to eat) more total calories without worrying about weight gain. The average runner training for a marathon and running 25 to 30 miles a week prob-

her to do the opposite: "At first you find yourself avoiding foods that don't digest properly and might make your next run unpleasant. Then you start checking calorie/fat content. Next you realize you're eating more bananas than an ape, drinking enough water to drown a camel. I can't remember the last time I was in a fast-food restaurant. None of this defined me 2 years before."

Brian Hann of Camden, South Carolina, remembers his past diet habits: "I would drink four to six soft drinks a day, skip breakfast, eat fast food for lunch, have three beers after work, and, before going to bed, eat some ice cream. I never exercised, but I never gained weight."

Nevertheless, Hann at age 34 felt old. He had high cholesterol, heart palpitations, and stomach problems. He felt tired all the time. "After starting to run," says Hann, "I eliminated the soft drinks, beer, and fast food. I eat tons of bananas, apples, yogurt, cereal, rice, chicken, granola bars, protein shakes, and drink about 2 liters of water a day." Hann suspects he eats twice as much food as before, but still has lost 10 pounds.

"I'm still tired all the time," says Hann, "but at least I know it's from running 40 miles a week."

ably needs a daily caloric intake near 3,000 to maintain muscle glycogen stores. As your mileage climbs beyond that, you need to eat more and more food, not less. In all honesty, this is why a lot of runners run, and why they train for marathons. Their common motto is "I love to eat."

That is why low-carb diets do not work for runners. The Atkins diet is a disaster for distance runners, as are any weight-loss diets that limit carbohydrate intake. Go on one of these fad diets, and you may experience a sudden reduction in weight, as measured by your bedroom scale. This weight loss, often dramatic, provides an instant boost to the dieter's ego and may cause the individual to stay on the diet and continue to lose weight. That's good. But the instant loss is artificial, since the shift in the protein/carbohydrate ratio causes the body

THE ATKINS DIET IS A DISASTER FOR DISTANCE RUNNERS, AS ARE ANY WEIGHT-LOSS DIETS THAT LIMIT CARBOHYDRATE INTAKE.

to lose fluids. Dehydration can be a danger for those training for a marathon, and particularly in the marathon itself. Add to that the discomfort caused by constipation, another low-carb side effect.

Someone who is clinically obese can lose 5 to 10 pounds within a few weeks simply through this process of dehydration. But that person will only continue to lose weight, and maintain that weight loss, if they restrict caloric intake. There are no magic diets when it comes to weight loss. It's calories in versus calories burned, and the weight-loss regimens that work best are those that burn calories through exercise, even something as simple as a mile or two a day of walking.

High-mileage athletes actually may need to supplement their diets with high-carbohydrate drinks to ensure sufficient energy for their daily long runs. But you also need more protein, says Liz Applegate, PhD, a professor at the University of California at Davis and author of *Eat Smart, Play Hard*. Dr. Applegate suggests that runners training for a marathon need a minimum of 70 grams of protein a day—more if you're a high-mileage trainer. Most important, she advises, you need that protein soon after you exercise, particularly after workouts longer than 10 miles.

"Eating a bagel or candy bar to quickly restore the calories you burned is not enough," says Dr. Applegate. "Better would be a tuna sandwich and piece of fruit. For the recovery meal, you need carbohydrates and protein in a ratio of about 4 to 1. The longer the run, the more important this becomes to promote rapid recovery."

Following the 4-to-1 rule is particularly important after the marathon itself. If you plan to use an energy bar before or after a long run, you need to read the labels, says Dr. Applegate, since some bars contain mostly carbohydrates, while others may include large amounts of protein. "You want the carbohydrate bar before you run," she says, "the protein bar after."

Nevertheless, carbohydrates still rule. You need 400 grams of carbohydrates a day if you're on a training program such as mine with weekly mileages above 30; 500 if your weekly mileage rises above 50; 600 if over 70; and so forth. Eating such a high-carbohydrate diet allows you to continuously restock your muscles with glycogen, the fuel that is as important in training as it is in racing. Because of the number of miles you run, you can also afford a somewhat higher ratio of simple versus complex carbohydrates in your diet—although some nutritionists might argue with me on this point.

Here's where I part company with the popular low-carb diets (Atkins, South Beach, Zone, etc.) that suggest food ratios near 40 percent carbohydrates, 30 percent protein, and 30 percent fat. People do lose weight following low-carb diets, although researchers suggest it is mainly because in following this regimen, they also cut calorie intake. When it comes to losing weight, all nutritionists agree that the best approach is to combine diet and exercise. And the most effective weight-burning exercise is running. You'll burn approximately 100 calories a mile. Run 36 miles (3,600 calories burned), and you can lose a pound. Follow my marathon training program, and you'll run approximately 500 miles over a period of 18 weeks. Theoretically, at least, you can lose 15 pounds by training for a marathon. This assumes that you don't increase your calorie consumption to meet your body's increased energy needs.

Some people seeking to finish their first marathons, however, are more than 15 pounds overweight—or they think they are. So they attempt to lose some additional weight by dieting. To a certain ex-

HIGH-CARBOHYDRATE FOODS

The traditional prerace meal for marathoners is spaghetti. With a wife of Italian origin, I also reap the culinary benefits of a tradition that literally demands frequent doses of pasta. But spaghetti (or macaroni or other forms of pasta) every day can become boring, particularly when you're trying to carbo-load the week before a marathon. Fortunately, there are many foods you can eat that will guarantee that your diet is high in carbohydrates both during training and before races.

In *Nancy Clark's Sports Nutrition Guidebook* (www.nancyclarkrd. com), the author, a sports dietitian in private practice in the Boston area, lists the following carbohydrate-rich foods.

FRUITS

Apples	Bananas	Oranges
Apricots, dried	Fruit Roll-Ups	Raisins

VEGETABLES

Broccoli	Green beans	Winter squash
Carrots	Peas	Zucchini
Corn	Tomato sauce	

GRAINS, LEGUMES, AND POTATOES

Baked beans	Potato, baked	Spaghetti
Lentils	Rice	Stuffing

tent, this isn't a bad idea, assuming you choose your diet prudently. Those who choose a fad diet that lowers carbohydrate intake make a major mistake. That's because most fad diets fail to provide enough energy for endurance activities. Follow the Zone diet, for example, and if you're eating 3,000 calories a day, according to Dr.

BREADS, ROLLS, AND CRACKERS

Bagel	Matzo	Submarine roll
Bran muffin	Pancakes	Waffles
English muffin	Pita bread	Whole-grain bread
Graham crackers	Saltines	

BREAKFAST CEREALS

Cream of Wheat	Grape-Nuts	Oatmeal
Granola	Muesli	Raisin Bran
(low-fat varieties)		

BEVERAGES

Apple juice	Cola drinks	Orange juice
Apricot nectar	Cran-raspberry juice	

SWEETS, SNACKS, AND DESSERTS

Cranberry sauce	Honey	Pop-Tarts
Fig bars	Maple syrup	Strawberry jam
Fruit yogurt		

Clark also warns that some foods that runners assume are high in carbohydrates may have a high percentage of their calories hidden in fat. These foods include croissants, Ritz crackers, thin-crust pizza (as opposed to thick-crust), and granola. When in doubt, Clark advises, read the labels.

Applegate, you'll ingest only about 300 grams of carbohydrates a day, much less than the 400 recommended. "One problem," says Dr. Applegate, "is that individuals following the Zone diet Monday to Thursday start running out of energy by the weekend, when they're about to do their long run. They need to take a day off on

Friday, not to rest from their running but to rest from their diets. These Zone diet runners either crash during the workout or binge on carbs to survive, which makes them feel guilty."

The only aspect of most low-carb diets that Dr. Applegate likes is their emphasis on protein. She feels that runners who graze on bagels and jelly beans and entirely avoid meats or other protein sources aren't doing themselves any good, either.

Frequently, I receive questions in my Inter*Active* forums from runners training for marathons who claim that they have no energy, that they have to struggle to get through their long runs, particularly as the mileage begins to escalate toward the end of their training plans. Not only do they find themselves struggling during workouts, but they're also tired at other times of the day. They aren't eating enough carbohydrates; they're starved for fuel. My advice is to avoid any kind of fad diet. Sound nutritional practices will get you to the starting line, and that includes eating plenty of carbohydrates, since they are the most efficient form of fuel.

Individuals training for a marathon and simultaneously on fad diets can get away with this double-dipping early in the training program, but they eventually fall victim to the low-carb fad. They run out of fuel.

You don't need to patronize Italian restaurants to ensure an adequate supply of complex carbohydrates. I sometimes choose a Chinese restaurant because rice is also high in carbohydrates. And Nancy Clark, RD, director of nutrition services for SportsMedicine Brookline in Boston and author of *Nancy Clark's Sports Nutrition Guidebook* (among the best books on the subject) points out that you can get plenty of carbs in most American restaurants. If you eat soup (such as minestrone, bean, rice, or noodle), potatoes, breads, and vegetables along with your main dish, and maybe grab a piece of apple cobbler off the dessert tray, you can end up eating more carbohydrates than fats or protein. (For a list of good high-carbohydrate choices, see "High-Carbohydrate Foods" on page 234.)

CHECKING OUT YOUR DIET

I don't spend a lot of time agonizing over what I eat, but on one occasion when a dietitian evaluated my diet, I averaged 12 percent protein, 19 percent fat, and 69 percent carbohydrates over a typical 3-day period. Fifty-two percent of my total calories came from complex carbohydrates, and 16 percent were from simple carbohydrates. (Dr. Applegate might argue that I was somewhat deficient in protein and a bit high on sweets, but I later corrected that in my diet.)

The nutritional analysis of my diet also showed I was getting more than the recommended daily allowances of vitamins and minerals, so I don't normally take supplements other than a daily multivitamin as an insurance policy. Also, my last cholesterol test indicated 147 total cholesterol, including 58 HDL (the good cholesterol), a very favorable ratio. If I have succeeded with my dietary goals, I believe there are two reasons.

A healthy breakfast. You can think of a good breakfast as a fast start out of the blocks. Each morning, I drink an 8-ounce glass of orange juice mixed with cranberry juice and usually eat a high-fiber breakfast cereal, with fat-free milk, piled high with raisins, bananas, and whatever other fruits are in season: strawberries, raspberries, blueberries. A couple of times when we were out of milk, I substituted orange juice on my cereal. Yes, it sounds disgusting, but don't knock it until you've tried it.

I used to add two slices of toast spread with margarine or butter, and sometimes a soft-boiled egg, although as my mileage totals declined over the past several years, I began to cut back on my calorie consumption to maintain a steady weight, and those items have dropped out of my diet. Sometimes on Sundays, between my long run and church, my wife and I will treat ourselves to a special breakfast with coffee cake (or pancakes, waffles, or French toast), bacon, and scrambled eggs with mozzarella cheese. Research suggests that if you are going to do any "dangerous" eating of high-fat foods, you're best off doing it on days when you burn a lot of calories and can quickly metabolize those foods.

Joanne Milkereit's refrigerator. Okay, this needs some explaining. Joanne Milkereit, RD, was the nutritionist at the Hyde Park Co-op, an upscale grocery store near the University of Chicago, when we collaborated to write the *Runner's Cookbook* back in 1979. (She now works as a nutritional consultant in Charleston, South Carolina.)

While we were working on the cookbook, Milkereit told me that all runners should tape the following words on their refrigerators: EAT A WIDE VARIETY OF LIGHTLY PROCESSED FOODS. Go back and reread this phrase. Think about it. By wide variety, she means you sample all the food groups. Milkereit says: "When you eat 'lightly processed,' not only do you get

EAT A WIDE VARIETY OF LIGHTLY PROCESSED FOODS.

all the vitamins and minerals, but you get the fiber in plant foods. It's amazing that after all the nutritional research done in the past 3 decades, those words of advice remain valid."

What does Milkereit mean by lightly processed? Beware of foods that come wrapped in plastic or that you can buy at a fast-food restaurant—although several restaurants have started to offer such fare as low-fat burgers, carrot sticks, and nutritious salads. "Frankly," says Milkereit, "I feel we sometimes dump on fast-food restaurants too much. There are good choices in fast-food restaurants and bad choices in other restaurants."

Another food rule comes from Pete Pfitzinger, a 1984 and 1988 Olympic marathoner. He once told me, "I don't put anything in my mouth that's been invented in the last 25 years." That may be a bit too extreme, but if you pay attention to these two messages, you probably can't go wrong with your diet.

Judy Tillapaugh, RD, of Fort Wayne, Indiana, believes that although runners understand the value of carbo-loading before a marathon, they don't give equal attention to day-to-day meal plans. "Endurance athletes need to continually replace energy stores with a diet high in carbohydrates, low in fat, and with enough protein to maintain muscle," says Tillapaugh. "Some weight-conscious runners don't eat enough."

And you need to spread your calories throughout the day by snacking, choosing healthy fare such as fruit, graham crackers, yogurt, or bagels. If you need 3,500 calories daily, you can't pack them into one or two meals. Athletes often neglect breakfast, then wonder why they're tired while running in the evening.

Fancy supplements, legal or illegal, cannot substitute for good nutrition. Excessive intake of vitamins is a waste of money and, in the case of fat-soluble vitamins (A, D, E, and K), raises the threat of long-term health problems. Dr. Applegate suggests taking a multivitamin that contains iron and zinc every other day as a minimum dosage. "Younger women need more iron than postmenopausal women," she says, "as do men who don't eat meat." Eating a single 3-ounce portion of lean red meat once a week can do a lot to make vitamin supplementation unnecessary; so can eating fish once a week.

Can certain supplements improve performance? Apparently they can, judging from all the effort that goes into detecting their use by athletes competing at the Olympic level and in most professional sports. Drug use seems endemic in many sports, but in reality probably only a relatively small percentage of athletes still try to steal an edge by using steroids or other performance-boosting drugs. Partly now it is a fear of getting caught. Testing at major events and also outside of competition is designed not only to catch cheaters for the benefit of drug-free athletes but also to prevent them from making mistakes that may shorten their life spans.

Scientists don't know or understand all the side effects of the so-called performance-enhancing drugs, but quite frankly I become suspicious when I hear of a champion athlete who dies at an early age.

I remember one middle-distance runner and member of the U.S. Olympic team who used steroids, according to one of his training partners. The Olympian died of a heart condition while still in his fifties. People do die of heart attacks at that age for reasons unrelated to drug use, but it makes me wonder. Would a midpack marathoner, knowing he or she would not be tested for drug use, resort to illegal drugs to set a PR, to qualify for Boston, or to achieve any seemingly unattainable goal? In my mind, that person would be very, very foolish.

Apart from supplementation, does following a good diet mean no treats? My measured intake of 16 percent of calories from simple carbohydrates might be considered high for "healthy" people, but not necessarily for a competitive runner. "Athletes are told to avoid junk foods," says Dr. Grandjean, "but the reality is that if you are eating 4,000 calories a day, once you have taken in those first 2,000 calories—assuming you've done a reasonably intelligent job of selecting foods—you've probably obtained all the nutrients you need. You don't need to worry about vitamins and minerals because you've already supplied your needs. You can afford foods high in sugar, so-called empty calories, because you need energy. Your problem sometimes is finding enough time to eat."

Sports nutrition thus comes down to a management problem.

SURFING FOR CALORIES

The importance of general nutrition—as opposed to prerace nutrition—is that you need adequate energy for training. And unlike the general population, you may need to eat more to help maintain your weight. If you're a 150-pound person running 30 miles a week to prepare for a marathon, you need approximately 3,000 calories a week more than a sedentary person, and most of those calories should come from carbohydrates. Since carbohydrates are bulkier than fats or protein, the sheer volume of food that high-mileage runners must eat can become a problem.

Dr. Grandjean says that among the athletes she advises, distance runners are most knowledgeable about nutrition because their energy needs are so high. And those most talented, the ones already on top, often have the best nutrition. Fred Brouns of the Nutrition Research Center at the University of Limburg in the Netherlands studied cyclists competing in the Tour de France, both in the laboratory and during the race. Brouns discovered that cyclists who finished near the front were those who were most successful at managing their diets. "Endurance athletes must pay close attention to food intake if they expect to keep energy levels high," says Brouns.

In the Tour de France, cyclists frequently burn 5,000 calories a day! There's no way these competitors can ride 5 or 6 hours a day and have time to eat that much, so they take much of their calories in liquid form while riding. Although most runners don't have anywhere near the energy requirements of a Tour cyclist, some high-mileage runners like to use high-carbohydrate drinks as a dietary supplement.

Nancy Ditz, the top U.S. finisher at the 1987 world championship and 1988 Olympic marathons, took an intelligent approach to diet. Between those two marathons, Ditz decided she wanted to leave nothing to chance when it came to race preparation. Following the suggestion of her coach, Rod Dixon (the 1983 New York City marathon champion and Olympic runner from New Zealand), she sought nutritional advice.

Ditz didn't go to a standard dietitian but spoke with Jerry Attaway, an assistant coach with the San Francisco 49ers. Attaway managed that team's strength training, rehabilitation, and diet programs. He determined that based on Ditz's energy expenditure while training 100 miles a week, she needed a higher percentage of carbohydrates than she was getting.

"Even though I was eating a pretty good diet, my carbohydrate intake still wasn't enough," Ditz recalls. She started using Exceed, a high-carbohydrate drink. (Such drinks are most effective when con-

DIET AND PERFORMANCE

Prior to the Olympic Games in Seoul, Korea, I wrote an article titled "What's Diet Got to Do with It?" that appeared in the October 1988 issue of *Runner's World*. With the cooperation of nutritional consultant Ann Grandjean, Ed.D., and the staff at the U.S. Olympic Training Center in Colorado Springs, we analyzed the diets of the six athletes (three men, three women) who had qualified for the U.S. team in the marathon.

Two of the women and one of the men clearly understood the connection between nutrition and performance, and another one of the men ate well somewhat instinctively. But the third man had a carbohydrate intake of only 44 percent, and the third woman scored only 33.8 percent and usually skipped breakfast!

I ended the article with predictions (based on diet) how the six athletes would do in the Olympics, ranking them how I expected them to finish relative to one another. But before publication, editor Amby Burfoot and I decided this would put too much pressure on those athletes. We eliminated my predictions, but it turned out that I got the rankings right. The male with the poor diet failed to finish, although because of blisters.

Nevertheless, he and the woman ran 2:12 and 2:30 respectively to win the Trials, beating runners who probably ate better. Nutrition is one element when it comes to success as a marathoner, but not the only one.

sumed immediately after exercise, when they can be most quickly absorbed.) Her calcium intake needed to be higher, so she also started drinking buttermilk with meals.

Ditz feared Attaway might ask her to cut out one of her favorite treats—cinnamon rolls at breakfast—but instead he eliminated mayonnaise on her sandwich at lunch. "That was a minor behavioral change for a major change in my ratio of fat to carbohydrate," she says. (In 2 tablespoons of mayonnaise, you get 202 calories that are 100 percent fat!)

Attaway identified foods that did the most damage to Ditz's diet, then asked, "Which do you really like?" He let her keep those, then eliminated the rest.

Ideally, long-distance runners interested in maximizing their performance in the marathon should find someone as knowledgeable as Jerry Attaway to tell them how to eat. If I had to offer a single piece of dietary advice to every person who reads this book—regardless of whether or not you have Olympic aspi-

> **IF I HAD TO OFFER A SINGLE PIECE OF DIETARY ADVICE TO EVERY PERSON WHO READS THIS BOOK, IT WOULD BE TO CONSULT A DIETITIAN.**

rations—it would be to consult a dietitian. (The American Dietetic Association's referral network can help you find a sports nutritionist. Dial 800-877-1600. Or check the ADA Web site: www.eatright.org.) Have that dietitian analyze your diet and recommend what to eat and what not to eat.

PREMARATHON NUTRITION

Pasta has become the ritual prerace feast for marathoners. No major marathon is without its night-before spaghetti dinner, which has assumed almost ceremonial aspects.

The spaghetti dinner, of course, has more than a ceremonial purpose. In eating high-carbohydrate pasta, we want to make sure our bodies have adequate glycogen, the fuel supply stored in the muscles that allows the most efficient form of energy metabolism. The more glycogen you can store, the faster you can run for longer periods of time, because when muscle glycogen is depleted, muscles contract poorly. But a well-fueled athlete also needs a full supply of glycogen for the liver, a "processing station" that sends fuel through the bloodstream to the muscles. So in addition to having your fuel tank full, you also need a full carburetor.

Various diets have been devised in an attempt to ensure maximum glycogen storage. The term carbohydrate loading, or carboloading, was originally coined to describe a dietary regimen that involved depletion and replenishment. This early form of carboloading became popular in the mid-1970s after research that was done in Scandinavia. The regimen began with a 20-mile run to exhaustion 1 week before the marathon, to deplete muscles of all available glycogen. For 3 days following that purge, the athlete followed a high-protein, low-carbohydrate diet designed to keep glycogen stores artificially low. Midweek, the athlete switched to a low-protein, high-carbohydrate diet to overload the muscles with glycogen during the final 3 days before the race. The theory was that if you depleted your body of glycogen, you would absorb more when you did eat carbohydrates—like a sponge that, squeezed dry, absorbs more water than a damp one.

I never could quite figure out how a sponge 100 percent saturated with water could absorb more than 100 percent after being squeezed dry, but this early form of carbo-loading seemed to work for some marathoners—at least sometimes. I experimented with it and had both good and bad results. (One problem scientists have in measuring anything as complicated as the effect of diet on performance is that so many other variables are present.)

Most experts today believe that runners should avoid the carboloading regimen featuring depletion and replenishment. The problems are the depletion part of the cycle and the 20-miler 1 week before the marathon. Enlightened coaches say that 20 miles is too long and hard a run so close to a marathon. They recommend more than a weeklong taper, which wouldn't allow any depletion runs. (All my training programs suggest a 3-week taper.) Also, the high-protein diet 3 days after the depletion run was so severe that runners often became depressed while following it. I certainly did. Eating became no fun—and because an upbeat psychological mood may be as important to performance as glycogen stores, the depletion phase soon lost favor.

Later research by Dr. Costill suggested that the depletion phase was unnecessary because you could achieve equally high glycogen levels with only the 3-day, high-carbohydrate approach. Forget about squeezing the sponge dry. We don't need to do that. Most of us shouted "Hallelujah" and never went back.

So the current advice is to concentrate heavily on eating carbohydrates the final days before the marathon. When someone says "carbo-loading" today, that's usually what they mean, not the 7-day depletion/replenishment cycle. For someone like me, used to following a high-carbohydrate diet, carbo-loading requires only a few changes in the regular daily routine. This is good because you don't want to subject your system to any radical changes just when you're about to run 26 miles.

If you're racing out of town, you may even want to take along some snacks to eat between the pasta dinner and the race the next morning. Dried fruits can be particularly useful, especially if you're competing in a foreign country where you're not used to the food.

LAST-MINUTE LOADING

Carbo-loading shouldn't stop with the pasta dinner; scientists tell us it should continue on the starting line to ensure maximum prerace nutrition. W. Michael Sherman, PhD, an exercise scientist and sports nutrition expert from Ohio State University, tested trained cyclists pedaling indoors, feeding them 5 grams of carbohydrates per kilogram of body weight 3 hours before exercising. Both power and endurance increased when athletes ate before exercising. (For a 165-pound cyclist, that would be about the amount of carbohydrates in 12 bagels or 7 baked potatoes.) Dr. Sherman explains: "The cyclists were able to maintain a higher output for a longer period of time before fatiguing."

Other studies have shown improved performance 4 hours after eating. "We can safely say that if you have a carbohydrate feeding 3 to 4 hours before a marathon, you can enhance performance," says Dr. Sherman.

Admittedly, marathoners do not tolerate solids in their stomachs as well as cyclists do. Dr. Sherman suggests runners either delay eating their prerace pasta until late evening, or rise early for a high-carbohydrate breakfast, such as pancakes or toast and orange juice. Liquid meals featuring high-carbohydrate drinks may work best for races near dawn. Dr. Sherman warns, however, that runners should try this first in practice or before minor races. You may find that if you eat too much immediately before the race, you may waste time standing in portable-toilet lines both before and during the marathon.

Actually, practice may let you adjust to a different type of prerace nutrition than you thought possible, including solid food an hour before the race. "You can train your body to do almost anything," says Tillapaugh, who says her favorite snack before races is a bagel or low-fat crackers.

Doug Kurtis, the Michigan elite runner who often ran a dozen marathons a year, most of them under 2:20, usually ate his last meal the night before. "Rarely will I eat anything the morning of a race," he says, "unless there's a late start, such as noon at Boston. I'd rather lie in bed an extra hour than get up just to eat. Some runners can eat and be ready to run an hour later, but I find I need 3 to 4 hours to digest my food before I feel comfortable running. I've experimented with eating 2 to 3 hours before, but it just didn't work."

"The main thing is not to do anything out of the ordinary," says Ed Eyestone, a 1988 and 1992 Olympic marathoner. "Yet you have to be flexible enough to go with the flow and eat what's available.

If you're programmed to eat pancakes precisely 7 hours before a marathon, you may be disappointed."

Experience has taught me that eating as close as 3 hours before a race gives my stomach sufficient time to digest the food and allows me to clear my intestines without the fear of having to duck into the bushes at the 5-mile mark. Closer to race time than that, however, and I'm asking for trouble. Timing can be a problem if you're running a race like the Honolulu Marathon,

> **EXPERIENCE HAS TAUGHT ME THAT EATING AS CLOSE AS 3 HOURS BEFORE A RACE GIVES MY STOMACH SUFFICIENT TIME TO DIGEST THE FOOD.**

with its predawn start. But I've gotten up as early as 2:30 a.m. to eat breakfast before that race, and I notice I'm not always alone in the hotel coffee shop.

I'll order orange juice, toast or maybe a Danish roll, and/or some applesauce along with a single cup of coffee. Some experts warn against coffee because it's a diuretic (and brings about water loss through increased urination), but it helps clear my bowels. If you're running an international race—and I've run marathons in Berlin, Athens, Rome, and other major cities—you may not be able to get a typical American breakfast, but the continental breakfast of coffee and rolls (with or without jelly) works quite well.

If the coffee shop doesn't open early enough, those snacks in the suitcase may come in handy. I'm less fussy. Practically every hotel has a soft drink machine on each floor, and frequently a can of pop is my last meal before a morning marathon.

I'll stop drinking 2 hours before the race, as it takes approximately that long for liquids to migrate from your mouth to your bladder. Another one to two cups just before the start will help you tank up for the race, and this liquid will most likely be utilized before it reaches your bladder. If you drink too much in that 2-hour period, however, you may find yourself worrying about how you

ARE CARBS STILL GOOD CHOICES?

"Good choice!"

Or, in certain extraordinary culinary circumstances: "Excellent!"

So utter waiters in trendy restaurants when my wife and I dine out on weekends. "Good choice" usually echoes my selection from the menu of fettuccini with a fresh basil sauce. "Excellent" comes in response to my adding a Shiraz wine from Australia's Yarra Valley that contained empty calories, but who was counting?

Were these paeans of praise sincere, or only to produce tips above the customary 15 percent? Were they true acknowledgments of my mastery of menus or crudely calculated by the management to insure our return? Perhaps some judgment was involved because it seems months since a server praised my choice of any carb-dominated meal. Nothing I eat lately elicits praise in this era, when the ghost of Dr. Atkins haunts our culinary choices.

All my once-healthy dining choices now seem obsolete. A believer in diets that combine carbohydrates, fats, and protein in a ratio of 55/30/15, I now discover my numbers all upside-down. Foods I choose at the grocery store stay the same but now have a different purpose. A brick of cheese identifies itself as a "low-carb alternative." Are we talking nutrition here or marketing?

will relieve yourself several miles into the race. Following his bronze medal performance at the 1991 World Championships, Steve Spence told *Runner's World* that he drank so much that he had to urinate three times during the race without breaking stride. Personally, I'd prefer to avoid that. Experience teaches you how.

In a visit to a fast-food restaurant recently, I noticed that one low-carb alternative was sandwiches without bread. But if you remove the bread, can it still be a sandwich? One current study suggests that carbohydrates cause cancer. Can a scientist have his PhD revoked for pandering to public tastes? One couple in Salt Lake City got kicked out of an all-you-can-eat restaurant when they went back for a 12th serving of roast beef because they were disciples of Dr. Atkins.

That's not quite as bad as what happened to Morgan Spurlock in the documentary film *Super Size Me*. Spurlock ate every meal for a month at McDonald's, gained 30 pounds, added 65 points to his cholesterol level, and exhibited symptoms of toxic shock to his liver. Plus, his girlfriend complained about their sex life. Were servers in that fast-food chain encouraging him with cries of "Good choice" and "Excellent?"

When I make food choices, should I worry about the opinions of people whose view of the economy is colored by the size of tips left after diners depart, picking flesh from their teeth? Thank you for telling me tonight's specials, but I have a 15-mile run scheduled tomorrow morning. Bring on the plate of pasta.

CHAPTER 17
ACHIEVING THE PERFECT PACE

"STEADY DOES IT" SPELLS SUCCESS

At the Chicago Marathon in 2000, Greg Castady of Homewood, Illinois, ran what he considers the near-perfect race in near-perfect pace. He covered the first half in 1:25.28 and the second half in 1:25:21—only a 7-second spread en route to 2:50:49. Still, Castady was not entirely satisfied. He says, "I crossed the finish line thinking that I should have picked it up sooner because I felt I had more in the tank."

Four years later at Chicago, a much better conditioned Castady ran a more aggressive race, running the first half in 1:20:19. Then, as winds picked up in the closing miles, he faded, covering the second half in 1:28:03. Nevertheless, his time of 2:48:03 set a new personal record, nearly 3 minutes faster than his previous, perfectly paced time. This caused Castady to wonder what he might have accomplished if he had gone out just a little bit slower: "I suppose that when I hit that mythical 'perfect race,' I can retire

> WE ALL SEEK THE PERFECT RACE, IN WHICH WE ACHIEVE THE PERFECT PACE.

from marathon running, but I'm not too worried about that happening anytime soon."

We all seek the perfect race, in which we achieve the perfect pace, crossing the finish line with no energy left—running on "fumes," so to speak—aware that we could not have run one second faster, gone one step further. That's not always easy to accomplish, but dreaming the impossible dream is part of what sends us to the starting line time and time again.

"The key," suggests Liz Reichman of San Antonio, "seems to be estimating your fitness accurately. That allows you to run even splits. Overestimate your ability, and you struggle the second half."

But how do you estimate fitness and pick the pace that's right for you? How do you determine a reasonable finishing time? These are vexing questions, not only for experienced runners but particularly for first-time marathoners, new runners with no background of past performances for guidance.

Unless you have some idea of the time you're capable of recording in a marathon, you won't know how fast to run each of the 26 miles. Run too slowly at the start, and you may find yourself too fresh at the end and with a slower finishing time than you had anticipated. That's all right if you're a first timer intent only on finishing, but not if you're a seasoned runner hoping to improve.

The other side of the competitive coin can be more a problem. Start too quickly, and you may find yourself struggling by the 20-mile mark, that mythical point that some runners refer to as "the wall." Twenty miles is about the time that many marathoners start coming unglued as they deplete their muscles of glycogen. The doors fall off. The bear drops onto their shoulders. Suddenly, running becomes much, much more difficult, and they may be forced to slow down or walk, or even stop. Running an even pace is the best way to avoid hitting the wall, or so goes the conventional wisdom.

Achieving that perfect pace, however, is not always easy. There are three ways to determine your marathon pace.

1. Workouts. If you chart your times during workouts—speed workouts as well as your long runs—you probably have an idea of how fast you can run. But only an approximate idea. It is not always easy to interpolate workout data in order to be able to predict performance. Just because you can run 8:00 pace for 20 miles, there is no guarantee that you can run that pace for 26 miles 385 yards. You may be forced to run slower, or—if you've paid attention to what I've said earlier and run your long runs at a comfortable pace—you may actually be able to run faster!

Predicting performance from workouts probably works better for experienced runners than for first timers. Particularly experienced runners who record their training in a log or diary. If you're running significantly faster on your easy runs, as well as on your hard runs, and perhaps logging more miles, too, that suggests you may have achieved a higher fitness level that may result in a faster time.

2. Short-distance races. A somewhat more accurate gauge of potential is your times in preliminary races at popular submarathon

NEGATIVE SPLITS

Runners love negative splits, where they run the second half of the race faster than the first half, allowing them to confidently pass others, better conditioned, who failed to hold an overly ambitious pace. "My best two marathons were both ones where I progressively got faster, not slower, in the last half dozen miles," says Judith Henderson of Denver. "You get an extra boost toward the end when you start passing people who look like they're on a death march."

Deena Drossin Kastor described that boost while being interviewed after winning a bronze medal at the 2004 Olympic Games. Kastor ran her first half in 1:15:40 and her second half in 1:11:40 despite a long hill in the second half of the Athens course. Paula Radcliffe's world records at Chicago in 2002 and London in 2003 were achieved by running negative splits. In contrast, Radcliffe dropped out in Athens on a very hot day, leading most of the way and pushing the pace.

If not negative splits, runners would like to run even splits, where with precise efficiency they click off each mile in a time nearly the same as the ones before and the ones after, first half equal to the second half.

distances from 5-K through the half marathon. First timers can get at least a hint of their potential, and build confidence, by running some races during their marathon buildup. Experienced runners can confirm whether what seems to be improved fitness is real or imagined. But this can work in reverse, too. If your fitness has declined since your last marathon, you'll want to know so you can set a somewhat lower goal.

Various performance charts (including one you will encounter later in this chapter) allow you to estimate how fast you can run a marathon.

3. Previous marathons. Better, at least for experienced runners, is

But realistically, how many succeed in their quest to achieve negative or even splits? And how many set personal records by doing so? Is this strategy best for a fast marathon, or is there any evidence that run-fast-and-crash works best?

I conducted a poll among those individuals who participate in my online bulletin boards and discovered that while many talked the talk about negative splitting, not all were able to run the run.

Among those responding, only 5 percent had achieved the admittedly difficult goal of running even pace. And while 22 percent had succeeded in running the second half faster than the first, 73 percent had run slower while still setting a PR. Ten percent of that group had run more than 5 minutes slower the second half of the race yet still succeeded.

Does this mean that negative splitting as means of achieving marathon success is an urban legend, like alligators in the New York sewers? Not necessarily. It just means that we all need to get better at predicting performance and pacing ourselves.

how fast you ran in previous marathons. If you ran 4:10 in your last marathon and have increased your level of training, you might have a reasonable chance of breaking 4 hours your next time out. Maybe. There's never any guarantee. Difficulty of the course, weather conditions, that cold you had last week may thwart your ambitions.

The more marathons you run, the easier it becomes to predict performance based on experience. If you're a first timer, the best strategy is to be conservative in your predictions, knowing that the most important goal is crossing the finish line, regardless of time. But sometimes that is true for experienced runners, too.

Alan Ford of Loganville, Georgia, has run eight marathons. He recalls: "My most successful race was not the one where I set my PR, but rather one where I went in seriously undertrained because of missing a month due to injury. That helped me make the decision to go out conservatively, then pick up the pace later in the race. I finished 10 minutes slower than my PR, but felt very good about it." Ironically, when Ford ran that aforementioned PR, he went out hard, slowed, barely hung on the last 8 miles, but finished with a smile when he looked up at the clock crossing the finish line and saw 3:27.

Although most runners will tell you that the best strategy is to run even pace or "negative splits" (second half faster than the first), a majority of those responding to an Internet poll I conducted admitted that in their PR races, they had slowed in the second half, a third of them by as much as 3 to 5 minutes.

Inevitably, predicting pace becomes a guessing game on the part of every runner. In some respects, the unpredictability of the marathon is what makes it such an exciting adventure. If you have run eight marathons,

IN SOME RESPECTS, THE UNPREDICTABILITY OF THE MARATHON IS WHAT MAKES IT SUCH AN EXCITING ADVENTURE.

like Ford, you can afford to take a risk by going out too fast and hoping to hang on. Nevertheless, runners can obtain some help from scientists and mathematicians in trying to determine just how fast they might run in a marathon, their first marathon or one in which they hope to set a PR.

PREDICTING PERFORMANCE

With the increased interest in fitness sports during the past several decades, there has been a simultaneous rise in the number of laboratories that are dedicated to measuring human performance. Scientists continue to exhibit an interest in why some athletes outperform others.

The most common measuring device found in any running-oriented human performance laboratory is the treadmill, a moving belt on which you can run in place while various measurements are made. The most common measurement is maximum VO_2, the volume of oxygen a person can consume during exercise. This relates both to the heart's capacity to pump oxygen-rich blood to the muscles and to how efficiently the muscles extract and utilize that oxygen.

Maximum VO_2, often referred to simply as max VO_2, is calculated according to the milliliters of oxygen that your body can absorb during 60 seconds per kilogram of body weight (ml/kg/mn). Within certain limits, the higher your max VO_2, the better you will be able to perform. A talented runner with a max VO_2 of 70 could be expected to run a 10-K in around 31 minutes, and a marathon in 2:23. An average runner—say, someone with the ability to run a 10-K in about 45 minutes—probably has a max VO_2 of around 45. Less trained or less talented or sedentary individuals would have still lower levels.

But other factors can also affect performance. One is running technique, or efficiency, what exercise scientists often refer to as "economy." Runners succeed only partly because of their superior cardiovascular systems and willingness to train hard. You need only look at the people near the front of the pack to understand that. Most of them are smooth, efficient runners who waste little energy covering ground. An economical runner might run a marathon 10 to 20 minutes faster than someone with an equal max VO_2 who is a less efficient runner. As an example, at our peaks Frank Shorter and I had near identical max VO_2 scores, just above the 70 mentioned above. My best performance was 2:21:55, good enough only for fifth at Boston. Shorter had a PR of 2:10:30, set winning the Fukuoka Marathon in Japan, but most important: He ran 2:12:20 at the 1972 Olympic Games in Munich, which earned him the gold medal.

In general, however, if you know your max VO_2, you can predict your performance. If you can improve your max VO_2, you may be able to improve your performance.

OXYGEN POWER

Alas, not everybody has the opportunity to determine their max VO_2. Most human performance laboratories are geared to doing research, not testing joggers. Most medical centers do what are known as "symptom-limited" exercise stress tests to diagnose heart conditions, but they usually stop short of testing for max VO_2. They don't—and usually won't—measure it for you. So how do average runners determine their max VO_2?

Jack Daniels, PhD, an exercise physiologist at the State University of New York at Cortland and coach of that school's highly successful cross-country team, developed what he described as "oxygen power" tables to help predict performance. Dr. Daniels, formerly a top-ranked pentathlete, is among America's most respected sports scientists and coaches. He also has worked as a coach/adviser to world-class runners such as Jim Ryun, Alberto Salazar, and Joan Benoit Samuelson. For several years in the 1980s, Dr. Daniels worked in Eugene, Oregon, for Athletics West, Nike's sponsored team.

Dr. Daniels developed his oxygen power tables in collaboration with Jimmy Gilbert, one of his former runners and a programmer for NASA in Houston. By doing treadmill and track measurements on runners of various abilities (and collecting available data on others), Daniels and Gilbert were able to relate max VO_2 scores to performances. The two researchers developed a set of tables, which they published in a book titled *Oxygen Power*. (Copies of the book can be obtained from Dr. Daniels at Box 948, Walden Pond Lane, Cortland, NY 13045.) With these tables in front of him, a runner can use any recent performance to predict something called VDOT. The Daniels/Gilbert approach combines max VO_2 with running economy into a single value that approximates max VO_2. The VDOT can be used to predict with some accuracy how fast you can run at distances from 800 meters to 50-K. A runner can also equate performance at one distance to a performance at another.

Charts such as those developed by Dr. Daniels, or based on his calculations, can be useful in predicting performance. If you know how fast you run a 10-K, or any other distance, you can predict your VDOT. If you run a 10-K in 49:00, you probably have a VDOT of 41.0. If you improve your time to 48:30, most likely your VDOT also has improved, to 41.5.

The table on pages 258–259 is an adapted and condensed version of the Daniels oxygen power tables for five commonly run distances: the mile, 5-K (3.1 miles), 10-K (6.2 miles), half marathon (13.1 miles), and marathon (26.2 miles). This oxygen power table includes 65 rows showing VDOT values that might be achieved by runners at various levels, from a beginning jogger to a world-class athlete. The first level (VDOT 30) shows someone capable of running 63:46 for a 10-K. The final level describes performances that are better than the current world records.

These tables still serve as a handy reference, but runners seeking to predict their marathon times now can do so using the Internet.

(continued on page 260)

OXYGEN POWER TABLE

VDOT	Mile	5-K	10-K	Half-Marathon	Marathon
30	9:11	30:40	63:46	2:21:04	4:49:17
31	8:55	29:51	62:03	2:17:21	4:41:57
32	8:41	29:05	60:26	2:13:49	4:34:59
33	8:27	28:21	58:54	2:10:27	4:28:22
34	8:14	27:39	57:26	2:07:16	4:22:03
35	8:01	27:00	56:03	2:04:13	4:16:03
36	7:49	26:22	54:44	2:01:19	4:10:19
37	7:38	25:46	53:29	1:58:34	4:04:50
38	7:27	25:12	52:17	1:55:55	3:59:35
39	7:17	24:39	51:09	1:53:24	3:54:34
40	7:07	24:08	50:03	1:50:59	3:49:45
41	6:58	23:38	49:01	1:48:40	3:45:09
42	6:49	23:09	48:01	1:46:27	3:40:43
43	6:41	22:41	47:04	1:44:20	3:36:28
44	6:32	22:15	46:09	1:42:17	3:32:23
45	6:25	21:50	45:16	1:40:20	3:28:26
46	6:17	21:25	44:25	1:38:27	3:24:39
47	6:10	21:02	43:36	1:36:38	3:21:00
48	6:03	20:39	42:50	1:34:53	3:17:29
49	5:56	20:18	42:04	1:33:12	3:14:06
50	5:50	19:57	41:21	1:31:35	3:10:49
51	5:44	19:36	40:39	1:30:02	3:07:39
52	5:38	19:17	39:59	1:28:31	3:04:36
53	5:32	18:58	39:20	1:27:04	3:01:39
54	5:27	18:40	38:42	1:25:40	2:58:47
55	5:21	18:22	38:06	1:24:18	2:56:01
56	5:16	18:05	37:31	1:23:00	2:53:20
57	5:11	17:49	36:57	1:21:43	2:50:45
58	5:06	17:33	36:24	1:20:30	2:48:14
59	5:02	17:17	35:52	1:19:18	2:45:47
60	4:57	17:03	35:22	1:18:09	2:43:25
61	4:53	16:48	34:52	1:17:02	2:41:08
62	4:49	16:34	34:23	1:15:57	2:38:54

VDOT	Mile	5-K	10-K	Half-Marathon	Marathon
63	4:45	16:20	33:55	1:14:54	2:36:44
64	4:41	16:07	33:28	1:13:53	2:34:38
65	4:37	15:54	33:01	1:12:53	2:32:35
66	4:33	15:42	32:35	1:11:56	2:30:36
67	4:30	15:29	32:11	1:11:00	2:28:40
68	4:26	15:18	31:46	1:10:05	2:26:47
69	4:23	15:06	31:23	1:09:12	2:24:57
70	4:19	14:55	31:00	1:08:21	2:23:10
71	4:16	14:44	30:38	1:07:31	2:21:26
72	4:13	14:33	30:16	1:06:42	2:19:44
73	4:10	14:23	29:55	1:05:54	2:18:05
74	4:07	14:13	29:34	1:05:08	2:16:29
75	4:04	14:03	29:14	1:04:23	2:14:55
76	4:02	13:54	28:55	1:03:39	2:13:23
76.5	4:00.2	13:49	28:45	1:03:18	2:12:38
77	3:58.8	13:44	28:36	1:02:56	2:11:54
77.5	3:57.5	13:40	28:26	1:02:35	2:11:10
78	3:56.2	13:35	28:17	1:02:15	2:10:27
78.5	3:54.9	13:31	28:08	1:01:54	2:09:44
79	3:53.7	13:26	27:59	1:01:34	2:09:02
79.5	3:52.4	13:22.1	27:49.9	1:01:14	2:08:20
80	3:51.2	13:17.8	27:41.2	1:00:54	2:07:38
80.5	3:49.9	13:13.5	27:32.5	1:00:34.9	2:26:57.5
81	3:48.7	13:09.3	27:23.9	1:00:15.6	2:06:17.1
81.5	3:47.5	13:05.2	27:15.4	59:56.6	2:05:37.2
82	3:46.4	13:01.1	27:07.1	59:37.9	2:04:57.8
82.5	3:45.2	12:57.0	26:58.8	59:19.3	2:04:18.8
83	3:44.1	12:53.0	26:50.6	59:01.0	2:03:40.3
83.5	3:42.9	12:49.1	26:42.5	58:42.9	2:03:02.2
84	3:41.8	12:45.2	26:34.6	58:25.0	2:02:24.5
84.5	3:40.7	12:41.3	26:26.7	58:07.3	2:01:47.3
85	3:39.6	12:37.5	26:18.9	57:49.9	2:01:10.5

"Most prediction calculators are based on the Daniels data," concedes Amby Burfoot, whose duties as executive editor at *Runner's World* include supervising that magazine's Web site. Surf into www.runnersworld.com, look for a section dedicated to tools and calculators, and you'll eventually come to a Race Time Calculator. It's simple to use. Enter your most recent time from a standard race distance, such as the 5-K. Ask the calculator to predict your time for any other standard race distance, such as the marathon. Click "Submit." In less time than it takes to read this sentence, the calculator predicts how fast you run.

I now more often use a calculator on the Web site www.mcmillanrunning.com, the work of Greg McMillan, a 2:31 marathoner from Austin, Texas. McMillan's Running Calculator operates somewhat differently from that of *Runner's World*. Input your running time at any one of 28 distances, from 100 meters to the marathon, and the calculator quickly estimates your potential at all those other distances.

McMillan studied under Russell H. Pate, PhD, chairman of the department of exercise science at the University of South Carolina in Columbia. For his master's thesis, McMillan correlated blood lactate levels with performance, the goal being to create a prediction equation whereby runners could use recent race performances to calculate training speeds. "From there," says McMillan, "I began to think about predicting race performances, too." He studied existing charts and equations plus rules of thumb. (Double your half marathon time and add 10 minutes to predict your marathon time, suggests one such rule.) McMillan felt all approaches were good, but flawed. He eventually created what he hoped would be a more perfect prediction calculator.

"Thousands of runners use it every month," says McMillan, "and while I think it still can be improved, it works well for most. And it fulfills my overall goal, which is to help runners succeed."

IS PREDICTION POSSIBLE?

How well do prediction calculators work? Very well—on average. Whether Daniels, McMillan, *Runner's World* or others, they offer a reasonable estimate to aid most runners in predicting marathon performance. But invariably in calculations involving humans with differing abilities, not everybody sits comfortably atop the bell curve. Some runners are born sprinters; others are born marathoners.

The world record for 200 meters set by Michael Johnson at the 1996 Olympics is 19.32. I was present in Atlanta, seated near the starting line, when Johnson set that record, and I still consider it the most riveting sports performance I have witnessed in my life. The McMillan calculator doesn't convert from hundredths of a second, but a 20-second 200 predicts for the marathon a mind-shattering 1:54.37! That's more than 10 minutes faster than the 2:04:55 Paul Tergat ran in 2003 when he set the world marathon record in Berlin. Tergat's time predicts backward to a seemingly more achievable 21.8 for 200 meters, but could he run that fast?

In truth, sprinters succeed because they possess muscular physiques and (substrata) a preponderance of fast-twitch muscles. Marathoners succeed because they are lean and light and have a preponderance of slow-twitch muscles. Ordinary runners who do not match these extraordinary athletes sit somewhere between, probably closer to the top of the bell curve. Everybody has a perfect distance, or range of distances, at which they perform best. For me, I've achieved some of my best performances and several national championships between 15 and 30 kilometers, an area where unfortunately no Olympic medals are awarded. If you fail to match a calculator's prediction, it may not be the fault of your training. In the meantime, take with a grain of salt how fast any coach or computer suggests you can run a marathon.

Though using similar data, each of the three calculators mentioned previously provides slightly different predictions. On the Daniels chart, a 45:16 time for 10-K predicts 3:28:26 for the marathon. *Runner's World* projects an only slightly faster 3:28:14 using that same time, whereas McMillan suggests a much more conservative 3:32:26. Which predicted time should you use? Are you a pessimist or an optimist? Is your glass half-empty or half-full?

Achieving success as a long-distance runner remains as much an art as a science. You need to apply both art and science if you expect to succeed.

ACHIEVING SUCCESS AS A LONG-DISTANCE RUNNER REMAINS AS MUCH AN ART AS A SCIENCE.

Pick a realistic goal, and for first timers, a conservative goal. Indeed, most of the reason many runners hit the wall at 20 miles may be the result of their not having accurately estimated their own abilities. If you train properly and pick a reasonable pace, there should be no wall.

THE RIGHT PACE

Once you obtain an estimate of your finishing time, you can determine the best means of achieving that time. Again, experts differ, and there are various ways to predetermine your race pace. The simplest is to run at the same pace, plus or minus a few seconds, mile after mile after relentless mile, for the full distance. That's the approach of the pacing teams, and it works!

Many major marathons now offer pacing teams to aid runners in their goals, whether those goals are to run a fast time or to finish. Pacing teams usually are led by experienced runners who promise to run an even pace to help other runners achieve a specific goal time. If the goal is a 4:30 marathon, the pace team leader will attempt to run a steady 10:18 pace, team members tucked behind him like goslings behind a goose, knowing that if they stick near that leader, they'll achieve their goals. Even if they drop off that pace, which often happens, they're reasonably certain of running at least a good time, or of finishing. I've led pacing teams at Chicago, Walt Disney World, and Honolulu, and it's a lot of fun for the leader and those following him.

Credit for developing the pacing team concept goes to Amby Burfoot, although I provided some of the spark because of an article, titled "Fast Train to Boston," that I wrote for the July 1995 issue of *Runner's World*. It was during a period when the goal of many runners was to qualify for the 100th running of the Boston Marathon the following spring, a landmark race that attracted a record 35,868 finishers.

Using data provided by 91 different marathons and convening an expert panel of five members of the Road Runners Club of America, I picked the 10 fall marathons whose courses seemed most likely to yield a qualifying time. Top of the heap was the St. George Marathon in Utah, whose mostly downhill course dropped 2,600 feet from mountains to the valley.

With that as inspiration, Burfoot gathered a group of *Runner's World* editors, most of them experienced marathoners, and traveled to St. George to help runners entered in that year's race qualify for Boston. They were enormously successful: 1,030 of the 3,207 finishing runners, nearly a third of the field, qualified for the 100th Boston Marathon.

Thus began the concept of *Runner's World* pacing teams, and in succeeding years, the magazine's editors traveled to Dallas, Chicago, Orlando (Walt Disney World), Honolulu, Tucson, and Portland to pace runners. I missed the first two team efforts, but when Burfoot et al arrived in Chicago, where I served as training consultant, I told race director Carey Pinkowski that we were going to steal their pace team idea the following year.

And we did, perfecting the concept because Chicago had more

available volunteer leaders than *Runner's World* had editors. And the pacing teams kept getting bigger and better. For the 2004 race, pace team coordinators Dennis Linehan Jr. and Ann Swayka recruited 95 leaders for 26 separate teams, aiming at finishing times from 2:50 to 6:00. "We've moved marathoning from an individual sport to a team effort," says Linehan.

"WE'VE MOVED MARATHONING FROM AN INDIVIDUAL SPORT TO A TEAM EFFORT," SAYS LINEHAN.

At Chicago in 2004, 3,572 runners, or 10.8 percent of the field, achieved Boston Qualifying times, less spectacular than St. George in 1995, but big-city marathons tend to attract a higher percentage of first-time runners, whose goal is mainly to finish and enjoy the experience rather than to run a fast time.

Each year at the 2-day expo before the Chicago Marathon, runners stop by the pacing team booth to register to run and talk to leaders about their race strategies the next day. Though some leaders run through aid stations, most walk to drink, or they may employ other strategies that it's good to know in advance. Registered runners receive numbers—such as 4:30 or 5:30—to pin to their backs, identifying them as members of that pacing team. "It helps keep everybody together in a field crowded as Chicago," says Linehan. "It's easy to get separated when you pass through an aid station, and the numbers on the backs help lost runners regain contact."

The morning of the race, leaders meet early and grab signs identifying their times. The signs atop tall poles are round, giving them the nickname "lollypops." The leaders march out to the starting grid, clutching their lollypops, and position themselves on the right side of the grid so runners can easily find them. They also wear identical uniforms and caps. Once they cross the line, they set aside the lollypops but continue to carry smaller numbered signs, sometimes for the entire race. "It's good that we have two or three leaders per team because it's not easy to run with a sign in one hand," says Linehan.

At Chicago in 2004, 6,221 runners signed up at the expo to attach themselves to one of the pacing teams. Even runners who are not members of a team benefit from their presence, since the teams act as a moving timepiece, allowing everybody to check pace. "Even though I didn't sign up for a team," said Andrew Smith of Omaha, "I used the teams to gauge my effort—at least until my legs stiffened at mile 18 and I sadly watched the 3:25 team slowly disappear in the distance."

John Carlson joined the 6:00 pacing team, where one of the leaders used a whistle to keep everybody together. "At first I thought his whistle would drive me crazy," Carlson recalls, "but later, as I became more focused on the race, the whistle became my security blanket, something that kept me going."

"The 3:00 pacer was on cruise control," remarked Tim Carter of Greer, South Carolina. "There is no way I could have run such a steady pace without him beside me." Carter lost contact in the final miles but still finished with a time of 3:05:23.

Whether inspired by *Runner's World* or Chicago, more and more marathons have begun adding pacing teams. That includes Columbus, Ohio; Houston; California International; and Salt Lake City. Clif Bar organized a traveling group of pace leaders who have run at Grandma's, Marine Corps, Dallas, Los Angeles, and the Flying Pig Marathon in Cincinnati. Many international marathons have followed suit. New York joined the movement in 2004, with 30 experienced marathoners leading pacing teams from 3:15 to 5:30 for each of its three starting areas. One of the leaders at New York was Linehan, who also has led teams at the New Jersey and Hartford marathons. "Being a pace leader," says Linehan, "has allowed me to help others achieve their goals while I work toward my own goal of running a marathon in all 50 states and the District of Columbia."

Maintaining the same pace for 26 miles is not easy, and as the

SETTING THE PACE

Until Frank Shorter won Olympic gold in 1972, marathoning in the United States had less status than Ping-Pong. Previously, Clarence DeMar had won bronze in 1924. During the half century between DeMar and Shorter, Boston remained the only American marathon to attract more than 100 entrants.

Top European marathons included the Polytechnic in England, Enschede in Holland, and Kosice in Czechoslovakia. I ran Kosice in 1963, the year Buddy Edelen, an American, won. Earlier that year, Edelen had set a world best time at Polytechnic, having run 2:14:28. Shorter achieved four consecutive victories at the prestigious Fukuoka Marathon between 1971 and 1974. That set the stage for the boom in American marathoning that by 1980 attracted more than 5,000 to Boston and 14,000 to New York. By then, Bill Rodgers had replaced Shorter as American hero, with Alberto Salazar and Joan Benoit about to move center stage.

American prestige soon would lag at the front of the pack as the focus shifted toward the back: the large number of much slower runners who transformed marathoning around the world. London, Paris, Berlin, and Stockholm soon began to attract fields in the tens of thousands. The Boston Marathon at its 100th running saw a record field of 35,868 finishers. The Comrades Marathon in South Africa became the world's largest ultramarathon, with 24,000 starters in its 75th anniversary year of 2000. (Comrades follows a devilishly hilly 55-mile course between

race continues, invariably some people lose contact, then more, then more and more. As a pace team leader, I've noticed that almost everybody can handle the pace through 10 miles and into the half marathon. They converse with one another and wave back at spectators. But beyond the half marathon point, people start taking re-

Durban and Pietermaritzburg, alternating directions every other year.)

The pacing team phenomenon, begun by *Runner's World* in the mid-1990s, quickly spread around the globe with editors from that magazine's international editions leading the way. "Pacing teams definitely are a worldwide phenomenon," states Adam Bean, an editor at *Runner's World.* Steve Seaton, editor of the UK edition, estimates that his staff paces as many as 6,000 runners at the London Marathon, roughly a fifth of the field. Seaton's crew also leads pacing efforts at several shorter-distance events, including the Great North Run, a half marathon that attracts 47,000 runners to a course between Newcastle, Gateshead, and South Shields.

Down Under, the magazine's staffers set pace at five marathons in Australia and New Zealand, including the scenic Rotarua Marathon, which circles a lake in the caldera of a 140,000-year-old volcano. In Spain, *Runner's World* editors do not organize the efforts, since the major marathons in the country—including Madrid and Barcelona—provide their own pacing teams.

The magazine's South African editors follow an ambitious schedule, pacing 10 marathons a year and turning down requests for their assistance at several more. "Our efforts at Comrades proved so successful that the Comrades Marathon Association wanted to buy the idea from us," says editor Mike Finch. "In the end they didn't, because they still needed us to set the pace."

ality checks related to pace. One by one, they start slipping backward. By 20 miles, usually the team is down to a small but tightly focused group that usually sticks together to hug one another in the finish chute. But invariably there is sadness about runners left behind.

George Myers, an engineer now retired in Sarasota, Florida, at one time designed a pacing chart with a fast beginning, a steady middle, and a fade at the end, under the theory that even the best runners sometimes finish slower than they start. In doing so, Myers offered several principles that make sense for runners of every level of ability.

- Choose a realistic goal.

- Carry your pacing schedule with you so you can figure out how close you are to pace at every point in the race.

- Believe in your pace chart: Check each mile, making no changes in the first 20 miles (no matter how "good" you feel).

- Be prepared to make the necessary adjustments if the course is especially hilly.

- Meet intermediate time goals. This gives you confidence and causes the miles to pass faster.

- At mile 20, if you feel good, go for it; if not, hang in there.

Myers usually wrote his pace carefully in large, clear numbers on a piece of paper, laminated the paper in plastic to protect it, then taped it to his race number, upside-down, so he could easily refer to it during the race. At my request, he provided such charts for me for several important races in which I wanted to closely control my time. I found it easy to flip the chart up each mile to see how close I was to predicted pace. Later, another friend, Keith Stone, a computer specialist from Winston-Salem, North Carolina, began producing laminated wristbands for *Runner's World* pacing team leaders. At many marathons today, you can obtain pacing bands for free or for small sums at the race expo. Another simple approach that I frequently take is to write my pace upside-down on the front of my race number.

One caveat concerning any pace chart: They are designed under the assumption that the course is flat, with zero wind. If the course is hilly or windy, you may need to make adjustments. A tailwind will make you run faster, sometimes as much as several minutes over the course of 26 miles. On a loop course, where the wind may hit you from different directions at different times of the race, you may need to make mental adjustments at midrace to stay on pace.

Temperature can also affect your pace. When race temperatures rise or fall much above or below your comfort level, you may need to throw your pace table away.

Any pace table can be a trap, a series of numbers that can lure you into trying to keep up a faster pace than your capabilities on that day. The best pace-setting device becomes your own mind. Experienced runners eventually know when to slow down and when to speed up. Of course, it may take them more than a few marathons, and there always remains room for improvement. That's part of the fascination of running 26 miles 385 yards and doing it more than one time.

CHAPTER 18

RACE-DAY LOGISTICS

GETTING TO THE STARTING LINE
IS THE NEXT STEP

After 18 weeks or more of training—after the mileage buildup, the long runs, the taper, the carbo-loading—what can you expect once you arrive at the race site and head toward the starting line? Most veterans usually follow a well-rehearsed routine that makes their marathons easy. (Well, easier than they might otherwise be.)

Here are some suggestions that may make race day easier for you.

Your "final" preparation begins just before you leave home, when you pack your bag. In this case, you need to heed one doctor's advice: the late George Sheehan, MD, who for several decades wrote a monthly column for *Runner's World* that focused as much on philosophy as physiology. Dr. Sheehan wrote that he virtually never left home without his runner's suitcase—a bag in the trunk of his car packed with gear in case he stopped somewhere and wanted to run. Dr. Sheehan once wrote in his local New Jersey newspaper column about the bag—then forgot it the next time he left for a 10-mile race in the New York City's Van Cortlandt Park.

"I had to borrow shoes, shorts, and a shirt," Dr. Sheehan recalled. "I was completely outfitted by other runners, who fortunately hadn't forgotten their bags."

But running clothes and shoes are only the minimum essentials, whether you're heading for a workout or a race. Smart runners cram their bags with numerous other items.

A RUNNER'S SUITCASE

Before packing that bag, consider the advice of Michigan's Doug Kurtis: "Break everything in before you race: socks, shorts, singlet, shoes." Kurtis recommends running one or two workouts in your racing gear to make certain everything fits and

> **BREAK EVERYTHING IN BEFORE YOU RACE: SOCKS, SHORTS, SINGLET, SHOES.**

there are no problem areas, such as an imperfection inside a shoe that could cause a blister. That may not bother you in a 5-K, but it can draw blood and bring you to a halt in a marathon. "One good way to work out the bugs and test your equipment is to enter shorter races before the marathon," says Kurtis.

Here are some items you might want to include in your runner's suitcase, not only for the marathon but for other long races.

The right shoes. The most essential item, obviously. Many runners (myself included) like to take training shoes for warming up, or for riding the bus to the start, then shift to a lighter pair of racing flats. On rainy days, you'll want dry shoes for afterward. For security, you may want to pack your racing shoes in your carry-on luggage. If the airline loses your bag, you can replace everything else, but not a well-broken-in pair of shoes. I've never forgotten or lost my running shoes, but one winter en route to a 30-K cross-country ski race in Ottawa, Canada, the airline lost my bag containing skis, polls, and boots. A friend lent me replacement equipment, including boots two sizes large, but it was not a very enjoyable race.

Shorts and singlet. Also obvious. Some people wear the cotton race T-shirt they've been handed the day before, but this is not a good idea. Cotton retains moisture: bad for both cold and hot weather. I prefer to test everything. Do the shorts fit? Will the singlet or T-shirt chafe? (A snug shirt or a brand-new, unwashed one might.) Also bring a warmup shirt to shed before you go to the start. You'll be most comfortable standing at the starting line if you wait

MARATHON SHOES

A frequently asked question to my online bulletin boards is "How many miles should you put on your race-day shoes?" Most runners recognize that wearing a pair of shoes bought at the expo the day before the marathon may not be a bright idea.

My general recommendation is to buy new shoes 3 to 6 weeks before the marathon so you have time to test them and obtain a different pair if the first pair causes problems. But I run in lightweight racing flats, whereas most runners prefer the extra protection offered by their everyday training shoes. Some first timers own only a single pair and need to change if their shoes have too many miles on them.

An Internet survey suggested that most runners put between 50 and 100 miles on their running shoes before the marathon. Here are the numbers.

Mileage before marathon	Percentage
25	3.8%
26–50	20.8%
51–100	47.1%
101–200	15.1%
201–400	13.2%
More than 400	0%

until after warming up to change into a dry racing singlet. Pin your number on the night before the race and check to make sure you haven't pinned the front of your singlet to the back.

Safety pins. Most races provide safety pins, but sometimes only two, and sometimes they run out. If you're like me, you'll want at least four to secure your number so it doesn't flap. A few races require two numbers. At Twin Cities, you wear a back number identifying your age group, a nice touch. If you're running in a marathon

As expected, different runners admitted to different mileages. "I prefer racing in new shoes," admits Cindy Southgate of Kanata, Ontario, "but invariably I can't afford them at the right time, or I'm too scared to shift too close to the race. I usually run marathons with about 200 miles on my shoes."

However, Ed Brickell of Dallas says, "For my last several marathons, I ran with pairs right out of the box—although a model I had trained with extensively."

David Harrison of Clitheroe, England, buys a new pair of shoes 6 weeks out. "I start using them for shorter distances," he says, "then do my last 20-miler in them. If something is going to rub, I want to know about it."

The more you know about the shoes on your feet, the less chance a blister will halt you midstride.

that provides pacing teams, you'll need four pins to secure the back number identifying your team. Pins also come in handy for other things, such as piercing blisters after the race (although podiatrists may not like my offering such advice, since you're supposed to use a sterilized pin). I usually take along four or more pins linked together and fastened to a snap on the outside of my bag or in my toilet kit.

Entry blank. If you got lost en route, would you be able to find the starting line? At most major marathons this is hardly a problem, but it's good advice for the 5-K or 10-K you might race to get ready for the marathon. There are other logistical problems to consider. Are you certain what time the bus leaves for the start and when that start is? The race may start at 7:45 a.m. to accommodate TV coverage, not the more logical 8:00 you seem to remember because it's an even number. Most major marathons either mail you informational brochures or include them in the bag you receive when picking up your number. On race day, use the time between the warmup and the start to read, one last time, all the directions you have been handed. You may learn some vital detail that will help you in the race, such as the location of aid stations or portable toilets.

Gloves and a cap. If the day is cold, you'll want these extra items. Whether or not you wear them in the race, gloves and a cap can help you stay warm before and after. If you start a marathon in the morning cold but you get too warm by midrace, you can always toss your gloves—or tuck them in the waistband of your shorts. A billed cap in summer will keep the sun off your face. As with other race gear, test each item for comfort during practice. Until companies began to provide high-tech caps for running, I used to wear a torn and battered cotton cap so formless and ugly that I wouldn't want to be seen in it anywhere else but the starting line of a marathon. Another old road-runner trick is to knot a white handkerchief at its four corners to wear on your head.

Varied-weight clothing. Don't assume the weather will be warm if the month is July or cold if it's January. If a freak cold wave or heat wave hits, can you cope with it? The Boston Marathon in April is notorious for unpredictable weather. I wear shorts

> IF A FREAK COLD WAVE OR HEAT WAVE HITS, CAN YOU COPE WITH IT?

and a regular race singlet if the temperature is going to be in the midforties. If it's much colder, I'll don Lycra tights and a long-sleeved shirt—a big improvement over the heavy cotton turtleneck top I had to wear for warmth in the cold and rainy 1964 Boston

Marathon when I set my PR. Don't forget gloves and a headband to cover your ears on really cold days. The 1995 Columbus Marathon featured temperatures in the twenties, but the sun was out, and I was comfortable because I had brought the right clothes.

Throwaway clothing. In large races, where you may need to stand on the starting line for a long time, it's important to stay warm. If you can't hand your discarded warmup gear to a friend at the last minute, take throwaway clothes that you won't mind having donated to the Salvation Army when you leave them behind. Garbage bags with armholes cut in them do protect against the wind, but they don't hold much warmth. Most major marathons arrange to both collect your bag before and deliver it to you after, but you may need to strip your warmup suit and tuck it into your bag a half-hour or more before the start. Also, be sure to determine what kind of bag-checking system will be in place before race day. At smaller

> DO NOT HURL ITEMS OF CLOTHING INTO THE AIR WHEN THE GUN GOES OFF.

races, there may be no system, meaning you are responsible for your own gear. Particularly in crowded fields, you may need to stand a long time on the starting grid. Fortunately, most marathons today are so well organized that they start precisely on time.

One important point for your benefit and for the benefit of runners behind you on the starting grid: Do not—repeat, do not—remove and hurl items of clothing into the air when the gun goes off. It looks good on TV, but it means that others behind will have to step over your discarded items. Discard your clothing on the curb or hand it to a spectator along the course, even if it means carrying the clothing for a while until you can move to one side. If you trip over a sweatshirt dropped on the course, it was probably dropped by some idiot who failed to read this book.

Money. Of course, you'll need money the day of the race for your entry fee, if you haven't preregistered. (Race-day registration is more common for smaller and shorter races than for marathons.) Cash also comes in handy after the race if a vendor is selling ice cream— or to take the subway home if you locked your keys in the car. Put a few extra dollars and some change in the bag that gets transported to the finish line just in case you need it. Is there a chance you might drop out? Tuck a $20 bill in your shorts pocket so you can take a taxi. It's not a wise idea to place your wallet or valuable items in the bags you check. Most races warn runners against this practice.

Extra little essentials. Pack these in a smaller bag: chafing lubricants, adhesive bandages, tape, sunscreen, aspirin, and other medication. Sure, you may be able to buy some or all of these items at the race expo, but don't leave any essential items home based on that assumption. You don't want to have to be told, "Sorry, we're all sold out."

Fluids and food. Need a final prerace drink, either water or your favorite sports drink? It's easier to sip from a bottle you brought along than to go searching for fluids. I like to go to the line with a 12-ounce can of pop and drink it a few minutes before crossing the line. Gels are handy for midrace carbo-reloading. If you don't have shorts with pockets (more common these days), you'll be happy I told you to pack extra safety pins so you can attach the energy gel packets to your singlet. Although most marathons will have bananas, yogurt, and other food items waiting for you after you clear the chute, if you finish too far back, you may find they've run out. Or—and this has happened to me more than once—you may stagger head-down through the finish area and retrieve your bag before realizing you've missed the food tables and need to go back. (Traffic coming out or security guards may make returning impossible to accomplish.)

Combination lock. This comes in handy if there's a dressing room where you can stow your gear in a locker, although access to lockers is more common at track meets than at marathons. Many races today are so large that runners come dressed to run.

RACE-DAY CHECKLIST

Before leaving home for your next marathon, use a checklist such as this one to make certain you haven't forgotten any essential items. This list was developed by Ron Gunn, athletic director at Southwestern Michigan College, when we used to lead groups of runners on tours to races such as the Honolulu Marathon.

CARRY-ON LUGGAGE

Racing shoes	Travel itinerary
Airline tickets	Toiletries
Passport and other documents	Credit cards
Toothbrush and toothpaste	Camera and film
Hotel and rental car confirmation	Wallet and money
Event schedule and information	

OTHER GEAR

Dress clothes	Race socks
Dress shoes	Throwaway cold-weather gear
Socks	Warmup suit
Underwear	Swimsuit
Coat	Gloves and hat
Gloves	Safety pins
Rain gear	Body lubricant
Sunglasses	Tape and adhesive bandages
Sunscreen	Medicine
Alarm clock	Special race drink
Race uniform	

Have I forgotten anything? Experience will teach you how to organize your own runner's suitcase.

Postrace clothing. Once you finish, you'll want to change into dry clothing, including socks. Make sure you pack a towel so you can dry off. You'll want to look and feel your best hanging around and chatting with other runners. This is important for workouts, too. I do most of my running from home, but when I climb in a car to drive to some scenic area, such as Indiana Dunes State Park, it's good to have a change of clothes, whether it is a hot or cold day. It's easy to get chilled driving home while wearing a shirt soaked with sweat.

Plastic bag. Bags—the kind they gave you at the store when you bought your last pair of running shoes—come in handy after the race to isolate your wet and sweaty gear from the rest of your clothing. A separate plastic bag for grimy shoes is also useful. A garbage bag into which you can punch armholes may be useful for keeping you warm and dry on cold or rainy days.

Miscellaneous. You'll want to record your finishing time, or splits, before you forget them. Or the phone number of that good-looking guy or gal you ran with for the last half dozen miles. Bring a notebook or pen. Cell phone to call home? That goes against my rule of packing anything valuable, but at least wrap it well to prevent it from being damaged.

Checklist. Have you forgotten anything? You won't know unless you also have a checklist of all the necessary items. Experience eventually will guide you. When you determine what items work best in your runner's bag, make a personalized checklist similar to the one in the "Race-Day Checklist" on page 277 to make sure you don't leave home without them.

THE MORNING OF THE RACE

For 5-K or 10-K races, I don't mind rising early and driving an hour or two to a race, and most runners feel the same. Not only do I want to avoid the extra expense of a hotel and meals away from home, but an overnight stay converts a fun race into an expedition requiring planning and commitment. Sometimes I like to just go, run, and go home (unless, of course, I've won an age-group award).

But a marathon does require commitment, and because I usually run only one or two a year, I prefer to stay overnight before the race. I've run the Sunburst Marathon in South Bend, Indiana, on several occasions. Even though South Bend is only 45 minutes from my home in Long Beach, I check into a hotel the night before the event to avoid having to drive even that far on race morning and to allow myself an extra hour's sleep before the 6:00 a.m. start. And for major marathons, particularly if you're bringing your family, you may want to arrive 2 or 3 days earlier to do some sightseeing and partake in numerous race activities. If you arrive in Chicago for the marathon later than Friday, you'll miss the party I throw that night for my V-Team, those who participate in my online bulletin boards.

Even if it costs a little more, I prefer to stay as close as possible to the race's start and/or finish. Usually race directors select their headquarters hotel with this in mind. One reason for the recent popularity of the Chicago Marathon is that runners began to realize that they could wait until the last minute in their hotel room before heading down to the start only a few blocks away. Having access to a last-minute restroom where the floor is tile rather than plastic is an important perk. Right after finishing the race, they're back in their room for a cleansing shower. For point-to-point marathons, most runners stay near the finish line so they can head to their rooms quickly after finishing. But make your hotel reservations early because the most desirable hotels at big-city marathons often fill up fast, sometimes a year in advance. If you run Grandma's Marathon in Duluth, Minnesota, and decide the next day to make a hotel reservation for next year, you're probably already too late.

GETTING UP AND GETTING GOING

You don't want to sleep through the start, or oversleep and have to rush your final preparations. This is particularly true at marathons that begin very early in the morning, such as Honolulu, with its

5:00 a.m. start. Usually my internal body alarm wakes me up a few minutes before the actual alarm sounds. (Maybe I don't want to hear its jarring noise.) Before important races, I'll set my wristwatch alarm, set the clock radio alarm, and even ask the front desk for a wake-up call. If you're a really heavy sleeper, have a friend at home call you on the phone and stay on the line until you've stumbled out of bed.

Your first assignment after rising is to complete your carbo-load by either going down to the hotel coffee shop or snacking on items brought with you for that purpose. My favorite prerace "meal" is usually a 12-ounce soft drink. (I got into this habit

> **YOUR FIRST ASSIGNMENT AFTER RISING IS TO COMPLETE YOUR CARBO-LOAD.**

because at international races, you were pretty sure what went into a Coke or Pepsi can was close to what you got at home.) Forget nutrition—what you need in the final countdown is something sweet, instant energy that will go straight to your muscles. Energy bars also can provide an effective last-minute meal, but be sure you eat a bar that is mostly carbohydrate. Some energy bars contain extra protein, good for postmarathon recovery, but not what you need before the race.

I often do a very short warmup at the hotel an hour or more early, for several reasons. First, going outside and testing the weather is more reliable than listening to weather reports on TV or radio. Second, a short run usually loosens my bowels; I'd rather use the toilet in my hotel room than stand in a long line for a porta-potty. A half mile or so jogging and walking usually accomplishes this.

Becoming toilet-trained is a necessity if you don't want to waste energy and time standing in long porta-potty lines. Hopefully you will have determined during your long runs in training what foods provide the least intestinal distress, but prerace nerves may trick your system. If I'm driving to the start, I sometimes arrive with a nearly empty gas tank so I'll have an excuse to stop at a gas station and use the restroom. I'm adept at locating toilets away from the start that I can visit during my warmup. Driving the final miles to the race, I keep my eyes open for a friendly fast-food restaurant close enough to jog to but far enough away so most of the other runners won't want to. That's one advantage of being a high-mileage runner: You can outrun the competition for an uncrowded toilet.

For my early-morning warmup, I don't usually wear my racing gear. After visiting the john and changing, I gather any extra gear I need—including my runner's bag, packed the night before—and head for the start.

REACHING THE STARTING AREA

Each race has its own protocol requiring careful attention (and some experience—yours or that of friends) if you don't want to get to the starting line too early or too late. At the Boston Marathon, runners board buses in downtown Boston by 8:00 a.m. for transportation to where the race begins at noon. After arriving near the start, they spend the next hour or two milling around outside the high school in suburban Hopkinton before being shooed to the starting line 30 to 60 minutes before the start. Until the Boston Athletic Association began providing outdoor tents at the 100th Boston, runners would cram into the gym so tightly no one could move, much less find a spot to lie down when the weather was cold or rainy. Weather can turn a good prerace experience into a bad one, so you need to learn each race's logistics to spare yourself discomfort.

At Boston and most other large races, the elite runners are supplied with transportation and a private dressing area near the start. It makes the final hour before the marathon much more comfortable, a necessity for runners seeking peak performance. Because race directors hope for fast times to please sponsors, they do what they can to make the prerace conditions comfortable for top competitors.

But most race directors do a good job for the rest of us as well. Particularly during the fall marathon season, there's a lot of competition among race directors to make runners entering each race comfortable so that runners will continue to return and provide the numbers the sponsors like. Fortunately, many race directors are marathoners (or former marathoners) themselves and remember the types of user-friendly practices that kept them comfortable and happy. In 2001, when I crammed seven marathons into 7 months to commemorate my 70th birthday and raise money for charity, I was struck by how well-organized each race was and how well race directors provided the back of the pack with a reasonable amount of comfort.

Runners without the privileges of the elite dressing room need to organize themselves as much as possible on race day to minimize the hassle caused by being part of a 35,000-runner happening. This requires preplanning. Often you learn how to cope with one specific marathon only by running it once and returning the following year better prepared. Or, if you're lucky, you attend the race with friends who were there the year before and who can tell you what to expect. It's called "networking," and it works in marathoning as well as in business.

ON THE STARTING LINE

Warming up is difficult—if not impossible—at large races because at the time when you normally might be doing some final strides or a bit of jogging, you often need to stay in place to secure your position on the starting line. At the really big marathons, such as Honolulu or Walt Disney World, runners are marched to the line well before the gun. It's the only way to handle the crowds of starters, but if you like to follow a particular warmup routine, as I do, this arrangement can wreak havoc with your preparation. The fortunate thing about marathons is that unless you're an elite runner planning a 4:30 first mile, you probably don't need as much warmup as you might for a 5-K race, where you need to run fast from the gun. You may lose a minute or two with a slow start, but this may not be that important over the length of a marathon. If you're a first timer, you probably won't warm up because you don't want to waste even the minute amount of energy it requires to jog in place standing on the line. Experienced runners, however, often have different agendas. The inconvenience of crowds is one reason you may want to try a small, intimate marathon when you attempt a new personal record.

At races where I planned to try for first in my age group, I used to position myself as close to the starting line as I could without blocking faster runners. I'm somewhat less competitive now and often line up at the absolute back of the pack, at races like the Gate River Run, a 15-K race I run every year at Jacksonville, Florida. One advantage of my last-row lineup scheme is that once the gun sounds, I can use a portable toilet without having to wait in a long line. The only time this got me in trouble was at the Comrades Marathon in South Africa, when I emerged from the toilet after taking too long a time and realized that the last runners were several blocks ahead of me down the street. It took me several kilometers to regain contact, during which time a police car pulled beside me and an officer asked, "Are you in the race?" (Fortunately, policemen in South Africa are much more polite these days than before the end of apartheid.)

Position on the starting grid is less critical today than it was a decade ago; in practically every major marathon, computer chips, easily laced onto one racing shoe, are used to provide runners with an official time that recognizes when they cross the starting line, not when the gun sounds. Leading a pacing team at the 1998 Chicago Marathon, I held the 5:00 group back until the starting line was nearly clear of runners. This meant crossing the line 8 minutes late.

Since those "lost minutes" would be subtracted from everybody's official time, it didn't really matter when we started.

At Chicago in 1998, my team experienced no delays caused by runners around us, and actually ran the first 2 miles somewhat faster than our planned pace. Several months later at the 1999 Walt Disney World Marathon, where I led the 4:30 pacing team for *Runner's World*, it took only 4 minutes to cross the line, but we lost a minute a mile for the first 3 miles because of a narrower course.

Each marathon is slightly different, so you need to approach each with a plan that is both flexible and well defined. Only by understanding race-day logistics can you both maximize your comfort and increase your chances of success.

CHAPTER 19

DRINKING ON THE RUN

FLUIDS ARE ESSENTIAL FOR TRAINING AND RACING

Paths along the Chicago lakefront stretch 18 miles from the South Shore Cultural Center on the South Side to Bryn Mawr Avenue on the North Side, encompassing Jackson, Grant, and Lincoln Parks. When you run on the lakefront, you encounter museums, one of the largest convention centers in the world, the football stadium where the Chicago Bears play, high-rise apartments, a lift bridge, several yacht clubs and golf courses, and numerous sandy beaches jammed each summer with swimmers.

Most important, there are water fountains—a total of 32, according to a map in the Chicago Area Runners Association's office. There are few places along Chicago's lakefront where you can run more than a mile without encountering a water fountain, called "bubblers" in some circles because of the way the water bubbles out of them. And each summer as the CARA training class does its long runs to prepare for the Chicago Marathon, we stop frequently to drink. It is our means of survival. Survival is merely one reason that runners need to drink when they run far. The other reasons are to replace lost energy and to enhance performance.

Before running became a mass participation affair, runners ignored fluids while running marathons because of a combination of arrogance, ignorance, and a lack of aid stations. Emil Zatopek, the great Czech runner, won the 1952 Olympic marathon without taking a sip. He was a world record holder in track who was running his first 26-miler, and probably didn't know how to drink on the run. He was his era's best distance runner and succeeded on talent, training, and toughness.

But Zatopek's time was 2:23:03, a performance so ordinary by today's standards that even I have bettered it. The time would hardly put him in the top ranks in many major races today—and wouldn't qualify him for the U.S. Olympic trials. The world record for women is now far faster than Zatopek's best, which seems astounding to those of us who are old enough to remember how the gritty runner totally dominated the distance runners of his era.

But today's runners know how to drink. They drink often—water as well as replacement fluids, such as Gatorade, Exceed, and defizzed Coke. They drink from paper cups handed to them by volunteers or from squeeze bottles with straws so they don't have to slow their pace. At the Comrades Marathon (an ultramarathon 55 miles long) in South Africa, runners are handed plastic bags that have to be torn open to get to the water within. One of the secrets to success at Comrades is to tear the top off the bags without spilling all the water inside.

At a nutritional seminar at Ohio State University in Columbus before the 1992 Olympic trials, Edward F. Coyle, PhD, of the department of kinesiology at the University of Texas at Austin, suggested that for efficient thermal regulation on a hot day, a runner may need to drink 1,000 milliliters of fluid an hour. That's a full liter! Nearly 1 quart! If you're a 4- or 5-hour marathoner, that would mean drinking 4 or 5 quart bottles; you could drown in that much water. I've drunk at that rate under controlled conditions in an exercise laboratory, running on a treadmill with someone handing me a plastic bottle with a straw every 5 minutes for 2 hours, and it's not easy. It took all my willpower to keep drinking as my belly filled with fluids and my mind sent signals that I was no longer thirsty. Yet that's what Dr. Coyle claims you need to do if you expect the best possible performance.

LEARNING HOW TO DRINK

We encourage participants in the CARA training class to drink on the run. Not only does drinking fluids make their weekend long runs more comfortable, but it teaches them how to drink and how often to drink. It underscores the importance of proper fluid replacement. Research also suggests that proper fluid replacement can help prevent cramps.

No tennis player would start a match without practicing lobs; no golfer would think a game complete without learning how to pitch from a sand trap. And no runner should enter a marathon without figuring out how and when to drink.

NO RUNNER SHOULD ENTER A MARATHON WITHOUT FIGURING OUT HOW AND WHEN TO DRINK.

Drinking while running definitely is not easy. Unless you grasp the cup carefully, you can spill half the contents on the ground. If you gulp too quickly, you can spend the next mile coughing and gasping. If you dawdle at aid stations, you can waste precious seconds. If you gulp down a replacement drink you aren't used to, it might make you nauseous. Lately, scientists have suggested that drinking too much during a marathon sometimes can be as dangerous on a hot day as drinking too little. Who are we to believe?

Drinking on the run is a science, and so we practice. Although there are ample fountains along the lakefront, the CARA classes in the northern, southern, and western suburbs aren't equally blessed. Class leaders at the first two locations must tour the course before weekend workouts and place jugs of water and Gatorade, along with paper cups, at strategic points along the way. On the Prairie Path, the Rails-to-Trails gravel path heading westward from the city

THE THINKING ON DRINKING

In the first two editions of this book, I encouraged runners to "drink, drink, drink." I modified that statement for this edition, suggesting only that runners learn to "drink on the run." The thinking on drinking has changed. Runners who walk around at expos the day before their marathons, sipping from plastic bottles, may now be drinking too much. Many major marathons with five-figure fields offer aid stations nearly every mile as one means of coping with the crowding. You can drown out there!

Excessive hydration may get you in trouble, today's experts believe. "Drinking too little is common," concedes Amby Burfoot, executive editor of *Runner's World*, "but drinking too much is more dangerous." Drinking too little is a performance issue: It slows you down. Drinking too much sometimes can kill you because of a condition known as hyponatremia, caused by excessive fluid consumption.

Many people believe they need to drink eight 8-ounce glasses of water a day because some fashion magazine told them so. But no scientific research exists to support the 8×8 thesis, wrote Burfoot in the July 2003 issue of *Runner's World*.

"Dehydration diminishes performance," Burfoot stated, "because it thickens the blood, decreases the heart's efficiency, increases heart rate, and raises body temperature. But a modest dehydration is a

limits, there are a few fountains, but most class members have been conditioned to run wearing water belts, carrying their own fluids with them. I never forget mine when I run with the class along the Prairie Path.

DRINKING FOR SURVIVAL

Drinking on the run is necessary for survival. When the weather is warm or humid, runners sweat. You sweat even during cool

normal and temporary condition for many marathoners and doesn't lead to any serious medical conditions. Excessive fluid consumption, on the other hand, can prove deadly."

The problem is not so much the elites, who run so fast that drinking becomes difficult and who are off the course in just over 2 hours. It's more the increasing number of slower runners, who may be running under the sun for 5 or 6 hours. They can drink all they want while walking past the numerous aid stations. That many of these runners are women compounds the problem, says Burfoot, because women only need 70 percent as much fluid as men because of lesser body mass.

Hyponatremia means low blood sodium. Excessive fluid consumption lowers the concentration of sodium in the blood. In extreme cases, hyponatremia can cause death through brain seizures, which happened recently at both the Boston and the Marine Corps marathons. As a result, organizations such as the International Marathon Medical Directors Association have lowered by nearly half their recommended race fluid consumption guidelines: from 20 to 40 ounces an hour to 13 to 27 ounces an hour.

Stay hydrated, goes the current advice, but do not overdrink. Sports drinks that contain at least some sodium may serve you an extra dose of protection.

weather, particularly if you are overdressed. If you sweat too much, you dehydrate. If you become dehydrated, body temperature rises and performance drops. Too high a body temperature can result in heat prostration, or—in extreme circumstances—death.

Most people sweat efficiently and adapt quite well to changes in temperature. It is only when you undertake extreme activities like marathons that you need to worry about taking in enough liquid to balance losses from sweat. The average sedentary person loses

2 quarts of water a day under normal temperature conditions, but a marathoner can sweat away that much in ½ hour, according to Lawrence E. Armstrong, PhD, of the University of Connecticut, who includes among his specialties the study of dehydration.

Some people sweat more than others. Alberto Salazar, for example, lost 12 pounds and placed a subpar 15th in the 1984 Olympic marathon, which he ran in the warm conditions of Los Angeles. "Without doubt, running marathons results in tremendous dehydration," states Peter B. Raven, PhD, a physiology professor at the Texas College of Osteopathic Medicine in Fort Worth.

Nevertheless, sweating is a natural effect of exercise. "Every muscle is a tiny furnace that produces heat," writes Gabe Mirkin, MD, in *The Sportsmedicine Book*. Muscles convert fuel to energy very inefficiently, resulting in excess heat that must be eliminated to keep the body from overheating.

A part of your brain called the hypothalamus detects the rise in temperature of the blood as it circulates, raising the body's core temperature. "The brain says sweat, and the body sweats," explains William J. Fink, a researcher at Ball State University's human performance laboratory in Muncie, Indiana.

Perspiration begins almost immediately when you start to run, emerging through glands so numerous that an area of skin the size of a quarter contains 100. (Our bodies have between 2 and 4 million sweat glands.) The rise in body temperature triggers the production and excretion of sweat. As sweat evaporates from the skin, you cool off. This process is called thermoregulation, and when it works right, it's an effective heating and cooling system.

Not everybody's system functions effectively, however. In a running class I taught in Dowagiac, Michigan, in the early 1980s, there was a woman named Joyce who essentially did not sweat. Some people might consider that an advantage, but it isn't if you're a runner. Joyce's inability to sweat normally caused her to overheat so quickly that even on a cool day she couldn't run farther than 3 miles. For Joyce to run a marathon would have been an impossibility. Later, as I began to answer runners' training questions online, I discovered that Joyce's problem was not unique. Rare maybe, but not unique. A number of individuals asked me online questions about their inability to perspire and cool their bodies as they exercised.

Alberto Salazar had another problem. He had tremendous willpower and could push himself past the point where lesser runners would quit. At the human performance laboratory at Ball State University in Muncie, Indiana, David L. Costill, PhD, found that Salazar kept running on the treadmill at the point of maximum oxygen uptake for much longer than any other runner. But that same drive got Salazar into trouble. On two occasions at the peak of his career—once at the Falmouth Road Race and another time at the Boston Marathon—he collapsed after winning fast races and had to receive fluids intravenously. I'm convinced that Salazar's career as an elite athlete was shortened considerably because of the impact of those two events on his system.

THE SCIENCE OF SWEAT

As Salazar discovered, what scientists refer to as effective thermoregulation occurs at the expense of body fluids. The hotter it is, the more you sweat. "If sweat loss is not replaced during exercise," says Robert Murray, PhD, an exercise scientist who serves as a consultant for the Quaker Oats Company, "the resulting dehydration compromises cardiovascular and thermoregulatory function, increases the risk of heat illness, and impairs exercise performance."

Dehydration reduces blood volume. This prompts the body to decrease both bloodflow and sweating in an attempt to conserve body fluids. Under these circumstances, the body's ability to cool

(continued on page 294)

PREVENTING MUSCLE CRAMPS

Jerry Wood of Fort Smith, Arkansas, has run half a dozen marathons and suffered muscle cramps in two of them. "Both races featured hot and humid weather," recalls Wood. "Even though I drank as much as possible, I could not replace the fluid lost through sweating."

Marathoners often suffer muscle cramps—calves, thighs, stomach, various other body parts—18 or 20 miles into a marathon. Conventional wisdom suggests that dehydration and the loss of various electrolytes, specifically sodium, causes cramps. Sometimes this is true, but not always.

"Dehydration can be a cause of muscle cramps," suggests Autumn Evans, a runner from Melbourne Beach, Florida, "but it's not the only cause." Lack of training can be a factor, adds Alan Headbloom of Midland, Michigan, who notes he only seems to cramp in marathons where his training has lagged, resulting in unstrengthened muscles. Going out too fast also can cause runners to cramp after being forced to slow down.

"Cramps occur at different times and for various reasons," says Nancy Clark, RD, director of nutrition services for SportsMedicine Brookline in Boston and author of *Nancy Clark's Sports Nutrition Guidebook*. She notes that people who sweat a lot of salt seem to cramp more often. E. Randy Eichner, MD, of the University of Oklahoma Medical Center and a member of the *Runner's World* Science Advisory Board, says the three roots of heat cramping are salt loss, dehydration, and muscle fatigue.

"Sodium is a key," says Dr. Eichner, "not only to maintain blood volume but also to help nerves fire and muscles work. Sodium depletion short-circuits the coordination of nerves and muscles as muscles contract and relax." The result, he suggests, can be muscle cramping.

Cramps are painful and can impede performance, but they can also be one of the signs of hyponatremia. While no cure-all remedy for cramps exists, these strategies may help prevent them in your next race.

1. Train properly for your marathon, specifically with long runs that build strength and muscle endurance.
2. Balance your diet with a good mix of fruits and vegetables and other foods that contain the vitamins and minerals you need, specifically sodium, potassium, magnesium, and calcium.
3. Learn to drink during the marathon, alternating between water and a sports drink containing sodium, such as Gatorade, but don't drink excessively, including before the race.
4. Check your biomechanics. If poor form or a poor foot plant places extra strain on certain muscles, they may cramp more easily.
5. Include stretching in your training routine. Your muscles need to be loose as well as strong.
6. Salt tablets (a quick source of sodium) may work for heavy sweaters. Experiment with extra salt during long training runs before trying them in a marathon. Drink at least 8 ounces of water with each tablet.

Nancy Clark suggests that runners learn their sweat rates by weighing themselves naked before and after a 1-hour run. "Losing 1 pound equates to losing 16 ounces of sweat," she says. "Drink accordingly on future runs—and in the marathon—to prevent dehydration and potentially cramps."

When you do cramp, what can you do to relieve the pain? Craig A. Horswill, PhD, a senior research fellow at the Gatorade Sports Science Institute, recommends both stretching and massaging the complaining muscles. "Rubbing the cramped muscle may help alleviate pain as well as help stimulate bloodflow and fluid movement into the area," says Dr. Horswill.

itself declines, and the body temperature can rise to dangerous levels unless you stop running—and it may not decrease even then if you fail to get out of the sun.

You can't adapt to dehydration, explains Dr. Murray, but living and training in hot environments can help you avoid dehydration. As you adapt to warmer climates, your blood volume expands and your sweat glands conserve sodium, he says. "This helps assure that cardiovascular and thermoregulatory function can be maintained during exercise in the heat," he says.

In other words, Dr. Murray is saying that we can train ourselves to utilize fluids more efficiently. Humans are homeotherms who need to maintain a constant temperature; we're warm-blooded, rather than cold-blooded. An internal temperature of 98.6°F is considered normal. Your body temperature drops below

> **WE CAN TRAIN OURSELVES TO UTILIZE FLUIDS MORE EFFICIENTLY.**

normal (called hypothermia) if you stay out in the cold too long or wear insufficient clothing. Your temperature rises above normal (hyperthermia) when you start to exercise. It also rises if you get the flu or a similar infection, one reason it's not a good idea to exercise to excess—or even at all—when you're ill.

Hypothermia normally is not a problem for marathoners—except occasionally on cold days when runners may feel less urge to drink. If forced to slow down because of fatigue or dehydration, they may experience a drop in body temperature. (Drinking helps keep you warm as well as keep you cool, as I've discovered while competing in cross-country ski races.)

Hyperthermia is more of a problem. There are two types of sweat glands: apocrine and eccrine. Apocrine glands don't concern marathoners. Those are the "nervous," or "sexual," glands that are located mostly in the armpits and around the genitals. Scientists don't entirely understand their function but suspect they serve some purpose related to sexual attraction. The eccrine gland, however, helps to keep us cool. Even though we begin sweating almost immediately as a response to exercise, it may be 10 minutes or more before our skin becomes moist enough to notice. On hot but dry days, you may not realize you are sweating because the moisture evaporates quickly.

Normally, sweat is very dilute, containing only about .10 percent electrolytes—mostly sodium chloride and some potassium. There has been some suggestion that perspiration is one of the body's means of ridding the bloodstream of waste products, including lactic acid. This is not true. The prime function of the eccrine glands is keeping us cool.

Cooling occurs when sweat evaporates from the body surface. "Evaporation is important," explains Dr. Raven. "The blood flows to the surface and transfers its heat by conduction."

During exercise, the body usually produces more heat than you can get rid of by sweating. A marathoner's body temperature gradually rises 3°F or 4°F to 102°F, an efficient level for energy utilization. At this point, your air-conditioning system is in sync with the environment and you perform well. If the weather is too hot or too humid, or you become dehydrated—resulting in a drop in sweat production—the body's temperature can soar to dangerous levels. Your muscles will not perform efficiently at temperatures that are too high (104°F and up), so that will slow you down. This is an important defense mechanism because if you fail to sweat and your core temperature rises past 108°F, you may suffer heatstroke, a potentially serious problem for which the early symptoms are headaches and dizziness, followed in extreme cases by convulsions, unconsciousness, and death.

The body's ability to safely regulate its internal temperature while exercising is influenced by four factors: the environment, exercise intensity, clothing, and the athlete's level of fitness and acclimatization. You can train yourself to resist both cold and hot weather, but extremes of either can cause problems.

EFFECTIVE SWEATING

Let's eliminate one myth. Although Joyce in my running class virtually did not sweat, in general women sweat as much and as well as men do. The suspicion that women's air-conditioning systems function less efficiently than men's was one excuse the International Olympic Committee offered for resisting inclusion of the marathon or any other long-distance race for women to the Olympic Games. As has been proved since 1984, women Olympic marathoners run just as hard as men do; their somewhat slower times being more a matter of genetic muscular efficiency than anything having to do with thermoregulation.

IN GENERAL WOMEN SWEAT AS MUCH AND AS WELL AS MEN DO.

One person who helped disprove the myth about women's capacity to sweat has a particularly appropriate name: Barbara L. Drinkwater, PhD, of the department of medicine at Pacific Medical Center in Seattle. In 1977, Dr. Drinkwater asked a number of female runners, including one world record holder, to exercise for 2 hours in an environmental chamber at 118°F. "They came out looking like they had climbed out of a swimming pool," Dr. Drinkwater recalls.

Yes, women sweat, and in fact they have more sweat glands than men do. In some studies involving men and women, men did sweat more, but Dr. Drinkwater suspects that's because the men and women compared didn't have comparable weights and oxygen uptake levels.

Regardless of your sex, conditioning improves your ability to sweat. Carl Gisolfi, PhD, an exercise physiologist at the University of Iowa, believes that we can increase our heat tolerance 50 percent by conditioning. According to Dr. Gisolfi, you train your sweat glands to function more efficiently by using them.

Acclimatization also improves our ability to tolerate heat. That is why marathoners experience more problems when the weather turns hot at Boston in April than at New York in the fall. By New York, they've had an entire summer to become acclimatized.

One year at the Shamrock Shuffle, a popular 8-K race held in Chicago each March, a freak warm spell raised the temperature to an unseasonal 70°F. I was astounded to see runners starting the race in tights and jackets, even cotton sweatsuits—clothing they had worn through the winter. Most finished the race sweaty and bedraggled, with jackets wrapped around their waists. Several overheated runners were taken to the hospital. A midsummer race with 70°F temperatures, however, would have caused few problems. Runners would have been conditioned both physically and psychologically to tolerate the heat.

Former world record holder Buddy Edelen, a graduate of the University of Minnesota, sometimes wore three sweatsuits while training for the 1964 Olympic marathon trials to simulate hot conditions. Sure enough, temperatures rose into the nineties during the May trials in Yonkers, New York, and Edelen soundly beat his rivals. Later, Olympic marathoners Ron Daws of Minnesota and Benji Durden of Colorado adopted Edelen's training strategy with success, as did Deena Kastor, bronze medalist at the 2004 Olympic Games in Athens. On a frighteningly hot day in August, while many of her rivals were outdoors, warming up on a track, Kastor stayed indoors, keeping her body temperature low by wearing an ice vest developed by one of her sponsors.

TIPS FOR STAYING COOL

Other than training in multiple sweatsuits or purchasing ice vests, what strategies can runners use to prevent heat problems? Let's talk first about training. Here are some training tips for proper hydration.

Drink before running. Drink adequately and drink often. Dr. Murray recommends drinking 16 ounces of water an hour before training: "Excess body water will be passed as urine before practice begins," he says. Marathoner Doug Kurtis says that he never passes a water fountain at work without stopping for at least a quick drink.

Drink while you run. For years, an old-fashioned notion among football coaches was that drinking was for sissies. They prohibited their athletes from going near water fountains during summer practices. Today's more knowledgeable coaches realize their athletes practice and play better if allowed time to drink. That was the motivation behind the development of Gatorade, a replacement drink formulated

> RUNNERS NEED TO DRINK FREQUENTLY WHILE TRAINING, ESPECIALLY DURING WARM WEATHER.

for University of Florida football players. Runners need to drink frequently while training, especially during warm weather. You'll run faster and recover faster. Most runners quickly become adept at locating available water in their neighborhoods. I sometimes carry coins in my shorts if I know I'll be passing a soft drink machine.

I live on Lake Shore Drive in Long Beach, Indiana, the area's most popular route for joggers, bikers, and walkers. When I added an extra parking space in front of my house, I asked the landscaper to install a drinking fountain. My popularity in the neighborhood soared as those exercising stopped to cool off. After George Hirsch, former publisher of *Runner's World*, mentioned my water fountain in his "Publisher's Letter," at least one runner coming from Detroit to run the Chicago Marathon told me at the expo that he had detoured off I-94 to drink from "Hal Higdon's fountain." I guess he wanted to sip from the fountain of knowledge.

Walk to drink. In preparing for the marathon at the 1981 World

Masters Championships in Christchurch, New Zealand, I experimented with walking through aid stations at several shorter races and discovered I lost only 7 seconds off my time if I walked to drink. That's inconsequential. In the race, I walked through every aid station (positioned at 5-K intervals) and figured I lost less than a minute en route to victory in the M45 age group with a time of 2:29:27. Many of the runners I beat that day had posted faster times coming into the race, but finished behind me on a warm day.

If you lose only 7 seconds each time you walk through an aid station running at a 5:30 pace, you'll lose even less running time at a slower pace. When I lead 4:30 pacing groups at marathons, we average 10:18 per mile. Most fit runners can walk 15:00 per mile or faster, so the drop-off between running pace and walking pace is little, but the gain is great.

Drink after running. Most runners don't need to be told this. Their natural instinct sends them immediately to the water fountain or refrigerator. But even after your initial thirst is quenched, you still may be dehydrated. One way of evaluating your intake is to check the color of your urine. If it's yellow, you probably need to keep drinking. Clear urine is a sign of good hydration. Another clue is body weight. If your weight is abnormally low after a long run on a hot day, don't congratulate yourself that you are losing weight; you're most likely badly dehydrated. Particularly after long runs, it's a good idea to use sports drinks to help replenish glycogen burned during your run. You'll recover much more rapidly and help prevent injuries if you do so.

Run when it's cool. Because of my flexible schedule as a writer, I can choose my running times. During the winter, I usually train at midday because it's warmer. During the summer, I switch to running at dawn, before it gets too hot. Running in the evening is slightly less satisfactory because it can still be hot and humid. And running in the dark has its own perils. You may need to do some hot-weather running to acclimatize yourself for races, but you don't want extreme temperatures to affect the quality of your training. I've run at 4:00 in the afternoon near my brother-in-law's house in Mesa, Arizona, when the temperature was 104°F. I didn't run far, and I didn't run fast, but I ran—partly to prove I could do it. But I was glad I don't have to run in those conditions every day.

Shift your training. The message in my earlier book, *Run Fast*, was "If you want to run fast, you have to run fast." Every coach will tell you that one secret to success—even in the marathon—is speedwork. The best time for speedwork is the summer, when the warm weather helps warm your muscles so you're less likely to suffer injuries. You can train on the track, never more than a short sprint from the water fountain. Short, intense workouts can get you just as hot as long, slow ones, but you'll be closer to home if you do overheat.

Beware of the sun. Wear a hat. Every runner should own a sloppy, floppy hat that can be used to douse yourself with water when you stop at water fountains. There are some excellent runners' hats on the market now, made of lightweight, breathable materials. Purchase one of those rather than using the standard, and heavier, baseball caps that are popular today. Particularly in spring, you may want to use sunscreen (for best results use a sun protection factor, SPF, of 15 or higher) to protect vulnerable areas, such as your face, your shoulders, and the fronts of your legs. Apply the sunscreen ½ hour before you run to give it time to be absorbed; then apply more. Wash your hands thoroughly to avoid rubbing the lotion into your eyes if you wipe your forehead; it can sting badly. For the same reason, you may want to apply the lotion only below your eyes, trusting your cap to protect your forehead.

I can't overestimate the importance of running covered when the sun is strong. I wish I had done a better job of protecting my skin while younger. I have a couple of scaly areas on my forehead that now make me nervous. My former coach Fred Wilt died of skin cancer. I could name another famous high-mileage runner recently diagnosed with that disease. Always—and I mean always—run with a hat when the sun is high overhead, specifically between 10:00 a.m. and 2:00 p.m.!

Don't overestimate your ability. Realize that you can't run as fast when it's warm. Learn your limits. Don't expect to achieve a pre-planned time, and don't be afraid to bail out early when you're starting to overheat.

I learned that lesson the hard way. During the prime of my running career, I set out one morning, determined to run at a 5:30 pace on a long run of 23 miles without realizing that the temperature was climbing through the eighties. I finished the workout, but barely jogging. Two days later, I came down with a knee in-

> ## REALIZE THAT YOU CAN'T RUN AS FAST WHEN IT'S WARM. LEARN YOUR LIMITS.

jury, which I attributed to my still-dehydrated state. I failed to make the Olympic team even though I had the second-fastest time that year among Americans. I'm convinced my body lacked sufficient fluid to lubricate the joints. Whether or not that theory is true, it's certain that you can't ignore Mother Nature while running in the heat. Warm-weather training must of necessity be a compromise. But if you learn to live with the heat, you can survive and condition yourself for any type of weather.

Still, it's sometimes difficult to gauge the weather. My oldest son, Kevin, qualified for the 1984 Olympic Trials with a time of 2:18:51. He was not a threat to make the top three, but the level of his training suggested that he might be able to shave several minutes off that PR in the trials race, which began in Buffalo and finished at Niagara Falls, Ontario. As his coach, I designed an even pace to achieve that goal. Carefully watching his splits, Kevin cruised past 10 miles right on pace, but he had to drop out a half dozen miles

(continued on page 304)

MARATHON MEALS

Unlike cyclists and skiers, most fast marathoners avoid solid foods when they run, for a simple reason: It's difficult to eat while moving faster than a 7:00 minute-per-mile pace.

But coach Bill Wenmark of Deephaven, Minnesota, recommends midmarathon snacks for people who take longer than 3 hours to finish. "If you're on the road 4 or 5 hours, you're running the equivalent of an ultramarathon," says Wenmark. "You need more energy than you can get from the drinks race directors provide. Someone running an 8:00 pace or slower can take time to eat. Digestion is less of a problem than for elite runners." Wenmark recommends saltines and high-energy bars for his back-of-the-packers and positions support crews along the course to provide this extra boost.

What do the scientists say? At Ohio State University, W. Michael Sherman, PhD, an exercise scientist, tested 10 cyclists who rode at 70 percent of their maximum capacity for 90 minutes, then did the equivalent of a 20-mile time trial. (Their total time approached 2½ hours.) In one trial they ate a specific amount of carbohydrates, and in the other they got the carbs in liquid form. "We found no performance difference in their response," reports Dr. Sherman. He adds that in warm weather, liquids certainly would be preferable to solids because the fluid would help combat dehydration.

Of course, Dr. Sherman admits that his study failed to explore the outer realm of endurance beyond 4 and 5 hours, where ultrama-rathoners (and slow marathoners) tread. Conventional wisdom among this breed suggests that food may be as important as drink—if only for the psychological reason that you want something solid in your stomach. First-time marathoners seem to have a stronger desire to eat solid food than experienced marathoners, who have adapted to a liquids-only diet while racing. Liquids high in sugar can cause stomach distress—nausea and diarrhea—if you are not used to them.

Solid food for energy replacement was more common in Europe a quarter century ago. When I ran the 1963 Kosice Marathon in Czechoslovakia (an invitational race with only a few finishers slower than 3 hours), I was surprised to encounter fruit and vegetable soup at the refreshment tables. This was in an era when you were lucky to get water at a U.S. marathon. Running the (54-mile) 1998 Comrades Marathon in South Africa, I found boiled potatoes at some of the aid stations. Knowing this in advance, I had used potatoes as an energy supplement during training.

Inevitably, runners must determine their own regimens. I usually stick with liquids when running races, but I have eaten solid food in other endurance events. In triathlons lasting 6 hours, I've experimented successfully with fruit and candy bars. In a 60-K cross-country ski race, several chocolate chip cookies provided a boost near the end. But during a snowshoe marathon, a combination of soft drinks and candy bars so nauseated me that I failed to finish.

Until recently, few American marathons provided anything other than liquids. If you wanted food and were unwilling to carry what you wanted in a fanny pack, you needed to enlist a support crew. Lately, manufacturers have provided gelatin supplements (gels) that can be carried easily in a pocket, pinned to a singlet, or carried inside your running gloves. I usually pin them to my singlet, positioning them near the waistband so they can be tucked into my shorts to prevent flapping. They are best taken with water as a chaser.

Most important: If you plan to eat on the run, experiment often in practice before you race.

later because that pace was too fast for that day's hot and humid conditions, which we had failed to recognize at the start. Meanwhile, the runners at the front of the pack ran against one another, not against their watches, and had far fewer problems—although their times were several minutes slower than might have been expected.

As a leader of pacing teams at various marathons, I warn runners of the danger of connecting with a team that is too fast, particularly on a hot or humid day. At the prerace clinics, I usually advise those who planned to join the 4:00 team to move back to the 4:10 or 4:20 team. Those planning 4:10 finishes move back to 4:20 or 4:30, and so forth. But runners often come to marathons preprogrammed to run specific times. It's sometimes difficult to realize that despite all your hard training, you are not going to achieve your time goal because of the environment.

DRINKING DURING THE RACE

Drinking during a marathon is almost a separate subject because in addition to your need to stay cool, you also need to adopt a strategy that permits you to refuel on the run. You need energy as well as fluid replacement.

Timing your prerace hydration can be tricky. I recommend that runners drink as often as possible until 2 hours before the race—then stop until just before they start to move (which in large races can be several minutes after the gun sounds). Otherwise, they may need to urinate at midrace, an obvious inconvenience. In the last 5 minutes before moving, I start drinking again, often downing a 12-ounce soft drink (usually a Coke or a Pepsi) while standing on the starting line, knowing it will be absorbed by my body before it reaches my kidneys. One advantage of using a soft drink is it comes nicely packaged and can usually be easily obtained in vending machines in most hotels. At international races, everything else about

CHOOSING YOUR BEVERAGE

Early research in fluid replacement suggested that drinks high in sugar content emptied from the stomach more slowly than water did. Then scientists fine-tuned their experiments and determined that fluids with a 6 percent sugar solution emptied from the stomach almost as fast as water, preferable if you want those fluids to get to the areas of the body where they're most needed. Most replacement drinks now offered in major marathons are formulated at that level. So don't bypass the replacement drink at refreshment stations (unless the sugar in the drink makes you nauseous).

My approach is usually to grab the replacement drink first, then wash it down with water, although many marathons offer water first, replacement drink second. Temperature usually dictates how much of each I drink. In warmer weather, I shade the ratio more toward water. I've found that too much replacement drink causes me stomach problems, but everyone is different in this respect.

Edward F. Coyle, PhD, of the department of kinesiology at the University of Texas at Austin, estimates that ingesting 30 to 60 grams of carbohydrates with each hour of exercise will generally help you maintain blood glucose oxidation late in exercise and delay fatigue.

You can reach this level by drinking between 625 and 1,250 milliliters (about ⅔ quart to 1¼ quarts) per hour of a beverage that contains between 4 and 8 percent carbohydrates. For races beyond the marathon distance, during which energy replacement becomes as important as thermoregulation, supersaturated sugar solutions (higher than 8 percent) may be necessary. (You can adjust the percentage by varying how much water you mix with powdered replacement drinks. Check the directions.)

the experience might be different, but you can usually find a Coke or Pepsi. Sipping a soft drink on the starting line works for me, but every runner has to experiment and come up with a workable drinking routine before practice and before races.

"Know what types of replacement beverages will be available during your race," advises Clark Campbell, a coach and professional triathlete from Lawrence, Kansas. "Then practice with that drink by using it during quality workouts and long-distance runs."

You should begin drinking early in the race. If you wait until you get thirsty, you may already have passed several aid stations that could have helped you avoid dehydration. Because of the crowds in the early miles, it may be difficult to get near the aid station for your first drink. But that drink may be the most important one you take in a race; it's worth losing a few seconds to grab at least a cup of water. One tip to remember is that it may be less crowded toward the end of the aid station than at the front. At the Chicago Marathon, the first aid station occupies an entire city block and both sides of the street in front of the Marshall Field's department store. "Our volunteers at the last table are a lot less busy than those at the first table," comments Pat Onines, coordinator for that first aid station.

Remember also Dr. Coyle's recommendation to drink a quart an hour. Keep that as your goal. Dr. Coyle says the largest factor affecting gastric emptying is volume. In other words, the more fluids you can force into your stomach, the faster fluids will empty from the stomach to be absorbed by the body. Dr. Coyle suggests that you may need to take in between 1,300 and 1,700 milliliters to force 1,000 milliliters to be emptied from the stomach during a marathon.

There are certain trade-offs to consider when deciding how much of what liquid to drink. One question is, Are the physical benefits of drinking large volumes of fluids worth the discomfort of making yourself drink so often?

On the hottest days, yes!

But the important goal is staying cool. "Any dehydration causes problems," says Dr. Coyle. "None can be tolerated." This is true not only in terms of safety but also in terms of performance. For every liter of fluid lost, your heartbeat will increase 8 beats per minute and your core temperature will increase accordingly. As a result, you'll be unable to maintain your race pace. If your goal is safety and performance, there's no question that the closer you match your intake of fluids to your rate of dehydration, the better.

In the closing stages of the race, water splashed on the body may help you more than water taken into the body. This is because it normally takes 30 minutes for water to migrate through the system to be released as sweat to provide an air-conditioning effect. One way to shortcut that system is to pour water directly on your body, permitting the water to evaporate. In the last few miles of the race, you're drinking for recovery after the race as much as for performance during it. My motto for the last half-hour of running is "Water on" as much as "Water in." Some scientists suggest that splashing water on your body will not cool you significantly. Maybe so, but it sure feels good—and the psychological boost is worth something.

If you're wearing a hat, pour water onto it and let the water drip onto your face. Rather than splashing yourself in front, pour water down your back, since it's less likely to flow downward into your shoes and cause blisters. If you pass someone standing beside the road with a water spray, consider stopping to stand under the spray for at least a few seconds rather than running through or around the spray.

The more attention you give to staying cool, the better you'll run. Once you get across the finish line, you'll want to begin drinking immediately to speed your recovery, but that's a subject for another chapter.

CHAPTER 20

MIND GAMES

THE MARATHON IS MENTAL
AS WELL AS PHYSICAL

Even in early October, the Twin Cities Marathon, between Minneapolis and St. Paul, can be chilly. One year when the temperature was just below freezing at the 7:00 start, I came prepared, wearing tights, a long-sleeved top, a hat, and gloves. Unfortunately, on the way to the starting line, I lost one of the gloves. To keep both hands warm as I ran, I switched the glove from hand to hand every third mile. It became a game for me, something to think about, something to help chart my progress. I could look forward to the switch each third mile.

If you think in those terms, a marathon is merely eight glove changes long.

Psychologists have long insisted that the mind is as important as the body when it comes to success in sports, particularly in an event like the marathon, where the mind must push the body to extremes. During the glory days of Eastern Bloc athletes, sports psychologists were as important as other coaches or trainers in preparing East German and Soviet athletes for competition. The U.S. Olympic Committee employs psychologists as consultants, as do many professional football and baseball teams. But anyone can use mind games to help get themselves through long-distance events.

I use mind games for survival in the marathon, physically as well as mentally. I divide marathons into fourths and thirds. At 3 miles,

I think: "Just done a 5-K. Piece of cake." At 6 miles, it's "A fourth of the race done." And at 8 miles, "A third." At 10, I console myself: "Double digits." At 13: "Past the half. Fewer miles ahead of me than behind me." At 16: "Only single digits remain." At 20: "I've passed the wall" or "Only a 10-K left now." By that time, you're close enough to count down like the liftoff of a rocket: "Six-5-4-3-2-1. I'm done."

Carolyn Warren of Tinley Park, Illinois, takes a slightly different approach, dividing the marathon into approximately 2-mile increments; it's simply 13 aid station stops. As marathoners, we play various mind games to get us to finish 26 miles 385 yards as fast as possible.

"Every marathon experience is different," says Cindy Southgate of Kanata, Ontario. "You need to figure out which mind games will work for that particular day."

When I was researching *Boston: A Century of Running*, I interviewed Dick Beardsley, who finished second to Alberto Salazar at the 1982 Boston Marathon. Coming off Heartbreak Hill in the lead, but with Salazar

> "ONE MORE MILE! ONLY 1 MILE TO GO!"

stalking him, Beardsley was toast. At 21 miles, he decided to adopt a strategy that ignored the fact that 5 grueling miles still remained. He decided he would run those miles one at a time, not caring whether there was another, not worrying whether or not there would be a tomorrow. "You can hold this pace for 1 more mile," Beardsley told himself. "One more mile! Only 1 mile to go!"

At 22 miles, Beardsley punched the reset button on his mental speedometer. "One mile to go!"

And at 23: "You're beating the world record holder. One more mile!"

Salazar eventually did outsprint Beardsley on the final straightaway, beating him 2:08:52 to 2:08:54. But it was Beardsley's mental strength that made their duel one of the closest in Boston Marathon history.

I've adopted that strategy in several races, including the 1999 Walt Disney World Marathon, in which I led the 4:30 pacing team for *Runner's World*. I arrived in Orlando undertrained, having failed to do any workouts beyond 13 miles in the months before the race. Though in respectable shape for a 5-K or a 10-K, I doubted my ability to keep the pace for a full 26. I told my coleader Leesa Weichert that I only planned to go 20; then she could take the group the rest of the way.

But at 20 I felt okay, so I tucked in behind Leesa, focused on the ears of the Mickey Mouse cap she was wearing, and told myself, "One mile to go. You can hold this pace for 1 more mile!" And like Beardsley, I reset my mental speedometer for each of the next half dozen miles. Although Weichert did pull ahead by 40 seconds in those closing miles, I finished in 4:30:27. That gave me more satisfaction than many races in which my times were several hours faster.

POSITIVE THINKING PAYS OFF

Marathon mind games are more than strategies for coping with pain and boredom. According to Charles A. Garfield, author of *Peak Performance*, 60 to 90 percent of success in sports can be attributed to mental factors and psychological mastery. Sports psychologist Thomas Tutko, PhD, quotes retired baseball player Maury Wills as saying that success is all mental. "There is nothing mystical about the emotional side of sports," claims Dr. Tutko.

Unfortunately, your mind can also work against you. One individual commented to me about a top-ranked woman runner he formerly coached: "It's her thinking that keeps her from winning."

Confidence is an important factor in the mind games athletes play: The power of positive thinking relates to more than success in business. One study of skiers training for the Olympic team showed that those who didn't make the team had negative or tentative feelings about their abilities, and successful candidates were more positive. Does confidence breed success, or were the less successful skiers simply being realistic about their talents? A little bit of both, probably, but consider the cocky attitude of Alpine skier Bill Johnson before he won the 1984 Olympic downhill in Sarajevo: Had Johnson known he had a lock on the gold medal, or had he simply been trying to psych himself up? The trash talk of NBA basketball players, as impolite as it seems, may serve some purpose.

If Johnson was only psyching himself up, he succeeded, as did British decathlete Daley Thompson, who also boasted of success before the 1984 games. Referring to his chief competitor, Thompson said, "The only way (Jurgen) Hingsen is going to get a gold medal here is to do another event—or steal mine." Thompson prevailed (defending his 1980 Olympic title), but Jamaica's Bert Cameron— who had claimed before the games that the 400-meter gold medal already had his name engraved on it—pulled a muscle in a semifinal heat and saw the medal go to another. There's a subtle line between confidence and overconfidence.

When we are confident, we can rationalize away any potential problems; without confidence, even slight threats become magnified.

Confident athletes can relax more easily than ones who feel threatened, but there are tricks to relaxing and eliminating fear. Robert M. Nideffer, PhD, a consultant for the U.S. Olympic Committee, recalled watching a diver about to execute a difficult $3\frac{1}{2}$ somersault in pike position off the 10-meter tower. The coach stood below, counting down: "Five, 4, 3, 2, 1. Go!" The counting, Dr. Nideffer explained, helped the diver redirect his attention away from his anxiety and fear. He likened it to a hypnotic state. Marathoner Tony Sandoval used a similar five-to-zero countdown when he went to bed each night. "It relaxed me and helped me to fall asleep quickly," explains Sandoval.

VISUALIZING SUCCESS

As a steeplechaser, I had my own presleep technique. I would visualize myself hurdling over barriers. It was better, I thought, than the more traditional counting of sheep, but it served another purpose beyond self-hypnosis. I was perfecting my hurdling technique through a technique known as "imaging."

In their book *Sporting Body, Sporting Mind*, authors John Syer and Christopher Connolly refer to this same technique as instant preplay. They describe one horsewoman who would lock herself in the washroom—the only place she wouldn't be disturbed—immediately before competition to focus on her event. That might not work in a major marathon with 20,000 runners waiting outside the porta-potties, but in *Golf My Way*, Jack Nicklaus described visualizing each shot before he hits it. He first pictures the ball landing where he wants it, then he "sees" the ball going there, and finally he visualizes himself "making the kind of swing that will turn the previous images into reality." Jon Lugbill, world champion kayaker, pictures himself paddling down whitewater rivers and feels this helps his ability to choose the best path through the waves during competition. Similarly, runners who want to improve their form can picture themselves running like the faster runners in our sport. Tom Grogon, a coach from Cincinnati, also suggests that runners mentally review the course before any distance race and think about how they will run it.

Another technique is instant replay, which Syer and Connolly describe: "The reverse of instant preplay, it is a visualized review of an action you have just performed." This enables athletes to imprint a perfect action more deeply in their sensory memory. Members of the U.S. weight lifting team preparing for the Olympics used these techniques. Each weight lifter had a videotape of his lifts at various meets and in training. As additional meets were filmed, the athletes added new tapes to their collection. With their library of tapes, the athletes could compare their recent lift styles with previous lifts or those of other top lifters filmed during competition.

THE POWER OF CONCENTRATION

One way to succeed in sports is to eliminate outside distractions. That way, you can more easily relax. Bryant J. Cratty, PhD, author of *Psychological Preparation and Athletic Excellence*, believes that relaxation and concentration can be improved in competition if an athlete erects imaginary walls to block off distractions. He suggests that a basketball player visualize partitions in front of the other players and behind the backboard before attempting to shoot a free throw. Dr. Cratty recommends that a gymnast imagine not only that the gym is empty but that there is a tent over each apparatus. So, too, should a long-distance runner focus on a narrow corridor of the road ahead.

Dr. Garfield says concentration is important for weight lifters: "The trained lifter knows that during the few seconds before a lift, total attention must be focused on the bar, and the degree to which this is done is largely determined by how much he really wants to make the lift." He found that if the lifter's confidence was lacking, and his will was not intensely focused, he would not be able to muster the control of muscle power necessary for success. The same is true in running.

> THE ABILITY TO CONCENTRATE IS THE SINGLE ELEMENT THAT SEPARATES THE MERELY GOOD ATHLETES FROM THE GREAT ONES.

"The ability to concentrate," says William P. Morgan, EdD, a sports psychologist at the University of Wisconsin at Madison, "is the single element that separates the merely good athletes from the great ones. Concentration is the hallmark of the elite runner." Elite runners succeed, he says, because they are totally in tune with their bodies, monitoring all symptoms from the nerve endings.

In contrast, Dr. Morgan found that middle-of-the-pack mara-

MIDPACK MIND GAMES

Although scientists suggest that tightly focusing on the task at hand (associating) allows elite athletes to extract the last ounce of energy from their bodies and win the race, midpack athletes often find themselves faced with a different challenge. They seek any strategy that will allow them to finish the race in a respectable time.

Don Pocock, an attorney from Winston-Salem, North Carolina, whose PR is 3:38, has a series of strategies, including a mantra, he uses when he runs marathons. The mantra is "Go the distance," which he chants repeatedly. "My track coach gave it to us back in high school to motivate us," Pocock recalls. "I now use the chant to keep my mind occupied with something else when every muscle in my body is screaming, 'Stop!'"

Pocock also spells words as another diversion. "Sometimes I get a sentence or a phrase in my mind and work it over and over to pass time," he says. "Sometimes, I even go over Russian vocabulary just to have something different to think about."

Finally, near the end of the marathon, Pocock pictures friends or family cheering him on, even if they're not there. "It works pretty well," says Pocock, "and folks usually like to hear that you were thinking about them during the race."

thoners more often thought of other activities (called dissociating) as a means of coping with pain. Dr. Morgan believes that in addition to possibly slowing them down, this tactic is dangerous: Runners could be ignoring important body signals and mindlessly run themselves into heatstroke or a stress fracture. For that reason, listening to music while running may unnecessarily distract you from the task at hand. Particularly at large races, I recommend leaving your music player at home because you'll miss a lot of the fun going on around you.

Owen Anderson, PhD, the editor of the journal *Running Research News*, defines dissociation as "ignoring the sensory feedback you get from your body while focusing your mind on something outside yourself." He claims that although dissociation blocks negative messages, prevents boredom, and diverts the mind from the pain and fatigue you experience in the muscles during strenuous running, it can create some problems if it causes you to fail to take in enough fluid, relax, or exert efficient muscle control. "It's hard to sustain a coordinated, quality pace unless you concentrate," says Dr. Anderson.

Researcher Kazuo Takai of the University of Tsukuba split 60 runners into groups at a 20-K race in Tokyo. Half of the runners used what Takai described as "attention" techniques to stay on pace; half used "avoidance" techniques and followed the pace of the others. Takai found that the attentive runners outperformed the avoidance runners in achieving their predicted goals. Attention means that you tune in to your body's signals midrace and let how you feel dictate your pace. Avoidance means that you tune out your body's signals and go with the flow.

Does this mean that joining a pacing team is a form of avoidance? It depends on your goals and how you hope to achieve them joining a team. Yes, if you just go with the flow and let the pace team leader do all the work for you. No, if you focus tightly on staying with the

> THE ATTENTIVE RUNNERS OUTPERFORMED THE AVOIDANCE RUNNERS IN ACHIEVING THEIR PREDICTED GOALS.

pace leader, monitoring closely how successful he or she is at keeping you on pace. That could be considered a form of attention. Avoidance is not always a losing strategy, however, and some pacing team members might choose avoidance at some parts of the race and attention at other times.

Takai's spin on the subject was to identify five attention strategies that contributed to good race times.

1. Body check. How does your whole body feel? Are you loose and relaxed? Any tight spots (such as a sore shoulder) might be a signal to slow down.

2. Tempo test. How's the rhythm of your running? Do you feel smo-o-o-th? You should flow along the ground as though this were an easy practice run.

3. Leg rest. Can your legs continue to carry you at this pace? Any cramps? Discomfort? Maybe by speeding up, you'll actually feel more comfortable.

4. Image replay. Remember your most successful races or practice runs. Do you feel as well now as you did then? Recapture the glory by picturing past triumphs.

5. Motion study. Are you running well? Move out of your own body and see yourself as though through a video camera. Now improve that picture.

Takai asked each of his subjects to indicate on a 7-point rating scale (1 = never; 7 = very often) how often they used these strategies to recall pace in a race. He then compared how close the runners came to their "predicted" time with their ability to run a 5-K. This permitted Takai to rate them as "accurate" or "inaccurate" recallers. Results showed that the accurate recallers were better pacers, capable of running steady through the race. "Overall," says Takai, "the accurate recallers ran with a steady pace throughout the race, while the inaccurate recallers were likely to decrease the pace after the first 5-K."

Maintaining a steady pace or even having the energy to pick up the pace late in the race can be a very effective strategy, since you will pass a lot of runners in the last half dozen miles who went out too fast. Deena Kastor applied that approach in winning a bronze medal at the 2004 Olympic Games. "The smartest way to race is to pick off runners," Kastor commented after her third-place finish. "I started to get an adrenaline rush every time I saw another girl in front of me."

When I ran marathons near the front of the pack, I always considered concentration to be as important an ability as a high max VO_2. I focused on every stride and was acutely aware of any signals my body was sending. I always liked the idea of running on scenic courses—except I almost never saw the scenery!

THE BETTER I RAN, THE LESS I RECALLED OF THE SURROUNDINGS.

Usually the better I ran, the less I recalled of the surroundings. I'd run the Boston Marathon 10 times and knew that the course passed somewhere near Fenway Park, where the Boston Red Sox played, but I was unaware how near until one year in the 1970s when I first covered the race for *Runner's World* as a journalist. After the lead runners had finished the race and offered their postrace comments, I decided to wander backward over the course to watch the remaining runners finishing. Less than a mile from the finish line, I came upon Fenway Park, home of the Boston Red Sox. I was startled. Intellectually, I had realized that Fenway Park was right on the course, but I had never seen it before. For me to have missed it while racing, my field of vision must have been very narrow.

WHAT TOP RUNNERS DO

Other runners agree on the value of concentration. Olympic marathoner Don Kardong states, "It's absolutely essential that you concentrate on your competition, monitor your body feedback, and not lose touch with what's happening around you. If you lose concentration in a good, competitive 10-K field, you immediately drop off the pace. There's never time to think those favorite thoughts you have on easy training runs."

Greg Meyer, who struggled to regain his form after winning Boston in 1983, ran several meets in Europe one summer. "I'd lose concentration for a lap or two," Meyer told me, "and that would get me out of the race. I'd drift off, get gapped, and never make it up."

Meyer felt that a series of injuries contributed to his inability to concentrate. "You start focusing on the injuries instead of racing," he said. But it's possible that in winning Boston, he had satisfied many of the inner demons that had driven him to success. He may have lost some of his will to win, and with it an ability to concentrate.

Dick Buerkle was top-ranked in the 5000 meters on the track in 1974 and set an indoor mile record in 1978. He noticed that in both years his ability to concentrate was at its highest. "I'd go for an 18-miler every weekend and be totally focused," he recalls. "Other years, I'd find myself daydreaming."

Kardong notes that some distance runners have difficulty switching from roads to track or cross-country. He suspects that the biggest factor isn't training but concentration: "When in an unfamiliar setting, you're distracted by it initially. Later, you adapt."

During a marathon, Bill Rodgers would think of specific things to help him concentrate: splits, competition, the course, the wind. If he has a chance to win, he thinks: "What's my best way to race certain individuals?"

Greg Meyer learned he could concentrate better in training if he ran fartlek, rather than straight distance: "Rather than doing mindless 20-milers, you vary the pace, which forces you to pay attention." Sue King, while training for the New York City Marathon, found she could concentrate more by running long runs alone so the conversation of friends didn't distract her.

"The physical training your body does during the 18-week buildup to the marathon can all be washed away if the mind wanders," says Frank Walaitis, a 3:02 runner from Carpentersville, Illinois.

Rodgers believes concentration must begin before a race. He avoids warming up with others, preferring to think of the upcoming race. He also believes that the clinics, dinners, and social events he's attended as part of sponsor commitments diminished his concentration. I agree. As a consultant to the Chicago Marathon, I have commitments in the weeks leading up to the race. I need to visit all five of the CARA training classes in five different areas of the city on 5 successive days. There are press conferences and social events to attend. At the expo on Friday and Saturday, when I am not talking to individual runners at my booth, I'm usually standing on a stage, talking to large groups. Race director Carey Pinkowski will usually ask me to say a few words at the pasta party. It's fun, and I love it until that time on Sunday morning when I have to get up and run the race. I have rarely run well at Chicago. My mind hasn't been in it. Recently, I've realized that I needed to either not run the race or run it at a low throttle setting, leaving my serious racing for elsewhere. Leading pacing teams, which I have done at Chicago and for *Runner's World* in other cities, also can be a draining experience because you're focusing on the success of others rather than your own.

Nevertheless, many runners are less interested in developing or maintaining their powers of concentration in order to run fast. They're more interested in keeping mind and body together long enough to finish!

Judith Henderson of Denver counts steps—almost for the entire length of the race. "If I count every left-foot plant," says Henderson, "it takes 440 left steps to run a mile. I keep the game up even through aid stations and brief conversations with other runners. It's like a mental metronome. In the final miles of the marathon, I keep my focus on just the numbers, and it's amazing how much this helps to keep moving you forward."

Tracy Musacchio of Philadelphia works out math problems in her head: "It's 70 degrees out. What's that in Celsius? How high can I name prime numbers? What's 86 squared? It seems silly, but it works for me."

While training for a marathon, Lori Hauswirth of Merrill, Wisconsin, keeps herself moving with what might be considered personal threats. "If I'm having a bad run, I tell myself that if I stop to walk, I won't qualify for Boston," says Hauswirth, who did so at Chicago in 2004 with 33 seconds to spare.

Autumn Evans of Melbourne Beach, Florida, uses a similar drill sergeant approach when it comes to the final miles: "I resort to telling myself, 'Suck it up, you weenie!' I don't want to disappoint myself by giving up or quitting."

Nicole Long of St. Louis used an omen to spur her to a Boston qualifying time. "I told myself around 19 miles that I'd qualify for Boston if I saw a beagle on the course. So I spent the next several miles looking for one. Luckily, I spotted a man with a beagle. Later I saw the same man and his beagle at the finish line. I thanked him for bringing it."

LEARNING TO CONCENTRATE

It might be risky for a runner to depend on the supply of beagles in the crowd for success. Inevitably, learning to improve your attention span and ability to concentrate for longer periods may prove the best strategy. But how can you learn to concentrate? How do you focus your mind on the business at foot?

At least one study shows that the average runner can learn to think like the elite runner. Researcher Hein Helgo Schomer, PhD, of the University of Cape Town in South Africa improved the concentration of a group of 10 nonelite runners over a period of 5 weeks. Before they were coached, the runners used association (being tuned in to their bodies) only 45 percent of the time. By the 5th week under Schomer's instruction, they were associating 70 percent of the time while running, and their average training intensity also increased.

Dr. Anderson states that the average runner probably associates about 30 to 40 percent of the time while running. He considers 60 to 70 percent optimal, and 90 to 100 percent necessary for supreme efforts. "Association is clearly a strategy you can use to reach your

true potential as a runner," he says. "Associative thinking can increase your ability to handle
strenuous workouts and cope
with tough races. While it
boosts your aerobic fitness, association probably also mini-

ASSOCIATION IS CLEARLY A STRATEGY YOU CAN USE TO REACH YOUR TRUE POTENTIAL AS A RUNNER.

mizes your risk of overtraining by keeping you in tune with how
your body is responding to your overall training intensity and
volume."

But learning to concentrate takes time. Each spring, once the
snow melts, I head for the track for weekly interval sessions to try
to regain speed lost after a winter of slow running. When I begin
running interval quarters, I know that to run my fastest, I have to
concentrate. Yet invariably I'll get on the backstretch and my mind
will wander and my pace will lag. Only after 5 or 6 weeks does my
concentration improve to the point where I can keep my attention
on running for a full quarter. My track times then start to drop, convincing me that the improvement results from both stronger muscles and a stronger mind.

To hone his ability to concentrate, Dick Buerkle would do long
repeats, rather than short ones, running repeat miles between 4:14
and 4:20. "It requires more effort to concentrate for 4 minutes than
for the 27 seconds it takes to run a 200," he says.

Like Buerkle, I've also found various forms of speedwork—
intervals on the track, fartlek in the woods, strides on the grass—to
be the most effective way of improving my concentration. Sometimes I would head to the golf course several times a week to run a
half dozen or more short sprints—not flat out, but close to the speed
I reach in a track mile. I do these "strides" to loosen my muscles for
other, longer and tougher workouts. Invariably I return from the
golf course running much faster, my mind totally focused.

I have difficulty concentrating during track workouts, and par-

---

THE FINAL 6 MILES

Past 20 miles is when mental strategies become most important. Conversation between friends usually has ceased by then. It's gut-it-out and head for the finish line. During the final 6 miles, concentration often spells the difference between a good and bad race. Here are some suggestions from marathoners who have used mental strategies to achieve success.

Jim Fredericks, South Milwaukee, Wisconsin: "I think about where I would be on my home training course. Six miles to go is the Grant Park Golf Course. Four miles to go is South Milwaukee High School. It makes the remaining distance seem somewhat shorter when I put it in that perspective."

Melissa Vetricek, Tampa, Florida: "It's too overwhelming to think of how many miles remain. I think minutes. When my body wants to walk, I tell it, 'Run for just 8 more minutes.' That's about how long it takes to cover a mile. When those 8 minutes are up, I say, 'Eight minutes more.' Sometimes when I'm really hurting, I say, 'One more minute.' Or 'Just take 90 steps more.' I'll bargain with the devil when it comes to those last half dozen miles."

---

ticularly on distance runs, but I usually manage to get my act together for important races: Competition tends to focus my mind. Maybe that's why I achieve speeds in competition that are beyond my reach in training.

TUNING MIND AND BODY

How do you get mind and body in tune to run long distances faster? Here are several tips to help you block out mind drift.

Prepare yourself to run. Have a game plan for workouts and particularly for important races. Where are you going to run? How fast? How far? Against whom? Get yourself in a running frame of

Colleen Gibbs, Carlsbad, California: "I use crazy ideas to counteract negative thoughts. Mick Jagger eating a banana on a unicycle worked one time. Just the distraction of conjuring up the visual pushed bad thoughts aside and killed a few of those last, long minutes."

Bob Winter, New Lenox, Illinois: "I dedicate each mile to someone, whether publicly or privately. Beginning with the next mile marker, I keep them in my thoughts. I use them for extra motivation, knowing that I'll have to report to them postrace about their mile."

Andrew Smith, Omaha, Nebraska: "I pick out a relatively close landmark and tell myself that I will run at least that far. Just before I arrive, I pick out another landmark farther down the road."

Barbara Mayer, Georgia: "I often dedicate marathons to a loved one or friend who has passed away. During the last few hundred yards of the 2001 Chicago Marathon (a month after September 11), I started to sing 'God Bless America' as loud as I could. Once I started, I couldn't stop because everybody was looking at me. I'm sure they all knew what was going through my mind."

mind. Learn to relax. Following a regular warmup routine before running can get you into the mood to perform. Find a routine that works best for you—whether chanting a mantra or stretching—and stick with it.

Discover how your body works. While running fast, try to be aware of what the various parts of your body are doing. Can you discover what it feels like to run smoothly? If so, you may be able to duplicate that feeling on other occasions. Remember: Given equal physical skills, the ability to concentrate separates the merely good runners from the great ones.

Practice instant preplay and replay. If you can imagine before running how top runners run successfully—preplay—you're halfway to emulating them. Practice running mentally as well as physically. Try replay as well. When you run well, remember how you ran. Fix that image in your memory, adding it to your mental video library.

Head for the track. Running against the clock and attempting to match preset goals forces you to concentrate. Learning to adjust to the track's rhythm—running turns, for example—also helps, as do fartlek sessions and other forms of speedwork done on trails and on the road.

Plan days of maximum concentration. Not every workout need be fully focused, but select one or more days each week to practice concentration. Racing, particularly track or cross-country races, may help focus your mind.

Avoid race-day distractions. Friends, traffic, or dogs (even beagles) can distract you from the act and art of running. Run solo when you can, to improve your concentration. If you want to succeed with your race plan, keep conversation to a minimum even if you're running with a friend.

Talk to yourself. Paul Thompson, MD, director of preventive cardiology at Hartford Hospital in Connecticut, believes runners need pep talks. "I talk to myself when I train," he says. "The year I ran best at Boston, I focused on what to tell myself during those last few miles, when it hurts." Thompson placed 16th at Boston in 1976 by telling himself, "Keep going" and "I'm a tough dude."

Landmark the course. What are the key points on the course you plan to race? Where are the hills? Where are the flats? What sections of the course will drain you, and what sections (such as by Wellesley College, where the women come out to cheer Boston marathoners) will give you strength? Don't wait until the course tour the day before the race to learn what you will be running.

Focus hardest when it counts most. If you find it difficult to concentrate during the full 26 miles of a marathon, save your focus for the miles when you need it the most. Kardong used to dissociate the first half of the race, then associate the second half. "My mind wanders at times," admits marathoner Doug Kurtis. "I like to look around and check the scenery, but I particularly try to focus late in the race, especially when I know a sub-2:20 is on the line."

Concentration can't compensate for lack of training or basic ability, but it can help you maximize your potential.

CHAPTER 21

MILE 27

YOUR RACE DOESN'T END
AT THE FINISH LINE

The most important mile of the marathon may be mile number 27, the one you walk to the hotel. Shortly after finishing the Boston Marathon one year, I sat huddled on a bench in Copley Square, wrapped in an aluminum blanket, in one hand a soft drink and in the other a cup of frozen yogurt that I was too nauseated to eat. I cursed having stayed at a hotel whose distance from the finish line would require that I walk another mile—a 27th mile, so to speak— before I could end that day's marathon experience.

Yet 15 minutes later, halfway to the hotel, frozen yogurt consumed, sipping a second soft drink, I felt my energy returning. I knew I would recover and eventually run 26 miles again.

That 27th mile is particularly important when it comes to speeding postmarathon recovery so that you can run and race again. Your actions during the first 5 seconds after crossing the line may be crucial to your recovery—as are the next 5 minutes, the next 5 hours, the next

> **YOUR ACTIONS DURING THE FIRST 5 SECONDS AFTER CROSSING THE LINE MAY BE CRUCIAL TO YOUR RECOVERY.**

5 days, and even the next 5 weeks. Postmarathon recovery is something many runners pay scant attention to. But by organizing your postrace plans as well as you organize your prerace plans, you can recover faster and more comfortably and minimize future injuries.

MINIMIZING DAMAGE

"Runners need to take responsibility for the health of their muscles, not just how fast they go," warns Linda Jaros, a massage therapist from Dedham, Massachusetts, whose clients have included Bill Rodgers and Joan Benoit Samuelson. "Recovery has to become an integral part of their training."

Indeed, recovery may be the toughest skill for a marathon runner to master. How do you snap back after more than 26 hard miles on the road? Are fatigued and sore muscles inevitable, or are there strategies you can use to make marathon recovery not only faster but less painful? What secrets can we learn from both elite and ordinary marathoners that will allow a quick return to full training—and the next starting line? What do scientists suggest based on laboratory research, not only for the morning after but for the week after?

David L. Costill, PhD, of the human performance laboratory at Ball State University in Muncie, Indiana, has researched, both in the lab and on the road, the damage marathons do to the body. In numerous studies, Dr. Costill has reviewed the postrace drinking, eating, and training habits of marathoners. His suggestions for recovery: Drink plenty of fluids, carbo-load after the race (as well as before), and don't start running again too soon. "A lot of things happen to the body as a result of running the marathon," he says. "You become overheated, dehydrated, and muscle-depleted. Your hormonal milieu gets thrown out of whack, and you traumatize your muscles. You have to bide your time to get your body back in balance."

Since 1974, Jack H. Scaff Jr., MD, founder of the Honolulu Marathon and author of *My First Marathon*, has supervised the Honolulu Marathon Clinic, a group that meets Sundays in Kapiolani Park to train for that marathon. After watching his group's recuperative efforts after the marathon one year, Dr. Scaff commented, "The runners felt so good about their achievement, they would bounce back too soon. The rate of injuries was exponential. We finally canceled the clinic for 3 months following the marathon to try to get the runners to take it easy."

Benji Durden of Boulder, Colorado, has observed the effects of marathon running on the body as a runner and as a coach of others, including 2:26:40 marathoner Kim Jones. Durden recalls running a 2:15 at Boston in 1978—cutting 4 minutes off his best time—then spraining an ankle the following week. "My body had not fully recovered," he notes. While conceding that total rest may be the best postmarathon prescription, Durden contends that runners may have conflicting psychological needs. "As a coach, I try to accept the best advice from the scientists and adapt it based on a combination of intuition and experience," he says.

KEEP MOVING

Want to recover as rapidly as possible following your next marathon? First, don't stop as soon as you cross the finish line. You may have no choice, particularly at major races where you will be prodded to jog and walk through the finish chute, after which you run a gauntlet that includes having various items pressed onto you: your medal, fluids and food, an aluminum blanket, and your gear brought from the starting line. Having accepted all this, you may need to walk what seems an unconscionably long distance to be greeted by friends and family.

Whether prodded or not, you need to keep moving to allow your stressed system a chance to gradually attain a steady state and also to avoid what Dr. Scaff calls "the postrace collapse phenomenon." This, he says, is when "a runner looks good coming across the finish line, sits down too soon, then 20 minutes later must be taken to the first aid tent with heatstroke or cramps." Blood pressure can drop too quickly, sometimes with disastrous results. "Walking around a bit seems to prevent this from happening," says Dr. Scaff.

How much you walk depends on your condition at the end of the

DEAD MEN WALKING

Most runners concede that walking for a mile or two after finishing a marathon probably promotes quick recovery. Forcing yourself to do so, however, is not always easy—unless you get lost, as did Matt Ferrara of Troy, New York, after the Buffalo Marathon. Despite staying in a hotel only one block from the finish line, Ferrara walked nearly a mile before realizing that he somehow had missed his hotel. "When I finally got back to the hotel," Ferrara recalls, "I was feeling good enough to drive to Niagara Falls for some sightseeing."

"Walking is a great way to cool down," suggests Michele Keane of Westlake, Ohio. "After the Chicago Marathon, I spent the rest of the afternoon walking and shopping up and down Michigan Avenue. It was great to have salesclerks and other shoppers ask me how I did, since I wore my medal proudly."

The size of many major marathons often forces finished runners to walk around, looking for loved ones and friends. At the Marine Corps Marathon, Mark Felipe of Arlington, Virginia, spotted his wife standing beside the course somewhere between miles 25 and 26. "I'll meet you here!" she shouted to him. Unfortunately, after crossing the finish line, Felipe couldn't remember where the "here" was. After 45 minutes, he found a pay phone and called his wife's cellular phone. "The walking around probably helped me keep my legs loose after the beating I gave them," conceded Felipe.

Paula Sue Russell of Findlay, Ohio, recalls finishing her first marathon with friends in Chicago: "We walked through the recovery area, gathering bagels, yogurt, water, and Gatorade. I was fine until we got to the Bud Beer area. Everyone sat down on the ground to drink their beer. By the time I got my stiff body down, everyone was finished and getting up to leave."

Russell found it most difficult to navigate curbs and steps. "I wish someone would have told me to turn around and go down them backward," she says.

race. "If your body is telling you to collapse in a heap, walking around is not easy," says Dr. Costill. "But continuing to move for a while will maintain your circulation, keeping the blood pumping through the muscles. This should aid short-term recovery."

Warning: Don't take the advice to keep moving to excess. Many compulsive runners feel the need to "cool down" by jogging a mile or two, even after a marathon. Although this may make sense following a 10-K race, it is not wise after a 42.2-K race. No scientific studies have shown any benefits from postrace running. You simply increase your chance of injury by continuing to run.

DRINK UP

As long as you're walking, head in the direction of the tables with fluids. All the experts—scientists and experienced marathoners alike—advise that you make an immediate and continuing effort to replace the several liters of liquid your system has lost during 26 miles on the road. Grab the first cup of liquid thrust into your hand and start sipping at once, no matter how nauseated you feel.

HUMAN THIRST IS NOT AN ACCURATE GAUGE OF DEHYDRATION.

Dr. Scaff recommends sipping at the rate of ½ ounce a minute. And while going about other recuperative activities for the next several hours, keep a drink in your hand and continue drinking.

Like most experts, Dr. Costill emphasizes that human thirst is not an accurate gauge of dehydration. "Drink more than you desire," he advises.

If the first cup thrust into your hand is water, accept it thankfully and sip on it, but look for the table where they have drinks with at least some dilute form of sugar, whether in a so-called replacement drink (such as Gatorade), a soft drink, or a fruit drink. Your primary need is to replace fluids, but you have also depleted your muscles of glycogen and need to replace that as well. "Try to get your blood sugar back to normal as quickly as possible," says Durden.

The best time for glycogen replacement, according to research by Edward F. Coyle, PhD, of the department of kinesiology at the University of Texas at Austin, is during the first 2 hours after the race. "The muscles absorb glycogen like a sponge," he says. "Four and 6 hours after the race, the absorption rate starts to decline." Nutritionists may argue that generally speaking, fruit drinks (because they contain vitamins and minerals) are superior to sugar drinks—and this certainly is true—but Dr. Costill claims that when it comes to glycogen replacement, the body doesn't know the difference between one sugar and another.

Doug Kurtis never minded having to undergo drug testing after winning a marathon. But in order to provide the necessary urine specimen, Kurtis found he had to drink steadily for 2 hours. "That forced me to ingest a lot of fluids," says Kurtis. "I feel that helped my recovery."

Two postmarathon drinks to avoid: diet soft drinks because they provide no glucose boost (having just burned approximately 2,600 calories, your goal should not be weight loss) and alcoholic beverages because they serve as a diuretic. That postrace beer may taste good, but it will eventually have a negative effect on fluid balance. If you drink a beer, do so only after you have already ingested twice the volume of other fluids.

Another good choice for postrace nutrition is an energy bar, but Liz Applegate, Ph.D., a professor at the University of California at Davis and author of *Eat Smart, Play Hard*, suggests that you carefully read the labels before deciding which energy bar to ingest prerace and which to save for postrace. "Not all energy bars have the same purpose," warns Dr. Applegate. "Before the race, you want a bar that is almost entirely carbohydrates. But after the race, your choice should be a bar with some protein added, which will promote recovery."

GET OFF YOUR FEET

After spending the first 5 to 10 minutes walking around and obtaining something to drink, get off your feet. Listen to your body. "Do what it tells you to do," says Dr. Costill. "Get horizontal." Pick a comfortable spot, preferably in the shade, and elevate your feet, easing the flow of blood to the heart. Dr. Costill speculates that some of the muscle soreness and stiffness experienced immediately after a race may be related to edema, swelling caused by the intramuscular pressure of accumulated fluids in the lower legs. "Elevating the legs may speed recovery," he suggests.

You can assist your recovery with gentle self-massage. But don't knead, advises my massage therapist, Patty Longnecker Van Hyfte of the Harbor Country Day Spa in New Buffalo, Michigan. Van Hyfte advises that you stroke your leg muscles gently toward the heart. Durden and New York City marathon winner Priscilla Welch recommend massaging with ice to reduce the swelling. Hosing your legs with cold water is another option.

Bill Rodgers, four-time winner of both the Boston and New York City marathons, likes to do some postrace stretching while lying down. If you choose to do the same, don't stretch excessively. Your muscles most likely are stiff and damaged; you don't want to traumatize them further.

Some experts even question the value of stretching. A study at the University of Texas at Tyler indicated that static stretching failed to prevent muscle soreness later. Researchers Katherine C. Buroker and James A. Schwane, PhD, concede that stretching helps maintain flexibility, but they say that stretching immediately after strenuous exercise is the wrong time for it. When Dr. Scaff surveyed members of his Honolulu Marathon Clinic, he discovered that those who stretched most also suffered the most injuries. Scientists remain divided on the value of stretching, so your best bet is to keep any stretching short and simple after a marathon.

While resting, continue to sip fluids—this is still your primary recovery strategy. Using a bent straw makes it easier to drink while horizontal. To guarantee a supply, place a bottle of your favorite postrace drink in your tote bag. If you don't have to use it, no problem. Better to have too much fluid available than too little.

BEGIN TO REFUEL

Your immediate concern after the race may be fluid replacement, but within an hour after the race, you should begin shifting to more solid foods. This may be particularly important if sugar from replacement drinks makes you nauseous, as food can slow down sugar absorption to help prevent the nausea. Ken Young, a top trail runner from northern California and the former coach of 2:11 marathoner Don Janicki, likes to eat saltines to help settle his stomach. Fruit is a good start, particularly bananas, because they are easy to digest and are a good way to replace lost potassium. Don't become obsessed with instant mineral replacement, however. Eating several well-balanced meals within the next 24 hours will take care of electrolytes lost through sweating.

"Food has real nutritional value, whereas sports drinks are just sugar," says Nancy Clark, RD, director of nutrition services for SportsMedicine Brookline in Boston and author of *Nancy Clark's Sports Nutrition Guidebook*. Clark recommends fruit or yogurt (frozen and otherwise) as a superior snack to cookies or candy bars. Research by Dr. Coyle indicates that 1 gram of carbohydrate per kilogram of body weight per hour is necessary for the most efficient glycogen replacement. That translates to 2 calories per pound, or 300 calories for a 150-pound runner. Clark suggests that a marathoner drink a glass of orange juice and eat one banana and a cup of yogurt the first hour, then repeat that the second hour.

As a practical matter, I'll grab anything handy, particularly those chocolate chip cookies at the end of the table. Immediately after a marathon, I'm like a shark feeding. Anything in close range of my mouth gets consumed.

CONSIDER MASSAGE

Many major marathons provide massage tents with teams of trained massage therapists ready to give a soothing rubdown. According to Jaros, massage helps push waste products from the muscles into the blood system for recirculation and elimination. Most runners find they feel better after a full-body massage.

Jaros cautions against getting a strenuous massage too soon after a marathon, however. Early finishers sometimes head straight to the massage tent to beat the crowd, but it's preferable to wait 45 minutes so you can give yourself time to rehydrate and cool down. And don't allow therapists to poke and probe your muscles as vigorously as they might during a regular session. The best postmarathon massage, according to therapist Rich Phaigh of Eugene, Oregon, begins with the lower back and the buttocks to relax those muscles and get intramuscular fluids flowing, then works gently on the legs with long, flowing motions toward the heart. If the massage hurts, ask the therapist to be gentler; if it still hurts, thank the therapist graciously and get off the table.

For those athletes with a regular massage therapist, the best time for a massage may be 24 to 48 hours after the race, the time when muscle soreness usually peaks. In preparing for marathons, I scheduled appointments with my regular massage therapist the afternoon before the race and 2 days after. When running in a different city— or a different country—I try to locate a massage therapist by networking with other runners. It's amazing how the Internet has made it easier to do this.

Avoid hot baths or showers, which may increase inflammation and unnecessarily elevate your body temperature. That bubbling whirlpool back at the motel may look inviting, but leave it to the kids. Opt for a cool shower. "Getting your body temperature back down will help you recover faster," says Dr. Costill. Jaros suggests a cold bath followed by a warm (not hot) shower.

Amanda Musacchio of Villa Park, Illinois, a regular poster to my online bulletin boards, strongly believes in ice baths. She has converted many runners into following this admittedly scary practice. You fill your bathtub with cold water, then add ice cubes to drop the temperature even further before sliding gently into the water. "Ice baths sound painful," says Musacchio, "but they really speed recovery by reducing swelling." Obviously, this is a strategy to employ only after returning home or to your hotel room. After long runs, I often chill my legs similarly, wading either into Lake Michigan or the Atlantic Ocean, depending on whether I am at home in Indiana or in Florida during the winters.

ICE BATHS SPEED RECOVERY BY REDUCING SWELLING.

Aspirin should be avoided, according to Tufts University research. Although it may reduce the pain of sore muscles, it also prolongs the time required to repair damage.

RECOVERING AT HOME

Most marathoners don't want to abandon the scene of battle too rapidly. Admittedly, part of the enjoyment of marathoning is hanging around to see old friends and rivals, cheering their finishes, and swapping stories about the miles just covered. Don't deny yourself the opportunity to wallow awhile in the joy of your accomplishment.

But after you've gotten home and showered, jump into bed. Even if you have difficulty sleeping, at least rest for 1 to 2 hours. Then get up: It's time for more food. Three to 4 hours after finishing, sit down to a full meal. Dr. Costill claims that carbohydrates should still be the food of choice. "Nutritionally, your first meal after the marathon should resemble your last meal before," he says. Sound advice, although many marathoners rebel against having to look at one more plate of pasta and instead indulge a sudden craving for protein.

"I'm not afraid to eat a hamburger after a marathon," confesses Kurtis. "It almost feels like a reward." Bill Rodgers recalls going to a restaurant one year after placing third in the Boston Marathon and eating a hamburger, followed by a hot fudge sundae. He also fondly recalls family victory celebrations at his store with picnic lunches of chicken sandwiches supplied by his mother.

But remember that spaghetti isn't the only source of carbohydrates. "Even high-carbohydrate diets have some protein," says Clark. "Your body needs to rebuild protein, so have your chicken or steak or fish, but start with some minestrone soup. Add some extra potatoes, rolls, and juice. The secret in anything you eat is moderation. Don't focus on the meat; focus on the carbohydrates that can accompany the meat."

TAKE A BREAK

Once home, too many marathoners make the mistake of resuming training too soon. They may fear getting out of shape or feel that some easy jogging will help speed their recovery. Kurtis always runs the next day, "even if only to limp through a mile," but most of us don't have his capabilities. The body of someone who's used to 105-mile training weeks and as many as a dozen marathons a year functions differently from that of an ordinary runner.

Research by Dr. Costill suggests that recovery is speeded

> "WHEN I SAY REST, I MEAN REST," SAYS DURDEN. "NOT NAUTILUS. NOT EXERCYCLING. NOT SWIMMING. NOT WALKING. YOU REST!"

and conditioning is not affected if you do nothing for 7 to 10 days after the race. Repeat: For the week after your marathon, *do nothing!*

Durden thinks it's all right to resume easy running by the 4th day.

He wouldn't recommend the cross-training used by some recuperating marathoners. "When I say rest, I mean rest," he says. "Not Nautilus. Not exercycling. Not swimming. Not walking. You rest! I've worked with a few athletes who thought rest meant everything except run."

Moving in the pool is another matter. It may comfort the muscles if you immerse yourself in water and use gentle, nonaerobic movements to stretch and relax your arms and legs. But don't start paddling because you will simply delay recovery by burning more glycogen.

EASE BACK INTO TRAINING

Once back with running, don't run too hard or too fast too soon. Dr. Scaff recommends the 10 percent rule: No more than 10 percent of your total mileage can be spent in racing or speedwork. "After you've run a marathon, you need 260 miles of training before you enter your next event or start doing speedwork," he says. "For someone running 30 to 40 miles a week, that means 6 to 8 weeks of recovery running. Someone used to higher mileage probably recovers sooner."

Rodgers took his time coming back after marathons. "Slowly, over a period of weeks, I'd build back to regular mileage. I'd stick with once-a-day training for a while. No speed or long runs for at least 2 or 3 weeks."

Particularly after a good performance, runners need to resist the urge to come back too soon. It's tempting to increase training under the theory that more work may mean still better times. "You end up pushing yourself too hard," warns Durden. "You may get away with it for 4 to 6 weeks; then you collapse, get injured, get sick, or feel stale and overtrained. The period immediately after a good marathon is when you need to be especially cautious about your training."

POSTMARATHON BLUES

Runners crossing the finish line of a marathon do so with a combination of exhaustion and exultation. For many, it is the most exciting moment in their lives; it may also be among the most painful. Yet runners raise their arms in victory—even though 10,000 or more other runners may have finished in front of them.

One day later, after the shining medal hanging from its colorful ribbon has been placed in a drawer, the same runners must face the question of what to do next. They encounter postmarathon blues.

"We focus our lives on this one event for 5 months—and then it's done," reflects Autumn Evans of Melbourne Beach, Florida. "Now what?"

For the immediate several weeks, runners like Evans can focus on repairing their bodies. On my Web site, I feature a postmarathon training schedule that involves 5 weeks of rest and easy running. That takes care of the body, but what about the mind?

One way to cope with postmarathon blues is to pick a new goal. Maybe it is another marathon. Maybe it is a faster time. Setting a personal record or qualifying for the Boston Marathon presents a challenge to many. Your goal need not be another 26-miler. Other runners add swimming and cycling to their fitness routines and point for a triathlon.

And your next goal does not need to be running-related. My massage therapist, Patty Longnecker Van Hyfte, decided in her midforties to learn to play a violin. Would taking a course in computer science improve your business skills? How about reconnecting with those people in your life whom you abandoned temporarily while doing 4-hour runs as part of your marathon buildup?

"I didn't train properly before my first marathon," confesses Cherie Robideaux of Hailey, Idaho. "My knees hurt so badly, I swore I'd never run again. I got over those postmarathon blues, and I'm already looking forward to my third marathon."

Russell H. Pate, PhD, chairman of the department of exercise science at the University of South Carolina in Columbia, developed a 2-week recovery method through trial and error. "I'd have very minimal activity for 2 to 3 days after the race, still modest running for the remainder of the 1st week, then, over the 2nd week, gradually build to near my normal training loads. By the 3rd week, I'd be ready to run hard again." But on one occasion when he felt good after 3 days and resumed heavy training too quickly, 3 weeks later he had a breakdown featuring minor injuries and fatigue. "I learned the hard way to put the brakes on," Dr. Pate recalls.

"Studies now show you do indeed damage the muscle, creating microtrauma in muscle fibers, with activities like marathon running," he says. "No one knows what we do to the connective tissue and skeleton, but I suspect there's trauma there also. Since scientists do not yet know precisely how much time is needed for such trauma to be reversed, it's smart for runners to give themselves plenty of time with minimal running to let that healing process occur."

None of the experts—neither scientists nor coaches nor experienced road runners—can offer an exact formula for marathon recovery. Too many factors are involved, from the condition of the runner going into the race to the conditions of the race itself. Hilly courses, particularly those with downhills near the end such as Boston, do more muscle damage than flat courses. Extremes of heat or cold slow the recovery process. And runners who start out too fast and crash usually have more difficulty recovering than do those who run an even pace.

"Nature takes care of us," says Dr. Costill. "Time heals most of the damage done in the marathon." Through careful attention to the 27th mile, most of us will be back on the road again, looking forward to our next trip to the starting line.

CHAPTER 22

FINISH LINE

WHAT THESE RUNNERS LEARNED
FROM THEIR MARATHONS

Runners do learn from their marathon experiences. They learn about themselves, and they learn about others. They learn how to strengthen their bodies, but they also learn how to strengthen their minds. And often they can apply what they learn finishing a marathon to other challenges that present themselves in life. In fact, few other activities offer as much a mind-changing experience as running 26 miles 385 yards for the first time.

To tap into this knowledge source, I contacted runners both slow and fast and asked a single question: "What did you learn from your first marathon, both training for it and racing in it?" Their answers will help you prepare for your next marathon, whether you are a first-timer or a veteran.

Advertising: Putting my name on my shirt was one of the smartest things I did. Everybody cheered me by name.
—*Mary Beth Winklejohn, nurse, Springfield, Illinois*

Aid: I learned in my first marathon that regardless of age, sex, race, creed, or physical ability, every runner has a single goal: to reach the finish. To that end, we help one another in our quest because that helps all of us reach our mutual goal.
—*Scott Hala, network engineer, Huber Heights, Ohio*

Biases: I admit a past bias against runners. As a cyclist, they always seemed grim and oblivious to others using the paths. But I discovered runners are rare for their supportive spirit. As for grim, that's me now, but my fellow runners and I exchange a smile when we pass. I'm a more courteous cyclist now, too.
—*David Kleeman, children's media consultant, Chicago*

Cockiness: I did my first marathon on a bet and hit the wall because of youthful cockiness. I now tell runners to take the marathon seriously and train to beat it; otherwise, it will beat you.
—*Bob Glover, coach, New York City*

Company: After passing and being passed by the same individual several times, I asked if he wanted company. In the last 3 miles, I learned how he had given up drinking and smoking and started running in his forties. He was now running his first race of *any* kind: a marathon. What a feeling: to share this moment with him. Suddenly I realized what I, too, had accomplished. I finished my first marathon and knew I'd be back for another.
—*Anthony Capone, 38, department head of a pharmaceutical firm, Carmel, Indiana*

Competition: I learned I love to compete: against the course, against the distance, against the other runners. I love the discipline of training for a marathon.
—*Nancy Ditz, 1988 Olympian, Woodside, California*

Confidence: When I started to train for a marathon, I had no confidence that I would finish. Through support from my husband, daughters, and running friends, I finally realized I could do it. That support got me through a lot of solitary miles.
—*Kaye Hastings, pharmacist, Clarkston, Michigan*

Control: Standing on the starting line, I realized I had joined those in the human race that actively seek out challenges, that push themselves to achieve goals, that are not satisfied with the status quo. I felt fully alive and in charge of my destiny.

—*John McCarthy, financial manager, Chicago*

Difficulty: The marathon was a much tougher event than I ever had encountered. Coming from a track background (10,000 meters), I was surprised by the training one had to do for the marathon. Then race day arrives, and suddenly it is over and you have to start again for the next one.

—*Elana Meyer, Olympic silver medalist, Stellenbosch, South Africa*

Distance: It is not the competition that you should fear, but the distance. I fell in love with the distance, and the marathon became my favorite event.

—*Khalid Khannouchi, former world record holder (2:05:42), Ossining, New York*

Easy life: Running with Team in Training, I realized that even with all the training, fund-raising, stress, and doubts, my life is easy compared to the honored patients we were running for.

—*Linda Leckrone, product development manager, Ann Arbor, Michigan*

Essentials: I ran my first marathon with 14 miles as my longest training run. I discovered the significance of long runs. I now consider them the single most important aspect of training for those who want to finish without too much pain.

—*Nels Nelson, publications manager, Plainfield, Illinois*

Family: I discovered a new love of family, including a brother-in-law who first inspired me to begin running, then took time out of his busy schedule to drive 130 miles so he could run the last few miles with me.

—*Brad Merrill, tax manager, Sandy, Utah*

Fears: I learned the joy of facing fear and conquering it. The fear of the first 6-miler was no less than the fear of the last 20-miler in training, yet I beat them both. Conquering the marathon itself then became merely an exercise in repeating what I had done before.
—*Pam Cooper, 35, accountant, Fountain Hills, Arizona*

Focus: A month before my marathon, I ran a half marathon. The result: several annoying injuries. I learned not to race too much while training.
—*George Christopher, consultant, Elmhurst, Illinois*

Foolishness: Midway through my training, I came down with a foot injury. My body told me to rest. My friends told me to rest. My podiatrist told me to rest. I went out for a 5-mile run to see if my foot was better. I lost another full week of training.
—*Patrick Ulman, consultant, Chicago*

The force: My decision to run my first marathon was very deliberate. After I made the commitment, I discovered I was being guided by an inside force that I never knew existed. When things got tough, I tapped into this force. I know now that I'll get through whatever life puts in my path.
—*Cindy Pepler, university relations manager, Seattle*

Friendships: Special friendships emerge during the course of 26 miles. These friendships may be fleeting but are no less real. No introductions, no conversations. You run together, pushing each other over many miles. Sometimes you separate, only to come together later on. When you're in the chute—if your new friend is still around—you look over and say, "Great race," and head your separate ways. It's a wonderful aspect of the marathon experience.
—*Jim Goodreau, chiropractor, Wheaton, Illinois*

Goals: Set very short term goals: water station to water station.
—*Michele Juliano, sales manager, Center Moriches, New York*

High heels: After my 18-miler, I spent the next dozen hours at a wedding in 4-inch stiletto heels. My calves felt like concrete the next day.
—*Cindyjo Blair, art teacher, Vernon Hills, Illinois*

Inner strength: Even when you have gone as far as you can, and everything hurts and you are staring at the specter of self-doubt, you can find a bit more strength deep inside you, if you look closely enough.
—*Thomas Davis, fire protection specialist, Baltimore*

Inspiration: I learned I could be an inspiration to others. This was shocking because I had never thought of myself as an athlete. Shortly before my first marathon, a couch potato friend of mine started running, following my lead. A woman I trained with had never run more than a half marathon but decided to run the full when I did. My parents, who were getting older and generally heavier, started exercising on a regular basis and felt better and happier than they had in years.
—*Linda Leckrone, product development manager, Ann Arbor, Michigan*

Kids: A high-five from an unknown child transfers enough energy and willpower to get you another few miles.
—*Roger Bottum, chief operating officer, Chicago*

Kindness: I discovered the kindness of spectators. Does this happen in any other sport? During a very hot 18th mile, a man stepped off the sidewalk and handed me a peeled orange. I was too worn down to even mumble thanks, but that random act of kindness got me back on pace and resulted in a strong finish.
—*Mike Kuykendall, finance manager, Spring, Texas*

Layers: I discovered who I was. As I pushed my body to levels I never had dreamed of, I felt the layers I hide behind peel away. I no longer was "the wife of," "the mommy of," "the daughter of." I encountered a strong, healthy woman who feels her best without makeup and with wet hair and blistered feet. When I return from a run and see my family, I know this is the Real Me. How I look, how clean my house is, all the other clutter in life has become unimportant. My true self shines through.

—*Edie Bourque, pediatric nurse practitioner, Crystal Lake, Illinois*

Learning: I'm still learning. Eat good carbs and cooked veggies until you're absolutely full. Don't look at the racecourse; what you don't know can't hurt you. Don't trust the pace charts. Get to the starting line with plenty of time on your hands.

—*Joan Benoit Samuelson, 1984 Olympic champion, Freeport, Maine*

Listen: I learned two things in my first marathon. One, listen to people who have run lots of marathons. They usually know what they're talking about. And two, no matter how fit you are, the last few miles are really going to hurt.

—*Don Kardong, fourth in the 1976 Olympic marathon, Spokane, Washington*

Mindset: After running my first marathon several years ago, I learned that I should never underestimate myself. No matter what anyone says, I can do anything I set my mind to!

—*Susan Henning, sales, Bartlett, Illinois*

Motivation: Watching my first marathon, I felt both joy and guilt. The joy was in seeing folks like me reaching their goals. The guilt was thinking I should be out there with them. The following year I ran a marathon myself. I not only experienced the joy, but I eliminated the guilt.

—*Paul Jankowski, banker, Valparaiso, Indiana*

My time: While training for a marathon, I discovered early-morning time was my time. It cleared my head, it tested my legs, it provided me with focus for the day. There's something very powerful about getting up every morning and getting out on the road before the world starts to stir. I've been running for 2 years now, and they have been the healthiest 2 years of my life, physically and psychologically.
—*Melanie Morrissey, education researcher, Austin, Texas*

Old shoes: I kept running too long on old shoes. The result was shin splints. I recovered, but for a while I feared I might miss the marathon. I now throw shoes away before they become a problem.
—*Rae-Ann Knaga Hopwood, operations manager, Independence, Kentucky*

Overtraining: I ran more than my schedule suggested. Luckily I was not injured, but it took a week of next to no running for my legs to feel better. The exhaustion was enough to tell me to apply the brakes.
—*Ronald Olech, marketing coordinator, Chicago*

Pain: Pain is very possible, but not impossible.
—*Diego Ponieman, physician, Fairmont, West Virginia*

Playground wisdom: Our 5 year old told me that I could win the marathon if I keep swinging my arms when I run. He said it works for him on the playground.
—*Joe Gow, programmer, Huntley, Illinois*

Power: Finishing a marathon was much more emotionally powerful than anything I could have expected. It was an exquisite combination of pain, relief, and pride. It was all I could do to keep from crying.
—*Pete Jones, finance manager, Denver*

Pride: The pride in finishing a marathon is much greater than all the pain endured during the marathon.

—Russell Allwein, financial specialist, Ellicott City, Maryland

Promises, promises: Never promise your husband before your first marathon that this will be the only time.

—Gail Johnson, director of continuing education, Rome, Georgia

Race day: Don't do anything in the race you haven't done in training, particularly in long runs. I put a new pair of insoles in my shoes and ran with them for most of the taper. However, what's comfortable for 6 miles can be torture by 26 miles. In the marathon, they blistered my feet badly.

—Steve Scott, computer software consultant, St. Charles, Illinois

Repeat: What started as a desire to run just one marathon became a desire to do more. The feeling when I crossed that finish line was so totally awesome, it was an experience that I wanted to repeat over and over again.

—Sherry Kent, loan officer, Hutchinson, Kansas

Saints: Volunteers on the racecourse are all saints for a day.

—Duke Karnes, sales manager, Overland Park, Kansas

Sense: Those summer weekends occupied by long runs, staying in on Saturday nights while my friends went out on the town, dragging myself out of bed hours before my body wanted me to—it all suddenly made sense as soon as I crossed the finish line.

—Ken Darlington, engineer, Toronto

Steadiness: Slow and steady wins the race. In my first marathon, two college buddies and I were setting what we thought was a reasonable pace. My dad thought differently. After a couple of miles, he declared, "You boys go on. Don't wait on me." About 16 miles later, he came chugging past and beat us all by 15 minutes.

—Mike McLaughlin, editor, Raleigh, North Carolina

Strangers: A few miles from the finish, I was whipped. This couple jogged a few strides with me, asked me how I was doing, and kept saying things like "You're almost there." I got so much from them and the crowds that I'm tempted to skip the marathon one year just so I can stand on the streets and encourage others.
—*Nels Nelson, publications manager, Plainfield, Illinois*

Stretching: I never took time to stretch before my first marathon. I'd jump out of bed, throw on running clothes, and charge out the door. I spent 2 months with ITB syndrome. Now I stretch when I get up and walk before starting to run. I now run without pain.
—*Barbara Tomasek, nurse, Darien, Illinois*

Support: When I decided to run Boston, I never would have gotten through all the training if it hadn't been for my coach, Arnie Briggs. He validated my perception of myself as an athlete. Sometimes we think we do everything on our own, but I realized then that support from others is essential.
—*Kathrine Switzer, Avon program director, New York City*

Surprises: Even though all the training runs go perfectly well, it does not mean that the marathon will go the same and one won't be faced with an unexpected challenge.
—*Ruchir Bakshi, technical support analyst, Atlanta*

Tourist: The marathon went by much quicker than I expected. The new scenery, the crowds, more runners than I had ever seen in one place. I felt like a tourist.
—*Joseph Hanson, management consultant, Wheaton, Illinois*

Training: The training was as memorable as the race itself. It wasn't always easy; it wasn't always fun. But I've seen more beautiful sunrises than I can recall, strengthened friendships in a way that can only be done through encouraging each other through rough runs and rejoicing after great ones. I reached deep within myself to discover the woman who will not give up, no matter what. The word "cannot" has been removed from my vocabulary. We are all winners.

—*Gail Johnson, director of continuing education, Rome, Georgia*

Trip: Training for my first marathon taught me that life truly is about "the trip" and not some final destination.

—*Rae-Ann Knaga Hopwood, operations manager, Independence, Kentucky*

Void: I often had wondered why people trained for and ran marathons. In fact, for most of my life, I thought it was a rather "extreme" sport and a ridiculous way to torture the body. I would hear people complain about their knees, ankles, calves, and parts of their body that you needed a medical dictionary to define. People would say they run marathons for fitness, weight loss, or endurance, but there are less arduous ways to get those benefits. Then, 2 years ago, my husband was diagnosed with and died of cancer. For the last year of his life, he had difficulty walking, much less running. He complained about his knees, shins, ankles, calves, and every other part of his body. His death left a big void in my life. What I learned from my first marathon is that the training can serve to fill the void and that running is the best antidepressant on the market, with virtually no cost or negative side effects. I learned to be grateful that I am healthy enough to be able to train for a marathon. So when I am asked why I am running a marathon, it's because I can!

—*Peggy H. Moore, marketing director, Madison, Wisconsin*

Vulnerability: Injury while training for my first marathon taught me that the human body can withstand serious punishment, yet is so vulnerable.

—*Russell Allwein, financial specialist, Elliott City, Missouri*

Walking: There is no shame walking through water stations—or any other part of the marathon, either. Doing so early can help you late.
—*Brad Merrill, tax manager, Sandy, Utah*

Waste: I realized how much time I wasted doing nothing. An hour spent watching TV became a 7-mile run. Time wasted daydreaming became time spent in the morning sun. It's about setting priorities.
—*Bob Winter, teacher, New Lenox, Illinois*

Will: I learned I can't run a good marathon off 10-K training. At the end of the marathon—if you haven't trained properly—there is a lack of will to run fast, or maybe even to finish.
—*David Morris, 2:09:32 marathoner, Missoula, Montana*

APPENDIX
TRAINING PROGRAMS

NOVICE, INTERMEDIATE, AND
ADVANCED SCHEDULES

The five training schedules that follow originally were designed for the CARA marathon training class in Chicago. As explained in Chapter 6, these schedules for novice, intermediate, and advanced runners evolved over a period of time with input from a number of people, but we also learned from the runners we coached.

Use these charts as your basic guides, being aware that even more detailed advice can be found on my Web site at www.halhigdon.com. I also offer the same five schedules in an interactive format, allowing you to sign up to get daily e-mail messages from me telling you what to run. Never before has training for a marathon been easier, but you still need to get out there and run the miles.

Before you start, here are a few preliminary words of advice as to which program might work best for you.

Novice. People differ greatly in ability, but I recommend that even experienced runners use the Novice program for their first marathons, choosing as a goal finishing, not finishing with a fast time. The key to the Novice program is the long runs, which build from 6 to 20 miles. You can skip an occasional workout, or juggle the schedule depending on other commitments, but do not cheat on the long runs. I suggest doing your long runs on Saturdays, following with some relaxing cross-training on Sundays. If that pattern doesn't work for you, feel free to adjust it.

As the weekend mileage builds, the weekday mileage also builds; midweek workouts on Wednesdays go from 3 to 10 miles. Tuesdays and Thursdays offer easy days, with workouts increasing from 3 to 5 miles. Novice runners rest on Fridays and Mondays, before and after the tough weekend training.

MARATHON TRAINING SCHEDULE: NOVICE

Week	Mon	Tue	Wed	Thu	Fri	Sat	Sun
1	rest	3-mi run	3-mi run	3-mi run	rest	**6**	cross
2	rest	3-mi run	3-mi run	3-mi run	rest	**7**	cross
3	rest	3-mi run	4-mi run	3-mi run	rest	**5**	cross
4	rest	3-mi run	4-mi run	3-mi run	rest	**9**	cross
5	rest	3-mi run	5-mi run	3-mi run	rest	**10**	cross
6	rest	3-mi run	5-mi run	3-mi run	rest	**7**	cross
7	rest	3-mi run	6-mi run	3-mi run	rest	**12**	cross
8	rest	3-mi run	6-mi run	3-mi run	rest	**13**	cross
9	rest	3-mi run	7-mi run	4-mi run	rest	**10**	cross
10	rest	3-mi run	7-mi run	4-mi run	rest	**15**	cross
11	rest	4-mi run	8-mi run	4-mi run	rest	**16**	cross
12	rest	4-mi run	8-mi run	5-mi run	rest	**12**	cross
13	rest	4-mi run	9-mi run	5-mi run	rest	**18**	cross
14	rest	5-mi run	9-mi run	5-mi run	rest	**14**	cross
15	rest	5-mi run	10-mi run	5-mi run	rest	**20**	cross
16	rest	5-mi run	8-mi run	4-mi run	rest	**12**	cross
17	rest	4-mi run	6-mi run	3-mi run	rest	**8**	cross
18	rest	3-mi run	4-mi run	2-mi run	rest	rest	**race**

Intermediate. Once you have completed one or more marathons, you may want to upgrade your training so as to improve. The Intermediate programs provide a step up in mileage and difficulty. The pattern is slightly different, with cross-training moved to Mondays and two runs scheduled for the weekends: a short run on Saturdays, most often done at marathon pace (as indicated "mi pace" on the schedules), and the long run on Sundays. Although you can change that order, it usually works best to do the faster run first, then follow with the longer run at a slower pace. Midweek mileage is somewhat different from that in the Novice program, but the pattern remains the same. Fridays are rest days in all my programs.

The difference between Intermediate-I and Intermediate-II is slightly elevated mileage, the logical next step as you move up the ladder of difficulty. In the former, you do two 20-milers; in the latter, you do three.

MARATHON TRAINING SCHEDULE: INTERMEDIATE-I

Week	Mon	Tue	Wed	Thu	Fri	Sat	Sun
1	cross	3-mi run	5-mi run	3-mi run	rest	5-mi pace	**8**
2	cross	3-mi run	5-mi run	3-mi run	rest	5-mi run	**9**
3	cross	3-mi run	5-mi run	3-mi run	rest	5-mi pace	**6**
4	cross	3-mi run	6-mi run	3-mi run	rest	6-mi pace	**11**
5	cross	3-mi run	6-mi run	3-mi run	rest	6-mi run	**12**
6	cross	3-mi run	5-mi run	3-mi run	rest	6-mi pace	**9**
7	cross	4-mi run	7-mi run	4-mi run	rest	7-mi pace	**14**
8	cross	4-mi run	7-mi run	4-mi run	rest	7-mi run	**15**
9	cross	4-mi run	5-mi run	4-mi run	rest	7-mi pace	**11**
10	cross	4-mi run	8-mi run	4-mi run	rest	8-mi pace	**17**
11	cross	5-mi run	8-mi run	5-mi run	rest	8-mi run	**18**
12	cross	5-mi run	5-mi run	5-mi run	rest	8-mi pace	**13**
13	cross	5-mi run	8-mi run	5-mi run	rest	5m pace	**20**
14	cross	5-mi run	5-mi run	5-mi run	rest	8-mi run	**12**
15	cross	5-mi run	8-mi run	5-mi run	rest	5-mi pace	**20**
16	cross	5-mi run	6-mi run	5-mi run	rest	4-mi pace	**12**
17	cross	4-mi run	5-mi run	4-mi run	rest	3-mi run	**8**
18	cross	3-mi run	4-mi run	rest	rest	2-mi run	**race**

MARATHON TRAINING SCHEDULE: INTERMEDIATE-II

Week	Mon	Tue	Wed	Thu	Fri	Sat	Sun
1	cross	3-mi run	5-mi run	3-mi run	rest	5-mi pace	**10**
2	cross	3-mi run	5-mi run	3-mi run	rest	5-mi run	**11**
3	cross	3-mi run	6-mi run	3-mi run	rest	6-mi pace	**8**
4	cross	3-mi run	6-mi run	3-mi run	rest	6-mi pace	**13**
5	cross	3-mi run	7-mi run	3-mi run	rest	7-mi run	**14**
6	cross	3-mi run	7-mi run	3-mi run	rest	7-mi pace	**10**
7	cross	4-mi run	8-mi run	4-mi run	rest	8-mi pace	**16**
8	cross	4-mi run	8-mi run	4-mi run	rest	8-mi run	**17**
9	cross	4-mi run	9-mi run	4-mi run	rest	9-mi pace	**12**
10	cross	4-mi run	9-mi run	4-mi run	rest	9-mi pace	**19**
11	cross	5-mi run	10-mi run	5-mi run	rest	10-mi run	**20**
12	cross	5-mi run	6-mi run	5-mi run	rest	6-mi pace	**12**
13	cross	5-mi run	10-mi run	5-mi run	rest	10-mi pace	**20**
14	cross	5-mi run	6-mi run	5-mi run	rest	6-mi run	**12**
15	cross	5-mi run	10-mi run	5-mi run	rest	10-mi pace	**20**
16	cross	5-mi run	8-mi run	5-mi run	rest	4-mi pace	**12**
17	cross	4-mi run	6-mi run	4-mi run	rest	4-mi run	**8**
18	cross	3-mi run	4-mi run	rest	rest	2-mi run	**race**

Expert. The final steps upward are the two Advanced programs. They're slightly more mileage than in the two Intermediate programs, but the main difference is the addition of speedwork: 1 day for Advanced-I and 2 days for Advanced-II. Cross-training has been eliminated because most fast runners like to focus on running first and running only. Fridays remain rest days leading into the tough weekend workouts. I cannot emphasize strongly enough that you should avoid doing your long runs anywhere near marathon pace. That adds too much stress, particularly when coupled with the speed sessions.

Hundreds of thousands of runners have achieved success using my marathon training programs. Follow them faithfully, and I know you, too, will succeed. Good luck.

MARATHON TRAINING SCHEDULE: ADVANCED-I

Week	Mon	Tue	Wed	Thu	Fri	Sat	Sun
1	3-mi run	5-mi run	3-mi run	3 × hill	rest	5-mi pace	**10**
2	3-mi run	5-mi run	3-mi run	30 tempo	rest	5-mi run	**11**
3	3-mi run	6-mi run	3-mi run	4 × 800	rest	6-mi pace	**8**
4	3-mi run	6-mi run	3-mi run	4 × hill	rest	6-mi pace	**13**
5	3-mi run	7-mi run	3-mi run	35 tempo	rest	7-mi run	**14**
6	3-mi run	7-mi run	3-mi run	5 × 800	rest	7-mi pace	**10**
7	3-mi run	8-mi run	4-mi run	5 × hill	rest	8-mi pace	**16**
8	3-mi run	8-mi run	4-mi run	40 tempo	rest	8-mi run	**17**
9	3-mi run	9-mi run	4-mi run	6 × 800	rest	9-mi pace	**12**
10	3-mi run	9-mi run	4-mi run	6 × hill	rest	9-mi pace	**19**
11	4-mi run	10-mi run	5-mi run	45 tempo	rest	10-mi run	**20**
12	4-mi run	6-mi run	5-mi run	7 × 800	rest	6-mi pace	**12**
13	4-mi run	10-mi run	5-mi run	7 × hill	rest	10m pace	**20**
14	5-mi run	6-mi run	5-mi run	45 tempo	rest	6-mi run	**12**
15	5-mi run	10-mi run	5-mi run	8 × 800	rest	10m pace	**20**
16	5-mi run	8-mi run	5-mi run	6 × hill	rest	4-mi pace	**12**
17	4-mi run	6-mi run	4-mi run	30 tempo	rest	4-mi run	**8**
18	3-mi run	4-mi run	3-mi run	4 × 400	rest	2-mi run	**race**

MARATHON TRAINING SCHEDULE: ADVANCED-II

Week	Mon	Tue	Wed	Thu	Fri	Sat	Sun
1	3-mi run	3 × hill	3-mi run	30 tempo	rest	5-mi pace	**10**
2	3-mi run	30 tempo	3-mi run	3-mi pace	rest	5-mi run	**11**
3	3-mi run	4 × 800	3-mi run	30 tempo	rest	6-mi pace	**8**
4	3-mi run	4 × hill	3-mi run	35 tempo	rest	6-mi pace	**13**
5	3-mi run	35 tempo	3-mi run	3-mi pace	rest	7-mi run	**14**
6	3-mi run	5 × 800	3-mi run	35 tempo	rest	7-mi pace	**10**
7	3-mi run	5 × hill	4-mi run	40 tempo	rest	8-mi pace	**16**
8	3-mi run	40 tempo	4-mi run	3-mi pace	rest	8-mi run	**17**
9	3-mi run	6 × 800	4-mi run	40 tempo	rest	9-mi pace	**12**
10	3-mi run	6 × hill	4-mi run	45 tempo	rest	9-mi pace	**19**
11	4-mi run	45 tempo	5-mi run	4-mi pace	rest	10-mi run	**20**
12	4-mi run	7 × 800	5-mi run	45 tempo	rest	6-mi pace	**12**
13	4-mi run	7 × hill	5-mi run	50 tempo	rest	10m pace	**20**
14	5-mi run	45 tempo	5-mi run	5-mi pace	rest	6-mi run	**12**
15	5-mi run	8 × 800	5-mi run	40 tempo	rest	10m pace	**20**
16	5-mi run	6 × hill	5-mi run	30 tempo	rest	4-mi pace	**12**
17	4-mi run	30 tempo	4-mi run	4-mi pace	rest	4-mi run	**8**
18	3-mi run	4 × 400	3-mi run	rest	rest	2-mi run	**race**

ACKNOWLEDGMENTS

Marathon: The Ultimate Training Guide, now in its third edition, has grown in breadth and depth because of hundreds, perhaps thousands, of people. If this is *the* text book for the marathoning age—and I think it is—I owe thanks to all of them, too many to name.

The first edition in 1993 owed its expertise to my own successful career as a runner and sometime coach, but also to more than 60 coaches who returned questionnaires sharing their ideas and training methods. You will find quotes from those coaches scattered through this edition. Let me specifically mention Ron Gunn of Southwestern Michigan College in Dowagiac, Michigan, and Bill Wenmark of Deephaven, Michigan, coach of runners preparing for the Twin Cities and Grandma's Marathons.

In the half dozen years between first and second editions, I became a training consultant to the Chicago Marathon, thanks to race director Carey Pinkowski. My duties included working with the Chicago Area Running Association's Marathon Training Class, which grew from several hundred to several thousand runners under the leadership of Brian Piper and Bill Fitzgerald and later Tom Moran. Working with the class certainly helped expand my knowledge.

For this third edition, I called on my friends on the Internet, the so-called "V-Teamers," who participate in my Inter*Active* Bulletin Boards, both asking me questions and helping me answer the questions of other runners. In reading this far, you have encountered quotes from nearly two hundred V-Teamers, but many more use my programs and contribute silently to my increasing knowledge. As a result, *Marathon: The Ultimate Training Guide* has grown from 208 pages in its first edition to 358 pages in its current edition. Thanks to all who have contributed.

Thanks also to my editors at the Rodale book division: Jeremy Katz, who agreed with me when I suggested a full updating and revision would make an already successful book even better; Heidi Rodale, who edited my words; Emily Williams, who guided the book through production; and Tony Serge, who provided the sparkling design. My agent Angela Miller has worked closely with me through all three editions.

Finally, my wife, Rose, who when I asked her to marry me nearly half a century ago must have wondered, "Do I really want to be married to a marathoner?" Fortunately for me—and for you—her answer was, "Yes!"

INDEX

Underscored page references indicate boxed text.